Small Money – Big Impact

Small Money – Big Impact

Fighting Poverty with Microfinance

PETER FANCONI
PATRICK SCHEURLE

WILEY

Registered Office
John Wiley & Sons, Ltd, The Atrium, Southern Gate, Chichester, West Sussex, PO19 8SQ, United Kingdom

For details of our global editorial offices, for customer services and for information about how to apply for permission to reuse the copyright material in this book please see our website at www.wiley.com.

Library of Congress Cataloging-in-Publication Data

Names: Fanconi, Peter, author. | Scheurle, Patrick, author.
Title: Small money big impact : fighting poverty with microfinance / Peter A. Fanconi, Patrick Scheurle.
Description: Hoboken : Wiley, 2017. | Translation from German of Small money-big impact, [2015] | Includes index.
Identifiers: LCCN 2017002364 (print) | LCCN 2017004723 (ebook) | ISBN 9781119338208 (hardback) | ISBN 9781119338192 (ePDF) | ISBN 9781119338246 (ePub) | ISBN 9781119351481 (ebk) | ISBN 9781119338192 (pdf) | ISBN 9781119338246 (epub)
Subjects: LCSH: Microfinance —Management. | Business enterprises. | Marketing. | BISAC: BUSINESS & ECONOMICS / Finance.
Classification: LCC HG178.3 .F3613 2017 (print) | LCC HG178.3 (ebook) | DDC 332.7—dc23
LC record available at https://lccn.loc.gov/2017002364

Cover design: Wiley

Set in 11/13 Times by SPi Global, Chennai, India

Printed in Great Britain by TJ International Ltd, Padstow, Cornwall, UK

10 9 8 7 6 5 4 3 2 1

Contents

Foreword   ix

Preface   xi

Acknowledgments   xiii

About the Authors   xv

CHAPTER 1
Introduction   **1**

1.1	Fighting Poverty	2
1.2	Investing in Financial Infrastructure	7
1.3	Content Overview	8
Notes		9

CHAPTER 2
Microfinance – the Concept   **11**

2.1	History	12
2.2	Definition and Goals	15
2.3	Double Bottom Line	18
2.4	Financial Inclusion	21
2.5	Market Participants	24
2.6	Impact Investing	25
2.7	Preliminary Conclusions	29
Notes		31

CHAPTER 3
The Microfinance Value Chain   33

3.1 The Protagonists and Their Tasks   34
3.2 Regulatory Environment   36
3.3 Development Finance Institutions   37
3.4 Market Overview   39
3.5 Geneva: Birthplace of Modern Microfinance   42
3.6 Preliminary Conclusions   46
Notes   47

CHAPTER 4
Micro Entrepreneurs   49

4.1 Definition   50
4.2 Needs and Requirements   52
4.3 Micro Entrepreneurs   59
4.4 Preliminary Conclusions   67
Notes   68

CHAPTER 5
Microfinance Institutions   71

5.1 Definition and Goals   72
5.2 Types of MFIs   73
5.3 MFI Funding   76
5.4 Services   85
5.5 Regulation   88
5.6 Preliminary Conclusions   94
Notes   96

CHAPTER 6
Lending Methodologies   99

6.1 Traditional Credit Theory and Microfinance   100
6.2 Lending Methodologies   101
6.3 Socio-Economic Factors   104
6.4 Late Payments and Over-Indebtedness of Clients   108
6.5 Default Prevention and Restructuring   110
6.6 Occupation: Loan Officer   113
6.7 Preliminary Conclusions   114
Notes   116

CHAPTER 7
Loan Pricing   **119**

7.1   Interest Rate Components   120
7.2   Setting Sustainable Interest Rates   127
7.3   Regional Differences   127
7.4   Loan Recipients' Willingness to Repay   129
7.5   Preliminary Conclusions   130
Notes   132

CHAPTER 8
Social Performance Management   **133**

8.1   Social Performance   134
8.2   Measuring Social Performance   135
8.3   Measuring the Outcome of Microfinance   149
8.4   Social Rating Agencies   151
8.5   Technical Assistance   153
8.6   Linking Social Performance with Profitability   156
8.7   Preliminary Conclusions   157
Notes   159

CHAPTER 9
Beyond the Reach of Microfinance?   **161**

9.1   Prejudices and Reservations   162
9.2   Preliminary Conclusions   171
Notes   172

CHAPTER 10
Investing in Microfinance   **175**

10.1   Market Development   176
10.2   Microfinance Investment Vehicles   177
10.3   The Investment Process   181
10.4   Loan Agreements and Pricing Policy   187
10.5   Microfinance in the Overall Investment
Portfolio   191
10.6   Incentives for Investing in Microfinance   195
10.7   Preliminary Conclusions   197
Notes   199

CHAPTER 11
Real and Financial Economy **201**

    11.1 Microfinance Is Crisis-Proof   202
    11.2 Real Economy and Local Influencing Factors   203
    11.3 Financial Economy   205
    11.4 Stability Mechanisms   207
    11.5 Preliminary Conclusions   208
    Notes   209

CHAPTER 12
Discussion of Results and Conclusions **211**

    12.1 Win-Win-Win   212
    12.2 Onwards and Upwards   212
    Notes   215

APPENDIX A
Example of a Loan Application   217

APPENDIX B
Due Diligence of Socio-Economic Impact Factors   221

List of Abbreviations **227**

Glossary **229**

References **233**

Photo Credits **243**

Index **245**

Foreword

One of the main goals of the World Economic Forum is to improve the state of the world. Improving the state of the world inevitably means improving the economic and social living standards of vulnerable and destitute segments of the population; with the help of collaborations and projects based on public–private partnership. Microfinance is unique and presents exceptional opportunities in achieving this goal.

Microfinance and impact investing – topics of interest for me for quite some time now – manage to generate financial and social returns at the same time and largely fall into the category of corporate social responsibility. The triple bottom line measures the economic, environmental and social returns of microfinance. Investors and enterprises that are committed to the triple bottom line contribute towards an environmentally friendly and sustainable economic development of poor regions of this world.

Small Money – Big Impact is comprehensive, and more importantly, informative and explanatory. Fanconi and Scheurle have successfully illustrated the nature and potential of the world of microfinance and impact investing, and displayed how social and financial interests can indeed go hand in hand and contribute towards the implementation of the United Nations' Millennium Development Goals. This book's detailed description of the loan granting processes of microfinance institutions outlines to what lengths private and public investors have gone over the last 15 years in their fight against poverty. Microloans foster financial integration and empower millions of people to progress economically. The results and the statistics are promising; however, we still have a long way to go.

This book is a standard reference that covers all the relevant information in the field of microfinance. It is an invaluable contribution towards the further development of current strategies in the fight against global poverty, and it aims to convince investors that both the financial and social returns that are generated by microfinance are attractive in equal measure.

Prof. Klaus Schwab
Founder and Executive Chairman of the
World Economic Forum, Geneva.

Preface

In 1990, when the world population was 5.2 billion, 36 per cent of the world lived in extreme poverty. Today – with 7.3 billion people – an estimated 12 per cent live in poverty. Over the past 25 years, the world has gone from nearly 2 billion people living in extreme poverty to fewer than 1 billion.

World Bank Group President Jim Yong Kim

Dear reader,

In our world, we witness on a daily basis, how *small money* can have a *big impact*. A microloan of just a few dollars empowers people in developing countries to be economically independent and therefore able to safeguard their own and their families' future.

Microfinance has established itself as a vital instrument with leading development banks in the fight against poverty. The geopolitical relevance of microfinance is undeniable. Institutional and private investors alike have come to realize the value of microfinance investment vehicles for their portfolios and appreciate the double bottom line of social and financial returns. Judging by the positive experiences and results of this asset class, the microfinance industry is emerging and breaking ground into impact investing, aiming to achieve a positive impact in areas such as education and climate change.

Microfinance and impact investing are a mega-trend and change the way we invest, offering unique investment opportunities that put the interests of investors and recipients on the same level and have a positive impact on the lives of millions of people. We have been able to witness these positive changes again and again, on numerous journeys to developing countries.

Small Money – Big Impact aims to share these developments with a broader public in an explanatory, illustrative and objective manner. It sheds light on the processes and investment vehicles in microfinance, and at the same time raises awareness and recognition of this asset class as a powerful tool in the fight against poverty.

Enjoy your journey through the world of microfinance.

Peter Fanconi
Patrick Scheurle

Acknowledgments

This book is the result of sustained efforts of our experienced BlueOrchard investment team. Ebony Satti, Maria Teresa Zappia and Chuck Olson, as well as many other individuals, have generously shared their wealth of experience in the fields of microfinance and impact investing. Our special thanks go out to our families, especially to Daniela, Chiara and Sera, for their unwavering support and understanding during the time of this book's creation.

About the Authors

PETER A. FANCONI is the Chairman and former CEO of Swiss-based BlueOrchard Finance, one of the leading asset management companies in impact investing. Peter demonstrated his entrepreneurial and social competences in various positions, including CEO of the Vontobel Private Bank, CEO of Harcourt Alternative Investments and managing partner at PwC. He also serves as Chairman of Swiss bank Graubündner Kantonalbank (GKB) and as board member of academic and charitable institutions worldwide. Peter is a renowned lecturer and published writer in the field of finance and impact investing.

PATRICK SCHEURLE is the CEO of BlueOrchard Finance. Prior, he acted as COO and CFO at BlueOrchard. His broad experience in finance includes senior positions at Bank Vontobel and Credit Suisse. He further served with a leading management consultancy focusing on governance and value creation. Patrick holds a PhD in finance from the University of St. Gallen, Switzerland, where he also held an assistant professorship. He is the author of several well-known finance books and regularly publishes on developments and research in impact investing.

CHAPTER 1

Introduction

Worldwide, almost 1 billion people have to live on less than $1.9 a day.

World Bank[1]

More than half of the world's population lives on an annual income of less than $2500 – the equivalent of about $7 a day. Africa, Latin America and South Asia account for the largest part of the population living below the respective national poverty line.

In the past, the limited offer of financial services has been one of the main pitfalls. There was a lack of financial infrastructure and products tailored to the needs of people and households living on a low income.

1.1 FIGHTING POVERTY

While less than 1.5 per cent of the world's population live on an annual income of over $20,000, more than half of the people around the world have to get by on less than $2500 a year (see Figure 1.1), the equivalent of no more than $7 a day. More than 2.5 billion people live on as little as $4 or less per day.[2] Such living conditions are officially referred to as poverty. The World Bank uses the term "extreme poverty" in cases falling below the $1.9 a day line – almost 1 billion worldwide are constrained to a life on as little as that.[3]

A look at the poverty levels of individual regions reveals that in many African countries more than 20 per cent of the population is living below the national poverty line. In most African countries, more than 40 per cent of people live below the national poverty line (see Figure 1.2). Latin America presents a similar situation, with Chile making a notable exception with less than 20 per cent of people living in poverty. Extreme poverty dominates in Central Asian states such as Afghanistan, Tajikistan and Kirgizstan. In South Asia and East Europe a staggering 20 to 40 per cent of the population are struggling below the national poverty line.

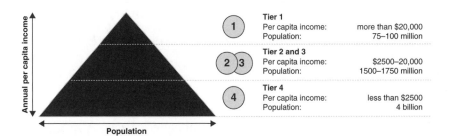

FIGURE 1.1   Economic Pyramid
Data Source: Prahalad and Hart (2002); World Bank (2001), adjusted according to World Bank (2016)

The pyramid shows the population distribution according to annual per capita income with respect to purchasing power parity. The majority of the population (4 billion) have to manage on less than $2500 a year, while 75 to 100 million people worldwide can rely on an annual income of more than $20,000.

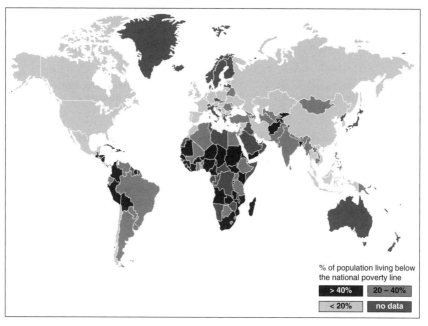

FIGURE 1.2 Prevalence of Poverty with Respect to Country
Data Source: CIA World Factbook (2008)

Africa and Latin America account for the largest part of the population living below the respective national poverty line, followed by South Asia and Eastern Europe.

Poverty is accountable for an insufficient dietary intake, causes famines and undeniably constitutes a health threat to anyone subjected to it. The poor are prone to illnesses, have restricted access to education, and women in particular are often victims of physical and psychological abuse.

The triggers and problems of poverty are well known. In efforts galvanized by the World Bank, the International Monetary Fund (IMF), the Development Co-operation Directorate of the Organization for Economic Co-operation and Development (OECD)[4], and several non-governmental organizations (NGOs), the International Community designed development goals built on this knowledge and out of this came the United Nations (UN, UNO) Millennium Development Goals (MDGs) in 2001. The MDGs

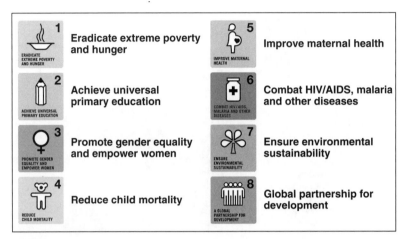

FIGURE 1.3   Millennium Development Goals
Data Source: McCann Erickson/UNDP Brazil

In their Millennium Declaration in 2000, the UN defined eight development goals that were to be implemented by the end of 2015.

were a set of eight goals designed to achieve and implement the targets of the United Nations Millennium Declaration by 2015 (see Figure 1.3).[5]

The first seven goals committed developing countries to employing financial means in their combat against poverty and corruption and to promote democratization and gender equality at the same time. The eighth goal obliged industrial countries to use their global economic authority in a bid to assist developing countries and achieve equality of all countries worldwide. Improving the situation of those afflicted by poverty, however, goes beyond merely devising goals, but should rather focus on effective measures. This in turn warrants an understanding of the underlying causes of poverty.

The problem is multi-layered, and people's economic and social situation is influenced by different factors. What has, however, become increasingly evident is that access to capital and financial services is pivotal in fostering economic growth.[6] And yet, individuals and households with a low income above all rarely have access to capital. Encouraging financial inclusion is therefore of the essence in the fight against poverty.

The implementation of the goals may be considered an overall success. The most important goal – the reduction of extreme poverty by half – has certainly been reached. Beyond this, the supply of drinking water has been improved, and considerable progress was made in connection with further objectives such as eradicating hunger and promoting gender equality. These are without doubt essential developmental steps.

However, albeit regarded as an overall success, the MDGs have been subject to criticism as well. Some critics maintain that their goals fell short of more general topics and focused on issues concerning developing countries exclusively, whereas industrial countries should be more willfully reminded of their commitment with respect to sustainability. Other voices argued that the partly flagging implementation of the MDGs was a result of the sustaining lack of political intent to create the necessary parameters in order to provide financing for development.[7]

In the wake of the criticism of the MDGs, the member states at the UN summit in Rio de Janeiro in 2012 agreed that a consistent and universal solution was indispensable in the battle against poverty. They furthermore concurred that sustainable development must no longer be regarded as a separate issue when fighting poverty, but that both goals are to be pursued simultaneously. Industrial countries for this reason should not only offer support to developing countries, but in turn commit themselves to sustainable development in their own countries at the same time.

With the lapse of the MDGs at the end of 2015, the Sustainable Development Goals (SDGs) have been devised with the target date of 2030. They also promote private sector investment. Developing countries alone are faced with a staggering annual funding gap of $2.5 trillion (see Figure 1.4) with the current level of investment in SDG-relevant sectors. Investments of the private sector are therefore indispensable, and consequently banks, pension funds, insurance companies, foundations and transnational companies should boost their investments in SDG-relevant sectors.[8]

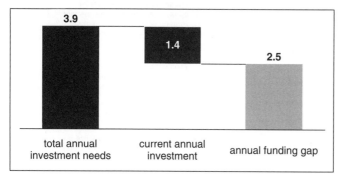

FIGURE 1.4 Annual Investment Needs (in $ trillion)
Data Source: UNCTAD (2014)

The United Nations Conference on Trade and Development (UNCTAD) published its World Investment Report in 2014. It accounts for \$3.9 trillion regarding the annual investment needs for SDG-relevant sectors in developing countries. With current investment in these sectors at \$1.4 trillion, the resulting funding gap amounts to \$2.5 trillion, a sum that needs covering from both the public and the private sector.

Figure 1.5 displays the 17 SDGs as defined and no longer confined to developing countries. Instead, they do apply to industrial states at the same time. The first eight goals are strongly reminiscent of the MDGs and

FIGURE 1.5 Sustainable Development Goals (SDGs)
Data Source: United Nations (2014)

With the lapse of the MDGs in 2015, the UN devised SDGs that are to be implemented over a course of 15 years. The new goals address all developing and industrial countries alike and urge them to adopt a sustainable approach in all their efforts.

challenge problems such as poverty, hunger, education and water supply. Environmental contemplations and action plans, justice, prosperity and food security newly join the ranks of the previous goals. It is evident that climate change is a core issue of these SDGs; 12 goals refer to sustainable development and climate change. Alarmingly, 14 of the 15 hottest years on record have in fact occurred in the twenty-first century.[9]

1.2 INVESTING IN FINANCIAL INFRASTRUCTURE

In retrospect, the limited offer of financial services almost made it impossible to access them altogether. There was a lack of both financial infrastructure and tailored products for the needs of people and households living on a low income.

Under the direction of the world's leading development banks, the financial infrastructure in development countries has experienced a remarkable surge in recent years. Together with private investors, financial institutions have been founded that efficiently serve people in developing countries and offer products that are tailored to their needs.

Microloans in particular are such tailored products. Owing to Muhammad Yunus, the 2006 Nobel Peace Prize laureate, modern microfinance has become a household name. Despite, or perhaps rather thanks to, a simple idea, its success has been truly remarkable: poor people receive a loan, fast and without collateral, which allows them to create employment to improve their livelihoods.

At present, 200 million people all over the world benefit from such microloans.[10] Development banks still are substantial investors and continue to play an integral part in the development of the microfinance sector. However, the sector has now reached a grade of maturity that increasingly allows for private investors. Private people and institutional investors alike thus have the opportunity to use their investment decisions to actively support inclusion of poor demographic groups and achieve an attractive return at the same time.

1.3 CONTENT OVERVIEW

This book offers an in-depth look at the concept and the effects of impact investing using the example of microfinance. Impact investing yields a financial as well as a social return.

Chapters 1 to 3 will introduce the reader to the topic and offer an overview of the industry, its agents and their roles. Chapters 4 to 7 in turn will focus on the different micro entrepreneurs and microfinance institutions (MFIs), followed by the principles of loan granting, the be-all and end-all of microfinance.

SHOE MANUFACTURE – BULACAN PROVINCE, THE PHILIPPINES

Jennifer Dalida produced her first children's shoes at the start of 2001. With a first loan with the Cooperative Rural Bank of Bulacan (CRBB), she bought different materials for her production. Before long, she began to instruct other family members in the production processes and her business soon went from strength to strength. With what now is her 15th loan she has bought new machines, employed additional workers and is able to turn out more than 240 pairs of shoes a day. Thanks to her business, she can provide for her family, send all the children to school and create new jobs for other relatives.

Source: BlueOrchard

Microfinance investment differs substantially from conventional investment. Chapters 8 to 10 will elaborate on those differences and closely inspect investment and diversification possibilities for investors. These chapters will also be dedicated to the question of why microfinance investment as such – particularly, however, in a portfolio context – can yield an attractive return. Chapter 11 explores the influence of real economy and global financial economy on microfinance and its protagonists. A summary of the main arguments and discussion thereof (Chapter 12) will conclude this book.

NOTES

1 World Bank (2016), database 2012.
2 World Bank (2016), database 2012.
3 Ravallion, Chen and Sangraula (2008), pp. 12–15, 23–24.
4 Development Assistance Committee.
5 United Nations (2001).
6 Schumpeter (1926), p. 494–495 and Gurley and Shaw (1955), p. 515.
7 Hofmann (2015).
8 UNCTAD (2014).
9 UN News Centre (2015).
10 Reed, Marsden, Ortega, Rivera and Rogers (2015), p. 8.

CHAPTER 2

Microfinance – the Concept

I believe in microfinance because it isn't just a path out of poverty. It's the road to self-reliance. By allowing people to team up and literally become their own bank, you can mobilize people and resources and alleviate poverty on the global scale.
Her Majesty Queen Rania al-Abdullah of Jordan[1]

The financial markets in many industrialized countries are a result of capital structures similar to those of microfinance.

Microfinance is a form of impact investing yielding not only financial but also social returns; a sustainable combination of economic performance and social impact.

Financial inclusion by means of facilitated access to financial products promotes higher income, leads to better health and education and reduces economic inequality.

2.1 HISTORY

Microfinance has become a household name and a story of success over the last few decades. However, its origins date back much further. Today's modern financial markets in many industrialized countries are a result of capital structures similar to those of microfinance. Deeming the concept of microfinance to be a relatively new one, and thereby confining its roots to the recent past, would not only mar its historical importance and overall impact but also neglect the consolidated findings of the past centuries. These invaluable experiences are the basis for any future development.

As early as back in the fourteenth and fifteenth centuries, Franciscan monks founded collective pawnshops (see Figure 2.1). Their aim was to assist poverty-stricken segments of the population to secure their economic existence at times of crisis. Typically, the pawnbroker would hold items of value for which a small fee was charged in return for safe custody. The resulting revenues would allow the monks to cover their operative costs. In Italy alone, the concept spread to 214 social institutions that were based on so-called monti di pietà (mounts of piety) as their capital base. Alongside the borrowers, there were sponsors who financially boosted the capital stock.[2]

At the beginning of the eighteenth century, the prolific Irish writer Jonathan Swift instigated credit funds that would issue smaller amounts of cash to people in need in Dublin. Initially, interest-free collective loans from donations were granted, and their weekly repayments were safeguarded by means of mutual monitoring. The introduction of a legal framework and regulations authorized for the calculation of interest and savings collection. As a result, and based on the Swiftian model, more than 300 economically independent credit funds were introduced by the mid-nineteenth century. They differed in size and client structure as well as in geographical focus, and covered a wide range of microcredits.[3] Returns and savings deposits led to tremendous growth in the various credit institutions, allowing more than 20 per cent of all Irish households to benefit from them.

At the same time, Germany saw the arrival of the credit cooperative system, with the foundation of the very first savings association in Hamburg in 1778 and the foundation of the first savings bank in 1801. Savings deposits were established and loans were granted to smaller enterprises and farmers. In 1846, Friedrich Wilhelm Raiffeisen and Hermann

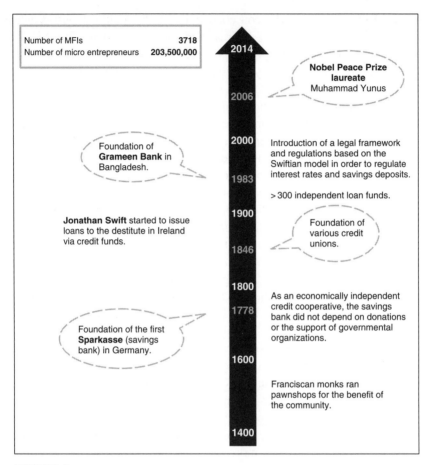

FIGURE 2.1   The History of Microfinance
Data Source: Becker (2010); Hollis and Sweetman (2004); Menning (1992); Reed, Marsden, Ortega, Rivera and Rogers (2015); Seibel (2003); savings banks, the Raiffeisen Group and cooperative banks

The beginnings of microfinance date back to the fourteenth century, when monks started operating pawnshops for the benefit of public welfare. In industrialized countries, a stable financial system has established itself to this day. In developing countries, there are currently almost 4000 microfinance institutions (MFIs), serving more than 200 million clients and thereby facilitating their financial integration.

Schulze-Delitzsch founded credit cooperatives that would establish savings deposits in both rural and urban areas and issue microloans. Shortly after their foundation, both cooperatives were able to operate economically independently, that is, entirely without the support of donations or governmental organizations.[4] To this day, the core of this business and financial model is inherent to the orientation of these organizations, which incidentally have all grown into major commercial banks.[5]

The beginnings of modern microfinance in developing countries are attributed to Muhammad Yunus and the positioning of his Grameen Bank in the mid-1980s. Yunus founded Grameen Bank to enable poverty-stricken members of the population to gain access to capital in the form of microcredits. In 2006, the economist, who had been trained in the USA, was awarded the Nobel Peace Prize for his efforts in the field. As a professor at a university in the south-east of Bangladesh, Yunus had been jarred by the unspeakable famine raging through his country, leaving tens of thousands dead. In 1976, he began to issue small loans to households in neighboring villages. The privately granted capital was enough to enable the villagers to set up basic business activities that provided a sustainable income.

Despite the fact that no collateral had to be provided, repayments were on time. Yunus expanded the concept in collaboration with the Central Bank of Bangladesh and founded Grameen Bank, which to this day continues to issue loans to low-income segments of the population nationwide. The bank's winning formula is their system of solidarity lending, where microcredit clients accept joint liability for their loans. By the early 1990s, Grameen already had more than one million clients. Today a multiple thereof, a staggering 8.7 million, profit from the bank's services.[6] Simultaneously, other financial markets all over the world started to develop, notably the microfinance service provider ACCION in Brazil and Bank Rakyat in Indonesia. A number of microfinance institutions (MFIs) have stood the test of time and safely established themselves. They are all based on the Grameen Bank business model and are continuously and successfully developing it further.[7]

Microfinance has grown impressively and rapidly since 1997. According to the Microcredit Summit Campaign Report in 2014, over 4000 microfinance institutions have reached more than 200 million clients with a standing credit (see Figure 2.2). In other words, each MFI on average serves 55,000 clients. More than 115.5 million clients count among the poorest of the poor when they enter a microfinance program.[8]

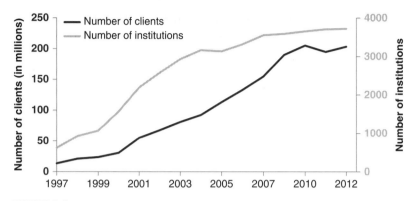

FIGURE 2.2   Growth of Clients and Institutions
Data Source: Reed, Marsden, Ortega, Rivera and Rogers (2015)

The concept of microfinance has experienced a tremendous growth over the last 15 years. In 2012, overall nearly 4000 microfinance institutions issued loans to over 200 million clients.

2.2   DEFINITION AND GOALS

According to estimates, about a quarter of the 500 million poor all over the world engage in micro enterprises and business activities, yet the majority do not have access to adequate and sustainable financial products.[9] Microfinance was primarily devised and conceived as a developmental approach that aimed to support those at the bottom of the pyramid. The term "microfinance" *sensu stricto* refers to the provision of financial services to low-income clients lacking sufficient funds for entrepreneurial activities.

The financial services mentioned above involve the granting of loans and savings deposits; however, insurance and payment services are increasingly being offered. In the broader sense, the term equally embraces the sundry non-financial and social services that are being provided by microfinance institutions, such as the imparting of financial knowledge, the development of intergroup leadership competencies, as well as educational and health services.[10] The definition of microfinance very often comprises financial as well as social services and is not limited to the realm of classic banking. Impact investing – a form of investment where both financial and social returns are generated – is a hypernym of microfinance and therefore has to be understood as a comprehensive developmental tool.[11]

From the point of view of MFIs, microfinance activities predominantly consist of the granting of microcredits intended to increase business capital, the assessment of borrowers and their planned investments, and the acceptance of savings deposits and credit control. Despite the fact that many microfinance institutions provide additional non-financial services, these activities transcend the definition of the traditional concept of microfinance. They may, however, be regarded as a progression that aims to steadily improve its products and broaden its range of services in order to meet client needs.

The exclusion of the poor from most parts of the economic and financial system is largely responsible for their desolate economic and financial situation. The inclusion of low-income segments of the population into the financial system is therefore a central objective of microfinance. This is all the more obvious as nowadays microfinance products and services have evidently broken the mold of what is known as the classic microcredit. The poor no longer only make use of financial services for business purposes, but increasingly invest in their health and education, in temporary financial relief or other cash flow requirements. By tapping a variety of financial services, the poor are given the chance to boost their household income, increase wealth and property, and considerably reduce their susceptibility to crises and unexpected shocks.

Access to financial services, furthermore, allows for a more balanced diet and better healthcare, which in turn reduces the transmission of diseases. Overall, people living in poverty may more easily plan their future and pay for their children's education. The participation of women in microfinance programs has bolstered their self-assurance and brought them a step closer in their battle for gender equality.

Microfinance for this reason is more than a form of development aid, as it also promotes self-determination: poverty-stricken segments of the population are given access to flexible and affordable financial services and are encouraged to be self-determined and at the same time develop strategies to gradually work their way out of poverty.[12] In recent years, the effects of microfinance with respect to the implementation of the MDGs have mostly manifested themselves in the fight against poverty, the improvement of school education and the health system, as well as in the socio-economic strengthening of female gender roles.

Thanks to their participation in microfinance programs, the poor can not only increase their income, but at the same time diversify it. This is paramount, as it is the basis for the fight against poverty. Taking a microloan means that business ideas can be funded, which is a boost to national economic growth in its own right. The combination of different financial services – including loans, savings deposits and insurance – facilitates the pooling of funds for business-related and private purchases. It additionally lowers income fluctuations over prolonged periods of time, so that the level of consumption can be stabilized, even in times of austerity. Microfinance therefore also acts as a buffer to secure both people's professional and private existence in times of adverse fortune.

Various qualitative and quantitative studies reveal a positive influence of microfinance on income and capital. Research by two microfinance institutions, Share Microfin in India and Crecer in Bolivia, suggests that three quarters of Share's clients in India safely attribute the rise in living standards to microfinance, while two thirds of Crecer clients in Bolivia reported a surge in income.[13] The variables considered were income, property, capital, housing situation and household expenditure. More than half of these clients managed to escape poverty.

Half of all Share clients further indicated that any surplus in income that was not used to cancel their debts was spent to fund additional expenditures.[14] Studies by the World Bank and Grameen Bank in fact yield comparable results that equally document a disproportionate increase in income of program participants. The studies furthermore disclosed that individual success stories of microfinance clients in many cases exert a positive influence on the economy of an entire village, largely because even non-participating households manage to record an increase in income.[15]

In many households, additional income is often invested in child education. Various studies have revealed that the children of microfinance clients are more likely to go to school and are less likely to leave school prematurely than children of families that do not seek relief with a microcredit. To further underline the advances achieved in education, many microfinance providers have developed a range of credit and savings services that are tailored to education as a whole. As a result, rates in children starting school have surged significantly and literacy as well as calculation skills in children from participating households have risen distinctly. In addition to this, consistent borrowing results in prolonged periods of school attendance.[16]

The improvement of healthcare is another declared goal of microfinance. Health issues and diseases often have dire consequences in poor families and lead to higher transmission rates than in wealthier households.

In the worst case, death or inability to work may result from any given illness. Ensuing expenditures in connection with ill health have a detrimental effect on income and potential savings, and in many cases lead to income consumption and over-indebtedness. Microfinance offers suitable products and services for the prevention of illnesses, mostly in the form of health credits that are granted alongside a micro loan. By doing so, microfinance consistently and substantially contributes towards a more balanced diet, better healthcare and the installation of sanitary infrastructure. In partnership with local insurances, MFIs offer their clients life insurances that in the event of death assume liability for outstanding microcredit repayments or funeral expenses.

Modern microfinance has always focused on empowering women. Women in fact very often handle money more responsibly than men, and they also yield a much higher repayment rate. Studies also suggest that women more readily invest higher incomes in the improvement of their family's standard of living and their households than male clients.[17] Providing them with access to financial services strengthens their powers of self-assertion and perseverance and involves them more actively in decision-making processes within their families and communities in general. Research into the socio-economic status of women reveals that their participation in microfinance programs leads to an increase in mobility and capital.[18]

2.3 DOUBLE BOTTOM LINE

The social goals of microfinance are critical in the fight against poverty. Regardless of this, financial profitability and independence remain core aspects. A sustainable and long-term alignment of the concept facilitates a comprehensive inclusion of the poor into the economic and financial system that goes beyond the limited possibilities of funds with the likes of donations and subsidies. Thanks to microfinance, public and private investors have the possibility to provide financial means without any local infrastructure and thereby to actively combat poverty.

Financial sustainability is key to any long-term success of a microfinance service provider. Coverage of any incurring costs enables more clients to profit from financial services. Distinctly, equal priority is given to purely financial aspects as well as to social impact on clients. This means that microfinance takes account in equal measure of financial and social services that are mindful of their environmental impact, hence the term "double bottom line".

Microfinance is an attractive investment class with a double bottom line. The combination of financial profitability for the investor and social commitment to the client's benefit make an investment in microfinance exceptional and one of its kind; for one thing, investors may generate an attractive and sustainable return by means of their investment. At the same time, it inspires the poor to assume more autonomy and independence, as the funding of their business activities actively combats poverty, which in turn encourages economic stability locally (see Figure 2.3). The term "triple bottom line" is often used when social impact and environmental impact are notably interpreted as separate entities.

While an investor's financial return is readily measurable, social performance and its impact are subject to interpretation. The Social Performance Task Force (SPTF) defines social performance as the effective

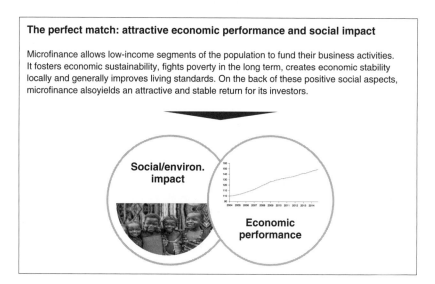

The perfect match: attractive economic performance and social impact

Microfinance allows low-income segments of the population to fund their business activities. It fosters economic sustainability, fights poverty in the long term, creates economic stability locally and generally improves living standards. On the back of these positive social aspects, microfinance alsoyields an attractive and stable return for its investors.

FIGURE 2.3 Double Bottom Line
Data Source: BlueOrchard Research

Microfinance is an attractive investment class. Its double bottom line results in an attractive economic performance and social commitment that are a perfect match.

translation of a financial service provider organization's mission into practice.[19] This comprises sustainability, better services to low-income segments of the population and those excluded from the financial system, advances in quality and efficiency of financial services, an improvement of clients' economic and social living conditions, as well as social responsibility in the face of the client, employees and affected communities.

Figure 2.4 illustrates the financial and social impact of a $1 million investment. With a 5 per cent return and a five-year maturity, a $1 million investment will yield $1.3 million. With an average loan of $500 and a one-year maturity, 2000 micro loans can be issued. Assuming that a total of five people live in the average household, 10,000 people will benefit from these 2000 microcredits. The second year will see 4205 microcredits flowing to 21,025 people – calculating on the basis of a default rate of 3 per cent or less. An investor's capital in fact issues multiple loans: over a period of five years, an investment of $1 million can issue a total of 11,504

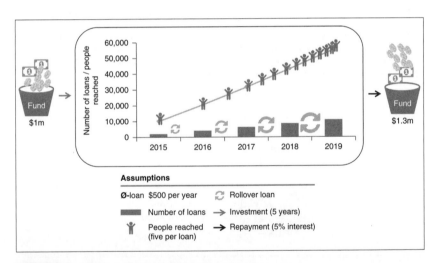

FIGURE 2.4   Effects of a $1 Million Investment

With a 5 per cent return and a five-year maturity, a $1 million investment will yield $1.3 million. After five years, the original investment of $1 million will have funded about 11,500 microloans and influenced the lives of over 50,000 people.

microcredits. An investor therefore generates a financial return of $300,000 on the one hand, and supports over 50,000 people in need in developing countries on the other.

2.4 FINANCIAL INCLUSION

The term "financial inclusion" refers to institutions such as banks, non-bank financial institutions (NBFIs) or NGOs and their resolution to extend their range of financial services to those segments of the population that traditionally do not have access to them. Reaching these mostly rural and underserved members of the population is a feat of innovation in terms of both products and distribution channels. Financial inclusion not only serves the individual client, but also encourages growth and fosters the dynamic development of potentially emerging economies. According to estimates of the World Bank, currently 2 billion people are excluded from the financial system, which means that 25 per cent of the people world-wide are unbanked. In developing countries, virtually half the adult population (46 per cent) have no access to the financial system.[20]

A look at financial inclusion with respect to levels of income renders an even more dismal picture. More than three quarters of all low-income adults do not have access to financial services, the reasons being costly access routes to a place where they can open an account, or onerous covenants that render it virtually impossible to access financial services or a simple current or savings account. Financial exclusion goes hand in hand with income inequality: adults in the financially strong OECD countries boast three times as many bank accounts as adults living on a low income.[21] Figure 2.5 illustrates unequal financial inclusion according to country: regions such as Latin America, the Caribbean as well as East and South Asia in particular have a comparatively higher inclusion rate into the financial system. Eastern Europe and Central Asia are the midfield players, followed by Sub-Saharan Africa. The Middle East and Northern Africa features the highest inclusion potential.[22]

Access to the financial system and sustainable financial services is of utmost importance and exerts a positive impact on various levels of society, most notably on all households and enterprises, as well as on overall economic growth.

Access to financial systems allows households, i.e. individuals and entire families, to build capital and deposit it safely. It fosters a sustainable

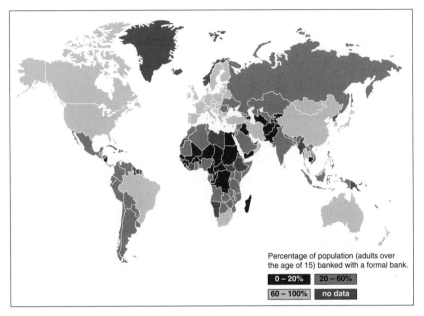

FIGURE 2.5   Financial Inclusion According to Country
Data Source: Demirguc-Kunt, Klapper, Singer and van Oudheusden (2015)

Half of all over 15-year-olds worldwide do not have a bank account, nor do they have access to the financial services of a formal financial institution.

and long-term approach in dealing with recurring risks and consumption smoothing in equal measure. By means of their economic contribution, micro entrepreneurs achieve higher social recognition, which is undoubtedly the source of more self-confidence and security.

Micro-, small- and medium-sized enterprises (MSMEs) are the major employers in many low-pay countries. They equally profit from financial integration. Often the growth of these enterprises is severely limited due to restricted access to capital and savings deposits, mostly as a result of a lack of funds to invest in capital assets or additional work force. With the help of savings deposits, adequate payment transactions and insurance products, businesses can manage their risks more sensibly and profitably.

Financial integration and the development into an integrated, universal financial system positively influence economic growth and contribute towards amending income inequality. On the initiative of the G-20, and their declaration of financial integration as a pressing economic policy, the Global Partnership for Financial Inclusion (GPFI) was set up. The GPFI is the result of the collaboration between the World Bank, the International Finance Corporation (IFC) and the Consultative Group to Assist the Poor (CGAP). Its declared goal is to greatly facilitate access to financial systems worldwide, particularly for segments of the population with a low income.

In many cases, due to soaring transaction costs, people at the bottom of the economic pyramid are beyond consideration as prospective clients for formal financial service providers (see Figure 2.6). The only option left for the poor is to borrow from informal financial service providers such as money lenders or relatives, often at hugely exaggerated interest rates. Numerous micro entrepreneurs are unable to develop their businesses further or improve their living standards as a frequent result of funding difficulties. Microfinance institutions bridge this gap and thereby manage to

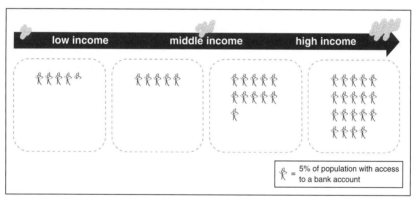

FIGURE 2.6   Access to a Bank Account Depending on Income Class
Data Source: World Bank (2015a)

Worldwide, 91 per cent of the population with a high income have a bank account, but only about 28 per cent of those with a low income have access to a bank account.

reach client groups that are yet to be included into the financial system. Hence, investments in microfinance foster a systematic development of the financial sectors in developing countries. The financial markets in developing countries, however, are still reasonably small in comparison to those in industrialized countries.

The steady increase in new client groups and the competition among MFIs may well lead to a growth rate of these small markets in the near future that will surpass the GDP of the countries in question.[23]

2.5 MARKET PARTICIPANTS

Ultimately, who profits from the concept of microfinance, and are there substantial differences between the different interest groups? The answer is remarkably simple: given professional and transparent conduct, all parties will benefit from microfinance; that is, individual borrowers, women, households, enterprises, microfinance service providers, microfinance vehicles, governments, sponsors and the economy as a whole. The following takes a detailed look at the different interest groups and the way they profit from microfinance.

Individuals and Micro Enterprises

As mentioned above, microfinance provides the poor with loans and access to financial services. This enables them to fund their investments. Savings services, too, are becoming increasingly important, even more so as they allow for wealth building that permits consumption smoothing but also serves as collateral for loans from formal financial services providers. Women experience the strengthening of their roles in the socio-economic framework and are thus better equipped to live autonomous and independent lives. Microfinance also improves access to education and healthcare and improves living standards. Businesses can fund their organic growth and create new employment thanks to microfinance.

MFIs, MIVs and Investors

Microfinance has advanced in record time over the last few years, and the original idea of the microloan has long been overhauled and has grown into the comprehensive microfinance we know today, with a vast range of financial services. The provision of such financial services to poor segments of the population in itself justifies the benefit of microfinance institutions. The collection of clients' savings allows for continuing growth of sustainable MFIs and reduces their dependency on governments, sponsors and loan providers.

MIVs profit from a regular fixed income from interest payments that are generated by loans that flow to MFIs. Investors, too, benefit from the properties of microfinance: their investments in MFIs give them access to an attractive investment class with stable and sustainable returns and, perhaps more importantly, they make an important contribution towards the fight against poverty in the world.

Governments and Sponsors

Local governments and sponsors benefit from microfinance, because the financial means that are generated can be used for further developmental projects. Governments profit on top of this from lower transfer payments and additional tax returns that are generated as a result of higher incomes and business profits. Microfinance boosts the efficiency of the economic system, which in turn has a positive influence on society as a whole.

The Economy

Growth of local microfinance sectors yields a positive influence on the development of any national financial system. Competitive constraints force MFIs into high market efficiency and safeguard their clients' needs sustainably. The mobilization of capital and ensuing investment activity generate growth within the national economy. An increasing number of people find their way out of poverty with the help of microfinance. Their business acumen raises the national income steadily.

2.6 IMPACT INVESTING

For a better understanding of the defined goals in microfinance and its suitable and deserved positioning in the order of the investment universe, impact investment needs to be differentiated from philanthropic and conventional investment (see Figure 2.7). These concepts are often muddled

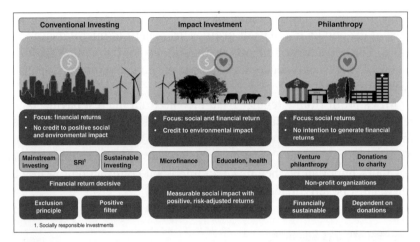

FIGURE 2.7   Differentiation of Impact Investing
Data Source: Impactspace (2014)

> Impact investing is a form of investment that combines conventional investment and philanthropy and yields both social and financial returns.

up and lack a clear-cut distinction with respect to motivation, impact and economic goals. It is of vital importance for investors in particular to know how they differ to avoid any misunderstandings.

Conventional Investments

Traditional investing employs capital in order to achieve a financial return. Social and environmental aspects are not focal points of a conventional investment strategy. Three different forms of investing can be distinguished: mainstream investing comprises all investments in businesses, regardless of their social or environmental impact. Contrary to that, socially neutral investing (SNI) can be divided into two categories: socially responsible investment (SRI) and sustainable investment (SI) (see Figure 2.8). SRI applies an investment filter that excludes investing in

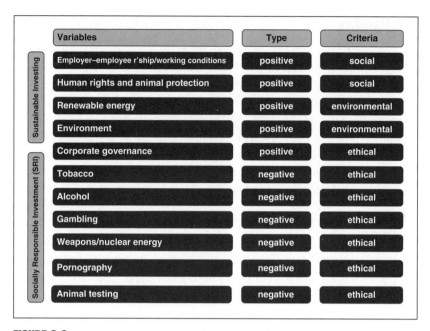

Variables	Type	Criteria
Employer–employee r'ship/working conditions	positive	social
Human rights and animal protection	positive	social
Renewable energy	positive	environmental
Environment	positive	environmental
Corporate governance	positive	ethical
Tobacco	negative	ethical
Alcohol	negative	ethical
Gambling	negative	ethical
Weapons/nuclear energy	negative	ethical
Pornography	negative	ethical
Animal testing	negative	ethical

(Left margin labels: Sustainable Investing; Socially Responsible Investment (SRI))

FIGURE 2.8   Filter for Conventional, Sustainable Investment Decisions
Data Source: Geczy, Stambaugh and Levin (2005); Meyer (2013); Renneboog, Jenke and Zhang (2008); Staub-Bisang (2011)

> Positive and negative filters are applied to identify SI or SRI respectively. The different variables are probed in terms of their social responsibility, environmental impact and ethics.

ethically problematic enterprises; investments in tobacco, alcohol and weapons production or in the gambling industry are consequently not encouraged. Sustainable investing identifies investment decisions with the help of a positive filter. It distinguishes businesses with a sustainable corporate governance that involve social and environmental aspects into their business activities. It considers companies, for instance, that are active in the field of sustainable energy production or with an environmentally friendly and socially responsible production run.

Impact Investing

While conventional and philanthropic forms of investment only consider financial or social impact respectively, impact investing is a combination of both approaches. Impact investing uses capital in order to generate social and environmental results as well as financial returns. The focus may meander between financial and social return.[24] Judging by the growing popularity and steady growth of impact investing, the double bottom line has become a buzzword and well-known concept (see Figure 2.9). Apart from microfinance, impact investing includes topics such as education, health, food security, supply channels and infrastructure.

Philanthropy

Impact investing denotes the socially motivated delivery of financial means with the intention to create a maximum social and environmental return (see Figure 2.10). The financial aspect of such investments fades

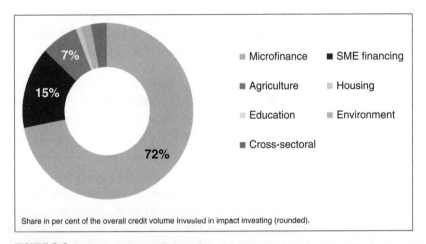

Share in per cent of the overall credit volume invested in impact investing (rounded).

FIGURE 2.9   Topics Impact Investing
Data Source: Forum Nachhaltige Geldanlagen (2015)

Microfinance constitutes the largest share of impact investing (72 per cent), followed by small- and medium-sized enterprise funding (15 per cent) and agriculture (7 per cent).

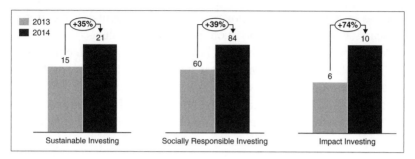

FIGURE 2.10   Growth of Sustainable Investment Strategies (Assets under Management in EUR Billions)
Data Source: Forum Nachhaltige Geldanlagen (2015)

In Germany, Austria and Switzerland, SI strategies have been hugely successful. In 2014, SI, SRI and impact investing have risen by 35, 39 and 74 per cent respectively.

into the background. We differentiate between venture philanthropy and donations to charity. Venture philanthropy has its focus on the funding of socially responsible enterprises that partly or entirely generate their income based on business activities.[25] Charitable donations, however, fund non-profit organizations that depend on those contributions.

2.7   PRELIMINARY CONCLUSIONS

Microfinance is instrumental in the fight against poverty and in fostering financial integration of destitute and low-income segments of society. More narrowly speaking, the concept of microfinance refers to the delivery of financial services to low-income clients who lack the necessary funds for business activities. These financial services comprise the granting of loans, the collection of savings deposits as well as insurance and payment services. Beyond that, many MFIs offer a variety of non-financial services that support microfinance clients' endeavors to establish business activities and more generally offer assistance in coping with day-to-day issues of life. Microfinance substantially contributed towards attaining the MDGs. Thanks to microfinance, major steps have been made over the last few years in the fight against poverty, the improvement of education and healthcare, as well as the socio-economic role of women.

Beyond all this, microfinance is an attractive investment class for investors with a double bottom line: it successfully combines profitability and social commitment. Investors, MIVs and microfinance institutions can generate sustainable and attractive revenues through microfinance. More importantly, however, microfinance encourages autonomy and independence

---

BAKERY – RUDAKI, TAJIKISTAN

Zohir Abdulov, 51, and his wife and children bake and sell bread. To increase his income and create a better life for his family, he launched his business in 2007, thanks to a loan of $2000 with The First MicroFinanceBank (FMFB). With the money, he purchased the necessary ingredients and equipment, and a factory. In 2008, he was granted another loan, this time of $4000, in order to construct an oven and employ additional workers. Today, this considerable productivity boost allows him to sell his bakery products in various quarters of town at a respectable profit.

Source: BlueOrchard

for those at the bottom end of the economic pyramid, by funding their business activities and combatting poverty in the long run.

Microfinance is a combination of conventional and philanthropic forms of investment. It is a fusion of two thus far separately regarded investment disciplines and manages to unite the goals of both approaches – financial return and social wealth – in one unique concept.

NOTES

1 Her Majesty Queen Rania al-Abdullah of Jordan since 1999, Director Emeritus of FINCA International.
2 Menning (1992), p. 661.
3 Hollis and Sweetman (2004), p. 4.
4 Seibel (2003), p. 10–11.
5 Credit cooperatives (Sparkassen), the Raiffeisen Group and people's banks (Volksbanken).
6 In September 2014.
7 Becker (2010), p. 46.
8 Reed, Marsden, Ortega, Rivera and Rogers (2015), p. 8.
9 World Bank (2014).
10 Education services comprise for example literacy programs; healthcare services include the communication and imparting of basic knowledge such as sex education and pregnancy counseling.
11 Ledgerwood (2000), p. 1.
12 Littlefield, Morduch and Hashemi (2003), p. 2.
13 MkNelly and Dunford (1998), p. 2; MkNelly and Dunford (1999), p. 27 and Panjaitan-Drioadisuryo and Cloud (1999), p. 769.
14 Simanowitz and Waters (2002), pp. 20, 23.
15 Khandker (1998), p. 148.
16 Desai, Johnson and Tarozzi (2015), pp. 77–78; Holvoet (2004), p. 30; Khandker (1998), p. 104; Littlefield, Morduch and Hashemi (2003), pp. 4–5.
17 Littlefield, Morduch and Hashemi (2003), p. 7.
18 Ibidem.
19 The Social Performance Task Force (SPTF) is the result of an initiative of the Argidius Foundation, the Ford Foundation and Consultative Group to Assist the Poor (CGAP), a coalition of 34 leading organizations that advocate for financial integration. The SPTF aims to pool the knowledge of different social movements in an effort to make financial services safer and more beneficial for clients. Today, the SPTF counts more than 150 microfinance

networks, rating agencies, financial service providers, sponsors and social investors among its members.

20 Demirguc-Kunt, Klapper, Singer and van Oudheusden (2015), p. 14.
21 Ibidem, pp. 83–84.
22 The Economist Intelligence Unit (2014), p. 20.
23 World Bank (2014).
24 Impactspace (2014).
25 Ibidem.

CHAPTER 3

The Microfinance Value Chain

Give a man a fish, [and] he'll eat for a day. Give a woman micro-credit, [and] she, her husband, her children, and her extended family will eat for a lifetime.[1]

Bono[1]

Highly specialized protagonists along the value chain of microfinance ensure an efficient distribution of the financial means to the various micro entrepreneurs.

Everyone involved, from investor to micro entrepreneur, is subject to supervision or is at least affected by this supervision in one way or another.

3.1   THE PROTAGONISTS AND THEIR TASKS

The microfinance sector has become professionalized over the years, which is amply reflected in the fragmentation of the value chain in highly specialized protagonists. Specialization of the different service providers along the value chain efficiently allocates financial means and at the same time raises the overall quality of the services on each and every level of the value added.

The value chain of microfinance typically consists of four levels (see Figure 3.1). Funds provided by the investors are bundled into fund structures to be supervised by a microfinance administrator. The administrator identifies, analyzes, selects and consequently supervises those MFIs that are the recipients of equity or debt capital. The MFIs in turn are in charge of issuing microloans to their clients and therefore perform all the associated actions.

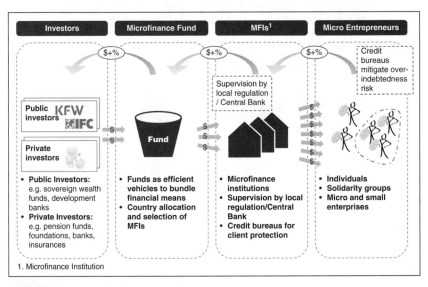

FIGURE 3.1   The Microfinance Value Chain
Source: BlueOrchard Research

Figure 3.1 shows the specialization of the individual protagonists along the value chain and the money flows. Whereas investors provide resources for micro entrepreneurs (indicated by the flow from left to right), interest rates and loan repayments flow from right to left. Thereby investors manage to achieve both a financial and social return.

Investors

Microfinance investors can largely be attributed to two groups. On the one hand there are public investors – mainly development banks such as the World Bank and Germany's Kreditanstalt für Wiederaufbau (KfW) – the recipients of financial funds from individual or several countries. Private investors, on the other hand, are becoming increasingly important. Private investors are large institutional investors such as pension funds, foundations, banks, insurance companies, but also private persons.

Microfinance Funds and Fund Administrators

Mutual funds bundle financial means effectively and provide even investors with considerably small investment volumes with a broad range of diversification. Due to the concentration of equity in a fund structure, for instance, more favorable terms for currency hedging and further transactions may be negotiated, as opposed to each individual investor having to take matters into their own hands. The fund administrator, moreover, ensures professional management of the finances and has the experience to select potential MFIs, invest in them and monitor them. The MFIs in turn benefit from the fact that instead of a multitude of individual investors they have a singular fund as their partner.

Microfinance Institutions

MFIs are the direct and personal points of contact for micro entrepreneurs and therefore bridge the gap between the clients and the funds. They are local financial intermediaries with varying legal structures and they are in charge of micro entrepreneur customer care. As one of their most important tasks, MFIs assess their clients' creditworthiness, grant and supervise loans, manage customer relationships and provide training to micro entrepreneurs.

Micro Entrepreneurs

Micro entrepreneurs are the recipients of microloans and usually are among the poorest of the poor. In general, micro entrepreneurs are granted loans in order to set up their business or expand it. These means are therefore invested in productive activities that secure repayment. This is even more important as these micro entrepreneurs are in most cases unable to provide financial collateral and their ability to repay the loan solely depends on their economic success.

3.2 REGULATORY ENVIRONMENT

The financial industry is strongly regulated, not least because of the international financial crisis that started in the wake of the events in the fall of 2008. Investment in microfinance is by no means an exception. Along the entire value chain each and every protagonist is carefully monitored, be it directly or indirectly. It is a much underrated fact that requires further scrutiny.

On the investor side, regulation differentiates between institutional and individual private investors. Institutional investors such as pension funds are often directly subjected to a regulatory authority that should ensure a meticulous administration and management of the funds entrusted to any given pension fund. When it comes to private investors, however, the regulator takes a more direct approach by supervising the distribution channels of the funds – for instance, banks or independent asset managers. In both cases, client protection is of utmost importance, i.e. investors should only invest within the limits of their personal risk profile. MIVs are readily available in most countries, both for institutional and private investors.[2]

The next level of the value chain – the funds and the fund administrators – is subject to tight supervision as well. Regulation of these entities generally is enforced by the financial markets authority.[3] The regulatory approach is more than evident in the fact that the simple launch of a mutual fund is subject to permit. The regulator must mandatorily grant permission for the launch of a fund and as a rule stipulates rigorous terms and conditions that the funds administrator has to abide by. The fund's management as such is an activity that is subject to permit in most countries and is governed by close and unremitting supervision. Regulatory authorities are particularly strict when it comes to a funds manager's substance. In many cases, specific standards in terms of both quality and quantity have to be obeyed regarding personnel. Furthermore, internal processes have to be sufficiently documented and remuneration systems must often comply with specific standards.

In the value chain of microfinance, MFIs are of great importance. They are the gateway to the client and therefore carry considerable responsibility, a fact that has led to particularly rigid and comprehensive regulation for MFIs. However, tight regulation can also incur considerable costs. Exaggerated regulation may markedly have two significant downsides for micro entrepreneurs. Firstly, regulation of the MFIs raises prices for the clients. Secondly, regulation may constitute an insurmountable challenge when it comes to market entry, which deters new service providers or even obstructs the introduction of new products for the benefit of micro entrepreneurs. This would inevitably lead to less competition among established MFIs and in all likelihood result in rising product costs. In addition to this, MFIs differ considerably in terms of their legal structures and their range of services. A universal approach is therefore hardly beneficial. The regulatory authorities should gauge the costs incurred by regulation and contrast their results with the overall goals of microfinance.[4] Today, international standards have been established that manage to deal with the challenges mentioned above. They principally tackle issues such as investment, minimal capital requirements, capital adequacy, liquidity requirements and customer protection (see Chapter 5.5).

Credit bureaus are another important instrument for credit users and customer protection. They collect information on previously issued loans. Loan offices are present in most significant microfinance markets today. In a first move, the regulator often compiles a loan register. Increasing market maturity, however, will also favor the emergence of private service providers. The information on a loan register typically comprises entries such as the type of loan, maturity, amount of loan and possible instances of late payment or payment default. Private loan offices will also gather information on their clients' payment performance – for instance on the local retail trade or whether their electricity and water bills have been paid. This allows for an even better appraisal of a borrower's creditworthiness (see Chapter 5.5).

3.3 DEVELOPMENT FINANCE INSTITUTIONS

Development Finance Institutions (DFIs) are financial institutions that belong to the realm between public development aid and private investments. DFIs are governmental or semi-governmental organizations and may be of a bilateral or multilateral nature (see Figure 3.2). Bilateral DFIs are governed by a single country. Examples are the German KfW, the Dutch Financierings-Maatschappij voor Ontwikkelingslanden (FMO), the Swiss Investment Fund

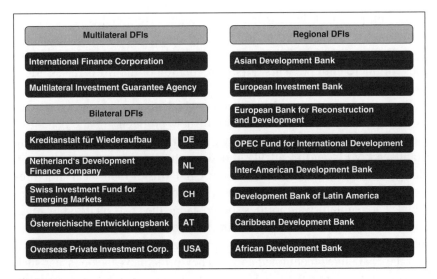

FIGURE 3.2   Selected Development Finance Institutions (DFIs)

There are multilateral, bilateral and regional public DFIs. Bilateral institutions are governed by a singular country and regional institutions are controlled by entire regions. Multilateral DFIs, however, in many cases are disguises of the World Bank.

for Emerging Markets (SIFEM) and the Austrian Development Bank (OeEB). Regional DFIs are communal institutions of several countries of a particular region – for example in Europe the European Bank for Reconstruction and Development (EBRD) or the Asian Development Bank (ADB). There are the multilateral DFIs that are positioned as international organizations. The best known example probably is the International Finance Corporation (IFC) that forms part of the World Bank.[5]

DFIs play a central and influential role in the fight against global issues such as poverty or climate change and are an integral part of the microfinance sector. In many cases, DFIs furnish the means for investments in developing countries. Typically, these are investments that still lack sufficient numbers of private investors, or projects to which private persons have limited access. Their mission, among other goals, is to create an investment environment for commercial investors – all the more reason for DFIs to closely collaborate with private organizations.[6]

DFIs invest in developing countries in three ways:[7]

1. They fund local financial institutions, which in turn finance local micro entrepreneurs and SMEs.
2. They provide funds to specialized private mutual funds to enable them to invest in local projects, businesses and institutions.
3. They invest in local businesses and projects directly.

DFIs go to great lengths to avoid direct competition with private investors. For this reason, their funding usually is not free of charge, but should yield a financial return. In some cases, DFIs manage to profit from their first mover advantage and create attractive returns. Those proceeds, however, are seldom distributed but generally reinvested in new projects.

As explained above, DFIs are weighty investors of specialized microfinance funds. Moreover, DFIs also invest directly in individual MFIs. Private investors thereby have the possibility to invest hand in hand with DFIs and in this manner profit from a risk-sharing mechanism.[8]

Beyond their basic funding services, DFIs often also provide services and equipment for technical assistance (TA). These services provide a comprehensive approach in a bid to further local institutions. TA might mean that an MFI may choose to make use of a DFI's consultancy services in matters concerning product development or design and improvement of business activities. In return, an MFI will usually in reasonable measure share responsibility for the costs incurred.[9]

Alongside development institutions, an increasing number of local governmental institutions have been known to position themselves on the market to improve the geopolitical stability of their region. Microfinance profits from the proximity to lenders of capital that such models provide, and by means of this, new paths open for further development in these countries.

3.4 MARKET OVERVIEW

The turn of the millennium has seen an ever-increasing emergence of impact investment funds and thereby a surge of fund administrators and consultants (see Figure 3.3).

A look at assets under management (AUM) reveals a significantly concentrated market. Figure 3.4 illustrates the share of microfinance fund managers in the total microfinance portfolio worldwide. The three largest fund providers manage 43 per cent of all AUM in microfinance. The five

Manager / Advisor	Inception	Head Office	
BlueOrchard Finance	2001	Geneva	CH
Cyrano	2000	Lima	PE
Developing World Markets	2003	Stamford, Connecticut	US
Finance in Motion	2009	Frankfurt	DE
Incofin	2003	Antwerp	BE
Oikocredit	1975	Amersfoort	NL
ResponsAbility	2003	Zurich	CH
Symbiotics	2004	Geneva	CH
Triodos	2000	Zeist	NL
Triple Jump	2006	Amsterdam	NL

FIGURE 3.3 Selected Managers of Microfinance Investment Vehicles

Most MIV managers were established at the beginning of this century.

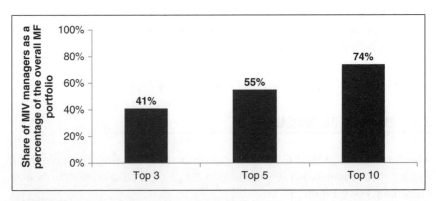

FIGURE 3.4 Concentration of MIV Managers
Data Source: Symbiotics (2015)

The three largest fund managers or advisors manage 41 per cent of all AUM in microfinance. The five largest alone constitute more than 50 per cent, and the ten largest MIV managers have a combined market share of almost 80 per cent.

largest alone constitute more than 50 per cent, and the ten largest MIV administrators have a combined market share of almost 80 per cent.

With providers such as BlueOrchard Finance, ResponsAbility and Symbiotics, Switzerland has more than one string to its bow in the field of impact investing. More than 30 per cent of all assets allocated in impact investing worldwide are either managed from Switzerland or monitored in an advisory capacity respectively (see Figure 3.5). Beyond Switzerland, another microfinance market has established itself in the tri-border area between Germany (Finance in Motion), the Netherlands (Oikocredit, Triodos, Triple Jump) and Belgium (Incofin).

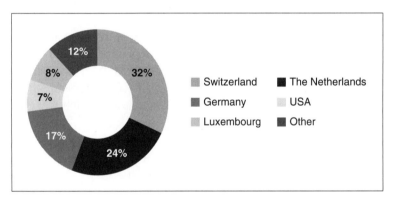

FIGURE 3.5 Managed AUM in Microfinance, According to Location of MIV Administrators
Data Source: Symbiotics (2015)

With BlueOrchard, ResponsAbility and Symbiotics, Switzerland is prominently represented in the field of impact investing. Further fund managers and advisors are located in the Netherlands, Germany, Luxembourg and the United States. More than 30 per cent of all assets allocated in impact investing worldwide are either managed from Switzerland or monitored in an advisory capacity respectively.

3.5   GENEVA: BIRTHPLACE OF MODERN MICROFINANCE

In Geneva in the late 1990s, the vision of a microfinance fund was born. The breeding ground for such productive thoughts was generated by the innovative partnership of the United Nations (UN), the United Nations Conference on Trade and Development (UNCTAD) and the private banking sector.

Circumstances

The exceptional circumstances in Geneva make the city a laboratory of sustainable economy. What are the reasons for this?[10]

1. Geneva is one of the most competitive financial centers in the world and a leader in the realm of transnational asset management. With its more than 200 years of tradition and history, the Geneva financial sector is renowned for asset management and its range of personalized services (see Figure 3.6).
2. The UN has their second subsidiary headquarters in Geneva, which has had its appeal for international organizations and non-governmental organizations (NGOs) for over a century.[11] Today, more than 30 influential international organizations have their headquarters in Geneva, not to forget the over 400 NGOs that advise the UN (see Figure 3.7).

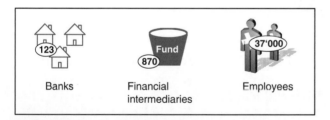

| Banks | Financial intermediaries | Employees |

FIGURE 3.6   Geneva Financial Center
Data Source: Sustainable Finance Geneva (2014)

Geneva's financial center comprises 123 banks and 870 financial intermediaries, with a total of 37,000 employees.

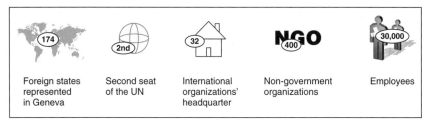

| Foreign states represented in Geneva | Second seat of the UN | International organizations' headquarter | Non-government organizations | Employees |

FIGURE 3.7 International Geneva
Data Source: Sustainable Finance Geneva (2014)

In Geneva, 174 nations are represented. The city is the second seat of the UN, and 32 further international organizations have their headquarters there. In addition, more than 400 NGOs operate in Geneva, and with them the 30,000 employees that work in these international organizations.

3. Switzerland is known as the epitome of innovation and has been leading the global innovation rankings for years. Such innovative spirit has propelled Switzerland to acquire a singular level of expertise in fields such as industry, biotechnology and in the financial sector – a knowledge that is travelling across the globe.

The fusion of two worlds – financial economy and international development – combined with the Swiss innovative spirit, makes Geneva a unique breeding ground and workshop of financial economy. For this reason, in Geneva many sustainable financial products, concepts and instruments of global relevance were conceived.

Switzerland counts 200 organizations that are actively involved in the sustainable financial economy (owners of capital, asset managers, investment specialists and so on). Moreover, the first global indexes for stocks of sustainable businesses (Dow Jones Sustainability Index – DJSI) and for microfinance (SMX – Symbiotics Microfinance Index) – used worldwide as reference indexes today – both have their origin in Switzerland.

The Emergence of Microfinance as an Asset Class

Geneva owes its role as a global leader to the cooperation of several specialized UN agencies with visionary private bankers – notably the International Labour Organization (ILO) and UNCTAD.

In 1997, the UN General Assembly decided to make 2005 the year of microcredit. As a result of this decision, the UNCTAD microcredit unit began its work on several projects in Geneva, with the aim of increasing transparency in the sector and fostering private financing for microfinance. The first milestone was set in 1998 with the introduction of the Dexia Microcredit Fund. The year 2000 saw the launch of a virtual microfinance market and a microfinance information platform devised by Infobahn, a Geneva-based IT company. A year later, the fund manager BlueOrchard was founded in Geneva. With the approach of the year of microcredit, BlueOrchard managed to raise an increasing amount of funds for its very first fund, mainly with the help of various Geneva-based asset managers and the structuring of a product by J.P. Morgan in New York, for which the US government acted as a guarantor.

These successes amply proved to the world that the combination of commercial financial economy and aid for poor segments of the population could indeed be a winning formula. In the following years, other Swiss fund managers established themselves alongside BlueOrchard. Their unique knowledge allows them to assume a leading position on the global microfinance market. In 2003, the company ResponsAbility was founded in Zurich, and a year later Symbiotics was launched in Geneva.

With its commitment to human rights and peace, Geneva has forged an impeccable international reputation for itself. Organizations such as the World Trade Organization (WTO), UNCTAD and the United Nations Environment Programme (UNEP) are a reservoir of the condensed knowledge of experts in both economy and finance.

The United Nations Finance Initiative (UNEP FI) was launched in the wake of the United Nations Conference on Environment and Development in Rio de Janeiro in 1992. The foundation of this specific initiative within UNEP relies on the significant role of the financial economy for the promotion of sustainable development. Banks and capital markets, which finance the economy, have the power as well as the responsibility to foster economically sustainable models. UNEP FI is a public–private partnership that aims to integrate the financial aspects of sustainable and social topics into financial institutions. One of its most impressive achievements is the introduction of the United Nations Principles for Responsible Investment (UN PRI or PRI for short). The UN General Secretary at the time, Kofi Annan, launched the initiative in 2005. UNEP FI and UN Global Compact – which argues the case for sustainable and ethical corporate governance – synchronize their development. Financial institutions that ratify the six

PRIs commit themselves to the common good of society. This was a truly extraordinary feat of ingenuity on the part of the UN and Geneva.

The PRIs have been a success story. To this day, more than 1300 asset managers and professional service providers have ratified them.[12] They thereby pledge to document their development for increased sustainability and to integrate the principles of sustainable investment into their daily business. The PRIs are set to permeate the entire industry.

The UNEP FI also cooperates with other institutions for synergy effects; for instance, the collaboration with the World Business Council for Sustainable Development (WBCSD), an association of companies committed to mutual topics in connection with sustainable development, or their cooperation with the World Economic Forum (WEF), the advocate of sustainability in economic, environmental and health policy worldwide.

The UN PRIs are one of the most significant initiatives for sustainability in the financial sector. Their top-down approach increases awareness in terms of sustainability in the financial sector on a large scale (see Figure 3.8). At the same time, national and local initiatives complement the large institutional PRI projects (bottom-up approach). The advantages are evident: more freedom of speech, more rapid responsiveness and more impact, thanks to their proximity to low-income segments of the population.

In 2008, 15 specialists pooled their energies and launched Sustainable Finance Geneva (SFG), a platform that allows interest groups to meet and exchange. Non-profit SFG fosters innovation and development in a sustainable financial economy. Its goal is to unite under one roof a multitude of personalities and collect a wealth of experience from fields such as asset

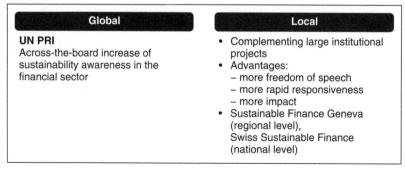

FIGURE 3.8 Sustainability Initiatives in the Financial Sector

management, fund management, microfinance, international organizations, as well as environmental, social and governance (ESG) criteria and philanthropy. SFG was developed with local organizations, such as the Genevan authorities and the Genève Place Financière, in order to further establish and continue to advertise Geneva and Switzerland as the number one sustainable center of the financial economy. SFG focuses on a regular exchange of information and conducts studies, but at the same time organizes numerous conferences and discussions with national and international experts.

The launching of the Swiss Sustainable Finance (SSF) platform in Zurich in 2014 hails a project on a national level. SSF aims at positioning and representing the topic nationally, for instance in dealing with various federal authorities. SFG is a networking partner of SSF. Both organizations collaborate closely and coordinate their activities.

3.6 PRELIMINARY CONCLUSIONS

Knowledge of the protagonists, and more importantly their roles along the value chain, is indispensable for a thorough understanding of microfinance. Their highly specialized activities lead to a bundling of financial means that in turn allow micro entrepreneurs to have access to valuable capital.

Investors provide microfinance funds with financial resources that fund managers or advisors invest in selected microfinance institutions. By doing so, MFIs can issue microloans to their clients.

More than a third of the funds invested in the entire microfinance sector are being managed from Switzerland. The three largest fund providers manage more than 40 per cent of the total AUM in microfinance. The vision to launch a microfinance fund was generated in Geneva, in the late 1990s. Geneva is one of the most competitive finance centers in the world and boasts a high presence of international organizations and NGOs. The close cooperation of these organizations with the financial sector, as well as the wealth of innovative force in Switzerland, make Geneva a laboratory for international financial economy. The center of the United Nations for sustainable financial economy in Geneva led to the foundation of the UN PRI, an admirably successful initiative established in the name of sustainability and responsibility in the financial sector.

RUNNING A KIOSK – MALOLOS, THE PHILIPPINES

Myrna Borota, 33, lives in Malolos. In 2002, she opened a small kiosk to generate an income alongside her husband's. She used her 13th loan of $1800 to expand her business and purchase goods. Some of her loans have been consumer credits that she used to acquire her house and a computer. The acquisition of a photocopier is a natural part of her continuing business expansion. Mrs. Borota now chiefly invests her sustainably generated income in the education of her children and their household.

Source: BlueOrchard

NOTES

1 Bono, singer and philanthropist.
2 Basel Committee on Banking Supervision (2015).
3 The Swiss Financial Market Supervisory Authority (FINMA) is the Swiss government body responsible for financial regulation.
4 Christen, Lauer, Lyman and Rosenberg (2012), pp. 8–9; Basel Committee on Banking Supervision (2010).

5 Dickinson (2012).
6 Massa and te Velde (2011), pp. 1–4.
7 Griffith and Evans (2012), p. 1.
8 See Chapter 10 "Investing in Microfinance".
9 See Chapter 8.5 "Technical Assistance".
10 Sustainable Finance Geneva (2014).
11 The headquarters of the United Nations are in New York City.
12 In January 2015.

CHAPTER 4
Micro Entrepreneurs

Small loans can transform lives, especially the lives of women and children. The poor can become empowered instead of disenfranchised. Homes can be built, jobs can be created, businesses can be launched, and individuals can feel a sense of worth again.

Natalie Portman[1]

The average micro entrepreneur has a low income that is generated from a self-employed activity in either craft or agriculture. Overcoming poverty raises fundamental needs such as education, health and consumption, which may all be satisfied with an extended MFI loan portfolio.

Most micro entrepreneurs live in regions such as Asia Pacific and Latin America. In many cases they operate a small business or work in agriculture.

4.1 DEFINITION

The most important protagonists in microfinance are the micro entrepreneurs, ultimately the recipients of an investor's capital. The effects of these funds on micro entrepreneurs are the very core of microfinance. What needs do these micro entrepreneurs have, and how can microfinance help to meet them? In which geographical regions do micro entrepreneurs live and in what industries are they active?

Micro entrepreneurs are the clients in microfinance. Without microfinance they would have no access to capital. The rural population in developing countries in particular is largely excluded from the financial system. The typical micro entrepreneur has a low income that is generated from a

Example of a Borrower: Noemi Marizano, the Philippines

Country: the Philippines
Sector: agriculture – rice cultivation
Number of loans: 2

Noemi Marizano, 42, has seven children. While one of her children has already entered into employment, her other six are still going to school. Mrs. Marizano is cultivating rice on a plot of land that she has inherited from her parents. She harvests twice a year. During the harvest season, other rice farmers support her.

Number of loans

1. Mrs. Marizano's first loan in 2005 was around 4500 Philippine Pesos ($100) and she used it as business capital for the purchase of fertilizer and other agricultural products.
2. Later she took a second loan of 18,000 Pesos ($400) to acquire a motorcycle for her husband's taxi business. By doing so, she created the basis for an additional family income.

The impact of microfinance

Making use of the microfinance services of the LifeBank foundations enabled Mrs. Marizano and her family to set up their business activities, expand them and increase their turnover and returns in a sustainable manner. Today, the family can fund their children's education and manages to satisfy elementary and individual needs at the same time.

Source: BlueOrchard Research

self-employed activity in either craft or agriculture. In order to sell their handiwork or agricultural product, they often operate small businesses or market stalls.[2]

Over the last few years, the microfinance sector has been professionalized. The breadth and quality of the products and services that are being offered by MFIs amply document this fact. Earlier models were designed to continuously increase the supply of microloans. The volume of loans may still be central; however, it has become increasingly evident that efficient financial services for poorer segments of the population must be tailored to the market and its clients to meet their needs.[3] A better understanding of the needs of the target group will inevitably lead to a more customized range of products. Micro entrepreneurs do not just want to take out loans, they want to save a part of their earnings or they may need special financial support for their children's education or their family's health.

4.2 NEEDS AND REQUIREMENTS

To best meet the needs of micro entrepreneurs, clients are segmented according to their economic circumstances. Demands within these different poverty levels vary and they therefore require different products and services. The following describes the different poverty levels and discusses the needs of micro entrepreneurs on their way out of poverty. With a second, third or further loan for education, health matters and consumption, successful micro entrepreneurs can send their children to school, make provisions against illness and smooth out their consumption.

Poverty Levels

Poverty has many faces and far-reaching consequences. Low-income parts of the population suffer from lack of food, lack of access to clean water and a lack of accommodation. Economically, they may be struck by unemployment, underemployment or exploitation of labor. Distressingly, people who cannot satisfy their most basic needs feel socially underprivileged and humiliated – a condition in which they incapacitate themselves both socially and politically. For this reason, many people afflicted by poverty frequently suffer from physical, mental and emotional disorders, have limited skills and a low level of education, which often goes hand in hand with feelings of self-consciousness and low self-esteem. The term "poor" is rather nondescript and includes all the aforementioned segments of the population. Yet there are significant differences within these segments of the population that need to be taken into consideration. There are the poor whose elementary needs are not at all or only partly satisfied – be it as a result of a food deficit or insufficient access to water – and whose income is barely enough to cover the loans they have taken. These people differ substantially from the poor who own minimal property – for instance a plot of land or real estate – and who either have a regular occupation or run a micro business. In many cases, the second group has successfully managed to raise themselves above the first group. Poverty as such does therefore not exclusively refer to a low income but rather denotes the fact that elemental needs cannot be met.[4]

We distinguish between three poverty levels – extreme or abject poverty, moderate poverty and economically active poverty (see Figure 4.1).[5]

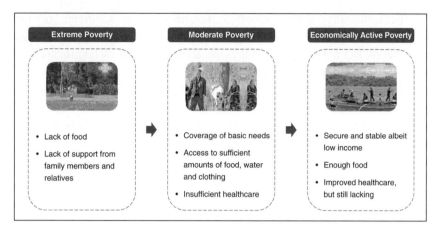

FIGURE 4.1 Poverty Levels

There are three poverty levels: extreme or abject poverty, moderate poverty and economically active poverty.

The World Bank attributes the term "extreme poverty" to segments of the population that live on less than $1.9 a day, which is below the breadline.[6] Extreme poverty describes those segments of the population that:

- Are either unemployed or underemployed and whose remuneration is so low that their spending capacity is insufficient to cover their daily caloric requirement
- Live in resource-poor regions
- Are either too young or too old to work
- Are too frail to work
- Have no prospect of employment because of their ethnicity, gender or political views
- Are fleeing from catastrophes that are caused by man or nature or
- Have neither property nor family members or relatives to support them.

The term "moderate poverty" refers to segments of the population that have an income that just suffices to cover elementary needs.[7] Basic requirements such as food, water, clothing and accommodation can therefore be fulfilled. However, they cannot provide for healthcare at this stage.

"Economically active poverty" describes those segments of the population that have a stable and secure income which allows for enough food, keeps sickness at bay, secures an adequate form of healthcare and allows for asset accumulation.[8]

The distinction of the different poverty levels is not conclusive. Households may change levels at any given time, e.g. when a qualified person has no employment for a while, or when the living standards of a particular household improve. Gender-related differences may be an issue too, as women often do not have the opportunity to acquire certain skills or pursue a particular profession. This may lead to discrepancies in poverty levels between men and women living under the same roof. Individuals with an occupation often remain on a lower poverty level because their income barely covers their basic requirements.[9]

And yet, from the point of microfinance, the distinction between extreme, moderate and economically active poverty is a useful tool. This differentiation allows for a factual assessment of the needs of the different segments of the population and paves the way for a sustainable availability of products and services. In commercial microfinance this distinction in terms of client structure facilitates the categorization of clients into those eligible or perhaps less eligible for a loan. The category of the economically active poor thereby refers to people on a low to slightly higher income. In this group there is a high demand for financial services that go beyond a microloan.

Requirements of Micro Entrepreneurs

Microfinance is a tool in the fight against poverty and improves the living standards of the low-income population in developing countries.[10] The escape from poverty is synonymous with a transition of the aforementioned poverty levels. The requirements of the different poverty levels are displayed in Maslow's hierarchy of needs. The hierarchy refers to an individual's survival, identity and self-actualization.[11]

Figure 4.2 merges Maslow's hierarchy of needs with the different poverty levels. The hierarchy, or pyramid in this case, comprises five levels. The first level refers to the physiological needs, elementary requirements such as food, water and air that need to be satisfied first. The second level represents an individual's need for security. Despite the fact that physical security takes priority, this category also displays economic security and stability in the wider sense, e.g. financial security, stable employment

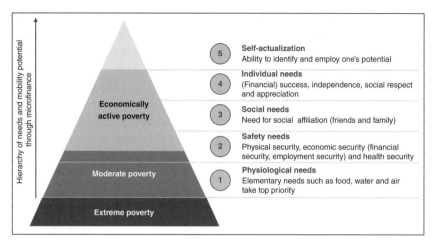

FIGURE 4.2   Poverty Levels and Maslow's Hierarchy of Needs
Data Source: Maslow (1943); World Bank (2014)

Maslow's hierarchy of needs displays an individual's needs, in ascending hierarchy (scale on the right-hand side). The poverty levels as defined by the World Bank are placed on top of the hierarchy of needs: extreme poverty, moderate poverty and economically active poverty. Microfinance service providers must tailor their services to the poverty levels in order to meet the different needs in a more satisfying manner.

and protection from illnesses. The third level reveals an individual's need for social affiliation (friends and family). Theoretically, this need is only generated when the first two categories have been largely satisfied. Such a rigid view, however, fails to do the different poverty levels justice. Social and societal exclusion often go hand in hand with extreme poverty, independently of the fulfillment of an individual's elementary needs. The second but last level on the pyramid displays an individual's need for success, independence and social appreciation. Finally, self-actualization is at the very top of the pyramid. It refers to an individual's ability to identify and consequently employ his or her own potential.

Merging the different levels of need and poverty reveals that the range of products in microfinance is crucial. The extremely poor are unable to meet their elemental health requirements. These segments of the population will benefit from their loans for the best possible start of their business activities that will cover most elemental needs such as food and water. In most cases, it is their first microloan. Although the moderately poor manage to satisfy their elemental needs, they do not have any economic security such as perhaps a stable employment, nor can they rely on adequate healthcare. Many on this level are on their second or third microloan. The economically active poor have already progressed to the upper levels of the hierarchy of needs and therefore are more likely to demand a wider range of services. These individuals are highly likely to have taken out microloans before, and successfully used them for business activities. Microfinance encourages individuals to rise within the hierarchy of needs by providing an adequate range of loans and further financial services. A tailored and client-oriented approach fosters this upward mobility and therefore constitutes an integral part of microfinance.[12]

Broader Range of Loans

A change in living standards inevitably leads to a shift in the needs of microfinance clients. The social and particularly the individual requirements go far beyond the traditional conceptions of microloans. As loans for education, healthcare and consumption do not primarily serve to generate income, they are limited to micro entrepreneurs with a stable income. Loans for healthcare lend themselves to any level of poverty. Education loans are only issued above a certain level of income, and consumer loans demand a stable income and business activity. Healthcare loans are particularly important for the extreme poor, because in the event of illness they are usually unable to work and consequently lose their remunerations. If they fail to repay a loan that has been taken for their business activities, any subsequent loan application will be rejected and severely hamper their rise in the hierarchy. An accommodation loan in times of illness, however, may restore their health and in turn secure repayment.

Quite often, micro entrepreneurs will invest their generated income in their children's education. The children of MFI clients are thus more likely to partake in an educational program than those of other low-income families. There also is a much lower risk that they will leave school prematurely.[13] Long-term and sustainable investments in education ensure that following generations can continue this upward mobility in the social hierarchy and that their acquired skills will allow them to generate a secure income and achieve economic stability. A rise in living standards will trigger the need for specific educational services in addition to the traditional types of loans – namely literacy programs and business development services. Training programs that provide basic economic and entrepreneurial knowledge promote local business networks to the benefit of micro businesses in their bid to position their business and develop it sustainably.

Bad health and insufficient access to the health system are both the cause and effect of poverty. For one thing, inadequate healthcare triggers a disproportionately high prevalence of illnesses in poorer regions. At the same time, the costs in connection with illness are soaring, and they involve the risk of further impoverishment. A bad state of health has a detrimental effect on a micro entrepreneur's productivity and severely compromises business development. Healthcare loans are an affordable and comfortable means of raising capital that offers protection against risks associated with illness.

As healthcare loans are not used to generate income, they bear certain risks for MFIs. Yet, inadequate healthcare in many cases leads to insolvency and subsequent exclusion from microfinance programs. Some micro entrepreneurs are known to have resigned due to illness, which has a negative effect on the repayment quota of traditional microloans.[14] In the world, an estimated 100 million people are forced below the poverty line as a consequence of significant and unexpected healthcare expenditures. The complex microfinance insurance products are not yet sophisticated enough. Healthcare loans thus present a viable option in a micro entrepreneur's attempt to avoid sinking into poverty and to reduce the business risk of MFIs.[15]

Consumer loans widen the range of products of MFIs. Ultimately, consumer loans aim to smooth out a client's cash flows, particularly because quite apart from their daily expenses, many households face substantial expenditures such as weddings, funerals and other exceptional situations. Requirements such as these are normally met by savings or intakes from business activities. Consumer loans, however, also satisfy individual needs and therefore go beyond the satisfaction of purely elementary requirements. There may be a demand for these loans, yet they are not offered by default, as many MFIs assess a client's debt capacity based on the cash flow generated by their microbusiness activity. Where no consumer loans are offered, business loans often take their place and are utilized for consumption purposes. The rising demand for consumer loans especially with economically active segments of the population,

Example of a Borrower: Maria Gutierrez, Peru

Country: Peru
Sector: small trade & business
Number of loans: 4

Maria Gutierrez, 69, lives with her husband Roberto and their ten children in a suburb of Lima. She has been a client of the MFI Edyficar for many years. She has been running a vegetable stall in San Gregorio market for 21 years. Her multiple loans have allowed her to steadily expand her business.

Number of loans

1. With her first loan of 1000 Peruvian Sol (approx. $360), Mrs. Gutierrez expanded her market stall and range of products.
2. She used her second loan of 1800 Sol (approx. $590) as further business capital and for the funding of her daughter's studies.
3. With her third loan of 3000 Sol (approx. $1000) she paid for the construction of a roof, an extension of her family home, and purchased some furniture.
4. With the surplus income generated from her business and a fourth loan of 7000 Sol (approx. $2500), she financed the repairs on her minibus that her husband uses for commercial purposes.

The impact of microfinance

Mrs. Gutierrez managed to set up a sustainable business with her very first loan. Her revenues amount to roughly $2500 a month, which is equivalent to a monthly profit of $500. Thanks to microfinance, she is not only setting up a successful business, but is able to finance her children's education and afford additional comfort for her residential house. Repairing the minibus means that her husband can offer public transport services into their neighborhood. It is an expansion of the family business into a new sector.

Source: BlueOrchard Research

however, also demonstrates that MFIs are indeed steadily developing their range of products and services.

4.3 MICRO ENTREPRENEURS

The number of MFI clients has risen rapidly over the last few years. Compared to ten years ago, clients who request the financial and non-financial services of microfinance have multiplied by around five. The success of this concept not only manifests itself in the rising number of clients, but in the proportion of people who have escaped poverty. When the MDGs were formulated in 2000, they stipulated that there were still two billion people living on less than $1.9 a day. Almost 20 years later, this figure has been reduced by half.[16] Financial integration empowers people to cast off the shackles of poverty and to operate and finance their business activities sustainably.

Regions

Over the last few years, microfinance has outgrown its idea as a local tool in the fight against poverty and has transformed into a global phenomenon with the aim of financially including all low-income segments of the population. Figure 4.3 shows the countries with the highest proportion of those living in poverty, with 30 per cent of the poorest of the poor living in India, 10 per cent in Nigeria and 8 per cent in China. Strikingly enough, particularly Asian and African countries seem to be afflicted most by poverty.

Example of a Borrower: Dogsom Tseden, Mongolia

Country: Mongolia
Sector: agriculture
Number of loans: 2

Dogsom Tseden, 42, and his mother live in Birvaa, near Ulan Bator in Mongolia. His mother supports him in his work as a cattle breeder. Mr. Tseden has a wife and three children, who all go to school. He was working as a veterinarian for more than 18 years. In 1999, he decided to start breeding cattle. He initiated his business activity with a stock of six cows.

Number of loans

1. He took his first loan of 1.2 million Mongolian Tugrik (approx. $825) with XAC Bank and bought additional cows for his herd.
2. Shortly after, the raised proceeds from his cattle breeding allowed him to take a second loan of 2.7 million Mongolian Tugrik (approx. $1900) for the purchase of yet more cattle for his herd.

The impact of microfinance

With the help of microfinance, Mr. Tseden has been able to increase his stock from 6 to 45 cows. Most of his proceeds are generated from the sale of milk and cheese to the region. He has plans to further expand his business. Microfinance empowers him to successfully operate a business that can satisfy his elementary requirements and finance his children's education at the same time.

Source: BlueOrchard Research

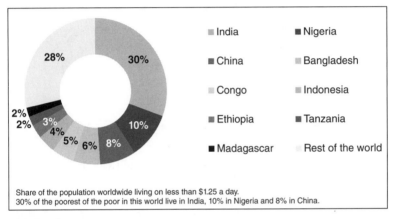

Share of the population worldwide living on less than $1.25 a day.
30% of the poorest of the poor in this world live in India, 10% in Nigeria and 8% in China.

FIGURE 4.3 Countries with the Highest Proportion of Poor People Worldwide
Data Source: World Bank (2016), database 2012

Figure 4.3 displays the share of the population worldwide living on less than $1.25 a day, with 30 per cent of the poorest of the poor living in India, 10 per cent in Nigeria and 8 per cent in China.

A look at the geographic distribution of the number of active borrowers (see Figure 4.4) reveals that more than half are from the Asia Pacific region (median), 11 per cent are in Latin America and the Caribbean,

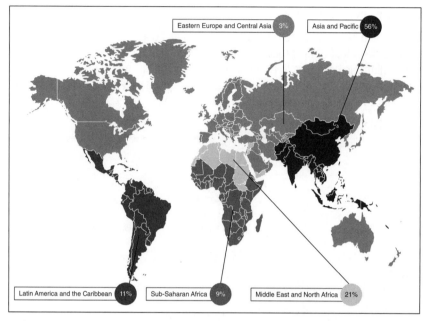

FIGURE 4.4 Percentage of Active Borrowers, According to Region
Data Source: MIX (2016), database 2014

Decoding client structure according to regions reveals that more than half of all clients come from the Asia and Pacific region (median), 21 per cent live in the Middle East and North Africa, 11 per cent in Latin America and the Caribbean, 9 per cent in Sub-Saharan Africa and 3 per cent in Eastern Europe and Central Asia.

30 per cent in Sub-Saharan Africa, the Middle East and North Africa. A total of 3 per cent of the active borrowers worldwide live in Eastern Europe and Central Asia.[17] Comparing these results with those of Figure 4.3, it becomes evident that in the future, microfinance programs have to be promoted much more effectively to reach the poorest of the poor, not just in Asia but particularly in Sub-Saharan Africa.

Figure 4.5 demonstrates that at $194 and $292 respectively, the poorest regions such as South Asia and Eastern Asia and Pacific have the lowest average loan (median). In more progressed microfinance markets such as

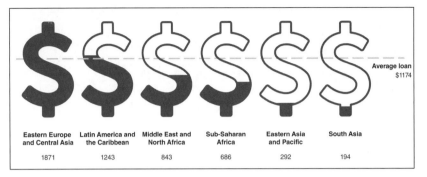

FIGURE 4.5 Average Loan Balance Per Borrower According to Region
Data Source: MIX (2016), database 2014

The average loan for all the regions is $1174 (median). The most substantial loans are granted in Eastern Europe and Central Asia ($1871), the lowest in South Asia ($194).

Latin America and the Caribbean, as well as Eastern Europe and Central Asia, the average loan is considerably higher at $1243 or $1871 respectively. The average microloan for all regions is at $1174.

Gender

In the microfinance industry more loans are granted to women than men on average (see Figure 4.6). In South Asia, an average of 99 per cent of loans were handed out to women. Distinctly, in regions such as Eastern Asia and Pacific, Latin America and the Caribbean, the Middle East and in North Africa as well as Sub-Saharan Africa, more than half of all loans are issued to women. Eastern Europe and Central Asia are the only exceptions, with the share of women dropping below the 50 per cent mark. Why women and not men constitute the larger target group of MFIs will be explained in Chapter 6.

Industries

The business activities of microfinance clients feature in different economic sectors and vary in terms of required capital resources and services. To an MFI, the distinction between rural and urban clients is central. The decision

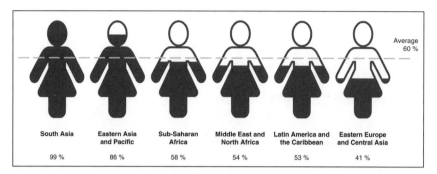

FIGURE 4.6   Percentage of Female Borrowers, According to Regions
Data Source: MIX (2016), database 2014

South Asia issues the largest number of loans to women by far (roughly 100 per cent, median). In Eastern Europe and Central Asia, however, only 41 per cent of loans go to women. In all the other regions, more than half of all the loans are handed out to women.

to serve the one or the other client group is decisive in their product development. If the sector is subject to a negative economic development, both microfinance clients and MFIs face a considerable business risk. Typical micro enterprises in urban regions are often part of the small trade and small businesses. They offer a specific product for the local trade or offer their services in one form or other. Micro entrepreneurs in rural regions mostly engage in agricultural activities, as well as in cattle farming, fishing or craft.

Figure 4.7 displays the share of the different sectors of the volume of credit of several MFIs into which a BlueOrchard managed fund has been invested: 32 per cent of this volume of credit flows to micro entrepreneurs that engage in trade, 28 per cent goes to agricultural enterprises, 21 per cent to service providers, 6 per cent flows to social housing and 5 per cent to industry. The majority of all loans are issued to the trade business because demand for business capital and the exchange of goods is particularly high. The agriculture and services sectors also demand high capital investments (cattle stock, localities and so on) that are mostly covered by external funding.

Balance Sheet of a Micro Enterprise

The balance sheet of a micro entrepreneur in Bangladesh (see Figure 4.8) clearly shows that people in developing countries lend money to one

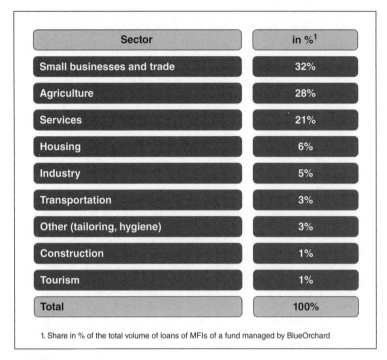

Sector	in %[1]
Small businesses and trade	32%
Agriculture	28%
Services	21%
Housing	6%
Industry	5%
Transportation	3%
Other (tailoring, hygiene)	3%
Construction	1%
Tourism	1%
Total	100%

1. Share in % of the total volume of loans of MFIs of a fund managed by BlueOrchard

FIGURE 4.7 BlueOrchard: Volume of Loan According to Sector
Data Source: BlueOrchard Research

another and take custody of each other's savings. Savings deposits and pensions (e.g. life insurances) are of great importance.

Assets		Balance Sheet	Liabilities	
Savings account	20	Microloan	100
Savings in custody	10	Private, interest-free loan	15
Savings at home	5	Wage advance	10
Life insurance	85	Savings of others	15
Money transfers to home country	10	Business owner loan	20
Loan	40	Rental arrears	10
Cash	5	Debt capital	170
Capital assets	175	Equity	5

FIGURE 4.8 Balance Sheet of a Micro Enterprise in Bangladesh (in $)
Data Source: Collins, Morduch, Rutherford and Ruthven (2009), p. 9

As an example, the balance sheet of a microfinance enterprise in Bangladesh reveals that people lend money to each other and also give custody to other people's financial means. A form of security such as a life insurance is of utmost importance. Micro entrepreneurs also put great emphasis on their savings.

Example of a Borrower: Saroam Toum, Cambodia

Most micro entrepreneurs come from the regions Asia Pacific (more than half of all borrowers) or Latin America and the Caribbean (approximately a tenth of all borrowers). The average credit volume received is $1174 and active borrowers are mostly females. The largest volume of loans is issued to micro entrepreneurs that engage in small businesses and trade as well as agriculture. For micro entrepreneurs it is vital to keep their savings and lend to each other. Other securities, such as life insurance, are of utmost importance.

Source: BlueOrchard Research

4.4 PRELIMINARY CONCLUSIONS

There are essentially three poverty levels: extreme, moderate and economically active poverty. The extremely poor fail to even satisfy their most elementary requirements. The financial means of the moderately poor only just cover basic needs and rudimentary healthcare. Economically active segments of the poor population have enough food and better healthcare. Aligned and adequate microfinance services allow and promote upward mobility within the different poverty levels. Micro entrepreneurs can satisfy their respective needs with the help of their business activities to elevate themselves from poverty, step by step.

A target-oriented satisfaction of needs is a key aspect in microfinance. It comprises a steadily growing range of financial services that include – among traditional microloans – loans for education, healthcare and consumption.

Most micro entrepreneurs have low income that is generated from a self-employed activity in either craft or agriculture. Geographical provenance and economic activity are further decisive factors.

Most micro entrepreneurs come from the regions Asia Pacific (two thirds of all borrowers) or Latin America and the Caribbean (a fifth of all borrowers). The average credit volume received is $502 and active borrowers are mostly females. The largest volume of loans is issued to micro entrepreneurs that engage in small businesses and trade, as well as agriculture. For micro entrepreneurs, it is vital to keep their savings and lend to each other. Other securities, such as life insurances, are of the utmost importance.

CULTIVATION OF VEGETABLES – PHNOM PENH, CAMBODIA

Sopha Keo, 75, lives in a village about ten kilometers away from the city center of Phnom Penh. Like most other people in her neighborhood, she has vegetable fields behind her house that she cultivates. She does not sell her vegetables in a market but instead sells directly to dealers who purchase from her and her neighbors locally. Over the years, she has received several microloans from ACLEDA Bank Plc. of between $150 and $200. Each time, she invested the money in her business, e.g. for the purchase of new seeding and working material. Her income supports her family and entire household.

Source: BlueOrchard

NOTES

1 Natalie Portman, actress.
2 CGAP (2014).
3 Rosenberg (2010), pp. 1–5.
4 Sen (1999), p. 87.
5 World Bank (2016), database 2012.

6 Ravallion, Chen and Sangraula (2008), pp. 12–15, 23–24.
7 Robinson (2001), p. 20.
8 Fairbourne, Gibson and Dyer (2007), p. 22; Sachs (2006), p. 20.
9 Robinson (2001), p. 19.
10 Annan (2005), Secretary-General tells Geneva Symposium.
11 Maslow (1943), p. 375.
12 Berg and Emran (2011).
13 Littlefield, Morduch and Hashemi (2003), pp. 4–5.
14 Leatherman, Geissler, Gray and Gash (2012), p. 10; Leive and Xu (2008), p. 849.
15 Xu, Evans, Kawabata, Zeramdini, Klavus and Murray (2003), p. 116; Xu, Evans, Carrin, Aquilar-Rivera, Musgrove and Evans (2007), pp. 977–982.
16 World Bank (2016), database 2012.
17 MIX (2015).

CHAPTER 5

Microfinance Institutions

The key to ending extreme poverty is to enable the poorest of the poor to get their foot on the ladder of development. . .the poorest of the poor are stuck beneath it. They lack the minimum amount of capital necessary to get a foothold, and therefore need a boost up to the first rung.

Jeffrey Sachs[1]

Microfinance institutions (MFIs) are of great importance in microfinance because they provide services to micro entrepreneurs. MFIs are a blend of a range of service providers that use their market position to supply small-scale financial services to people who are usually excluded from the benefits of a sound financial system.

MFIs employ savings deposits and loans as well as donations and subsidies for funding purposes. They primarily provide financial services in the form of microloans and savings deposits. Often, however, they also offer services such as micro insurance and micro pensions.

Credit granting, deposit taking and a wide range of non-financial services foster the financial integration of the poorest of the poor and promote the fight against poverty in a sustainable manner. By means of provident loan granting, optimal asset allocation can be achieved. This boosts productivity and at the same time allows individuals to benefit socially and economically, ultimately much to the benefit of the entire national economy.

5.1 DEFINITION AND GOALS

The term "microfinance institution" is rather general as it refers to a large number of financial institutions. So far, no standardized definition has prevailed. This perhaps explains why many institutions interpret both the mission and services of MFIs in different ways. In the past, MFIs were often understood as private organizations that were offering financial services but were not commercial private banks. When it comes to MFIs, the United Nations distinguish between microfinance and inclusive finance. This takes into consideration that the industry is changing – in a shift in paradigm – by moving away from classic microfinance towards more efficient and more comprehensive financial sectors.

While microfinance can be defined as the supply of different financial services to poorer segments of the population, it is becoming increasingly difficult to unite the growing number of providers in this market segment under one term. Variety is the issue: there are NGOs, private commercial banks, state banks, postal banks, non-bank financial institutions (NBFIs), credit cooperatives, savings cooperatives, as well as several associations and organizations.[2] Most of these institutions have attracted a large clientele and offer a range of diversified financial services. Technically, their rather general market orientation, however, qualifies them more as MFI in the broader sense. The term "MFI", therefore, more strictly speaking denotes formal and semi-formal financial service providers whose main purpose is the provision of financial services in the lower market segment.

The choice of a potential target market depends on the goals of these MFIs and the expected demand in connection with them. There are numerous households and businesses that are either only partly served or not at all. They range from the extremely and moderately poor to the economically active segments of the population that create employment locally. This range ultimately represents the demand side for microfinance financial services. In many cases, however, the supply side lacks the necessary products to meet this need. MFIs are indispensable as they bridge this gap in supplies and include parts of the population and businesses that have been excluded from the financial system. Quite apart from that, MFIs must also be classified as development organizations whose ultimate aim is to reduce poverty, increase productivity and income of the poor, and strengthen the role of women.

MFIs create work places for the underprivileged segments of the population and foster economic growth. Any market entry requires careful examination and assessment of the different local conditions against the backdrop of the long-term goals of MFIs and microfinance in general. Generally, financial inclusion and economic and social sustainability are an integral part of it. The financial situation of an MFI therefore depends on its target market and influences decisions concerning their goals and how they can be attained. For this reason, MFIs have to assess carefully in which markets there is a demand for financial services and which of the client groups are in line with their long-term goals if they want to implement their business models sustainably. An MFI that aims to supply financial and non-financial services to the most destitute segments of the population will therefore be substantially different from one that exclusively focuses on financial services for the economically active poor. Targeted goals on the other hand can also be reached by purposely putting a focus on selected economic sectors or activities.[3]

5.2 TYPES OF MFIs

Microfinance institutions consist of private, public or charitable organizations and usually have social and financial goals, which is why they are often described as organizations with a double bottom line. Figure 5.1 displays the distinction of microfinance service providers into regulated, non-regulated and member-based institutions as well as NGOs. The following in short describes the most important institutions with respect to their international funding.[4] No further notice will be given to non-regulated and member-based MFIs, as they do not qualify for international funding. NGOs can be split into two groups: those that predominantly supply microloans and those that additionally offer healthcare and education services alongside their more elementary financial services. NGOs are subject to civilian and commercial law and are largely funded by donations and subsidies. The main focus of their business activities is the financial

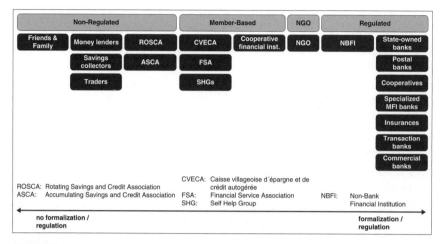

FIGURE 5.1 Different Forms of MFI Organizations
Data Source: Ledgerwood (2013)

Figure 5.1 shows different forms of MFI Organizations, which are arranged by their degree of formalization and regulation. Loans from families, money lenders, etc. are not subject to regulation and are informal. Transaction banks or commercial banks, on the contrary, are mostly strongly regulated and are referred to as formal institutions specializing among other things in the lending of financial means.

integration of the poor and the improvement of their living standards. Unlike banks, NGOs are neither regulated nor under continuous supervision. As a result, they are unable to take and manage deposits of microfinance clients.

Non-Bank Financial Institutions (NBFIs)

This group of institutions consists of, for instance, former NGOs that have undergone a transformation process. Their range of services is usually limited to loans and services (mostly group loans) without collateral. Some institutions – in certain cases and under certain supervision – are capable of taking deposits.

State Banks and Postal Banks

State banks were founded by governments in order to promote particular sectors, such as agriculture, and to reach poorer segments of the population that had been left unbanked by commercial banks. These banks served as a vehicle in transfer payments. Despite the fact that some amply fulfill their mandate, many had to close as a result of mismanagement. Postal banks are able to use the infrastructure of the largest distribution network in the world. In many countries they offer savings and transaction services and are market leaders, particularly in rural areas.

Financial and Credit Cooperatives

This group of finance providers comprises communal savings and credit cooperatives as well as credit unions. They are defined as charitable organizations and are usually owned by their respective members. The proceeds that are generated beyond the operative costs are paid out as dividends, capital stock, increased interests on savings deposits, reduced credit rates, insurance rates or other services. Within the framework of these organizations, micro entrepreneurs are to be understood as stake holders who can profit from both their access to financial services and the resulting proceeds.

Specialized MFI Banks

MFI banks are rigorously regulated also via legal and institutional parameters. These MFIs are either independent or work as a subsidiary of a larger bank. The business model of these banks respects a social component and understands microfinance as a profitable core activity. Unlike commercial banks, the offer of MFIs is designed to target microfinance clients and serves a broad segment from the lowest to the highest income bracket.

Insurance Companies

Insurance service providers increasingly offer their products in developing countries. Profit-oriented and charitable organizations, government organizations as well as insurance companies are all among these providers. Sales figures in the lower income brackets are relatively low as yet. Insurance products have not been established in most places and are regarded as additional services more than anything else. In addition to this, insurance companies do not offer their services to the clients directly, but often act as re-insurers for MFIs that in turn offer insurance services such as buildings or life insurance, or credit risk insurance.

Transaction Banks

Enterprises specializing in transactions dominate the simple and secure transfer of financial means between countries for the low to middle income brackets. Further providers of transaction services are commercial business banks and postal banks, but also MFIs and NGOs. Their services comprise, for example, the transfer of money or the backing of a credit limit of bank cards of foreign relatives. These services are profitable thanks to the fees that are charged. This is clearly an incentive to recruit more clients, who in turn benefit from access to credit and savings deposit services.

Commercial Banks

The supply of services for households with a low to middle income can present a profitable business model to commercial banks. The variety of services stretches from savings accounts and transaction services to loans. A presence in this market segment either depends on a government mandate, competitive pressure or expectations of potential future growth.

5.3 MFI FUNDING

According to estimates, there are nearly 4000 MFIs worldwide.[5] Although many of these institutions offer similar services, they differ considerably in type, funding and regulation. The funding of MFIs deserves further investigation.

Financial Sources

Originally founded as charitable enterprises, the activities of MFIs were mainly funded by donations and subsidies of governments, development organizations, foundations and private people. Over time, some of these organizations have developed into formal financial service providers or

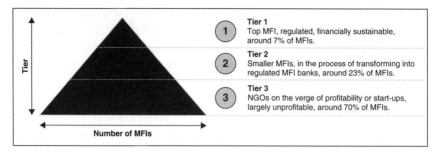

FIGURE 5.2   Types of MFIs
Data Source: Microrate (2013a)

The pyramid displays the degree of commercialization of different types of MFIs. Tier 1 MFIs are tightly regulated, whereas tier 2 MFIs are in the process of developing into banks. Tier 3 MFIs are largely unprofitable. 90 per cent of MFIs on the market are tier 2 or tier 3 institutions.

regulated banks, increasingly so in recent years. Formal financial institutions are better equipped to achieve financial independence and sustainability, as they are able to refinance on the capital market and can take deposits.[6] Moreover, in many countries only regulated MFIs are authorized to offer certain services.

The financing strategy of an MFI depends on its profitability and development. By and large, MFIs can be put into three categories: Tier 1, tier 2 and tier 3 institutions, as shown in Figure 5.2. Tier 1 and tier 2 MFIs are distinguished by their economic stability and are increasingly state-regulated. Tier 1 institutions are predominantly state-regulated banks that are rated by rating agencies. They are funded by savings deposits, loans and equity. Tier 2 institutions consist of smaller and younger MFIs. They are predominantly organized as NGOs aspiring to be regulated banks or they are already undergoing the transformation process. For this reason, tier 2 MFIs can also fund themselves via loans and equity. Depending on how far this transformation process has progressed, they may also take deposits to fund their activities. Most MFIs are classified as tier 3 institutions. They constitute roughly 70 per cent of the microfinance sector, but are yet to be financially independent or sustainable. Tier 3 institutions are on the one hand MFIs on the verge of profitability but still lacking the necessary funds. On the other hand, this group also comprises NGOs and startup MFIs that are mostly unprofitable and have a purely social agenda.[7]

Many financial institutions and organizations – such as microfinance vehicles, local and international banks, development and supranational organizations, as well as international capital markets and sponsors – facilitate the funding of microfinance institutions. Tier 1 MFIs on the whole are given more attention by commercial banks and institutional and private investors, as these MFIs not only reveal a great degree of economic stability, but usually also have rather experienced managements that put their social mission into action. Hence, from an investor's point of view, these MFIs efficiently and effectively channel means to micro entrepreneurs. Tier 1 MFIs in particular thus have better access to both local and international capital markets and investment funds. For this reason they are able to take out loans in addition to their equity capital in order to reach more entrepreneurs. Many of those MFIs are holders of a banking license, and are authorized to take deposits. Some tier 2 MFIs also receive funding from international investors, albeit much less funding than tier 1 institutions. The vast majority of all MFIs in tiers 2 and 3 lack a comparable professional and commercial business structure and therefore have limited access to the capital market. Their microloans are funded via loans from development organizations or sponsors.[8]

Figure 5.3 shows that the assets on the balance sheet of an MFI represent the loans issued to micro entrepreneurs, whereas the liabilities depend on their form of funding, legal structure, regulatory framework and the supply of services.[9] Equity, international or local capital markets, savings deposits, as well as subsidies from governments, supra-national organizations and private persons are particularly adequate sources of funding. The left-hand side of Figure 5.3 represents the assets of an MFI that are open to competition and not subsidized. It can therefore fund itself via savings deposits, loans from the international and national capital market or via its equity. The balance sheet on the right represents an MFI that can only employ subsidies and donations to fund its business activities.

However, not all institutions follow this funding pattern in their development. There is thus no conclusive overall capital structure that would fit every stage of their development. More importantly, their funding structure depends on internal factors such as the expansion of the loan portfolio

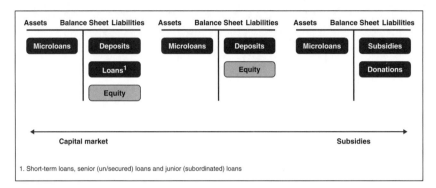

FIGURE 5.3   Forms of Financing of MFIs
Data Source: Becker (2010) and Dieckmann (2007)

The assets on the balance sheet of an MFI represent the loans issued to micro entrepreneurs. The structure of the liabilities on the balance sheet depends on their form of funding, their legal structure, the regulatory framework and their range of financial services.

and the taking of deposits. It also depends on external factors such as the regulatory framework, the availability of sponsors or commercial credit institutions and the development of the local financial system. Finally, the costs and maturities of the various sources of funding are also decisive in the choice of optimal structure.

International Equity

The volume of the portfolio of outstanding microloans has surged in the last ten years. This development can largely be explained by a facilitated access to commercial funding via international loans and local savings deposits. This trend is reflected in the foreign investments made in the microfinance sector. They almost doubled between 2007 and 2012 to around 17 billion dollars.[10]

An average MFI mainly funds itself via local sources (see Figure 5.4). Deposits from microfinance clients contribute around 45 per cent of the balance sheet of MFIs. In addition to this, microloans are financed via local debt capital at 20 per cent and local equity at 10 per cent. This means that foreign investments only constitute around 25 per cent of the overall

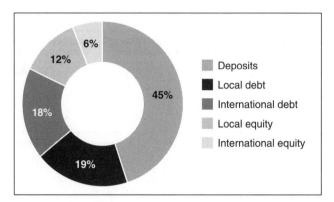

FIGURE 5.4   Funding Structure of MFIs
Data Source: Becker (2010)

MFIs refinance themselves to a great extent via local sources. Microloans issued to micro entrepreneurs are funded by savings deposits at 45 per cent, local debt capital and equity at 30 per cent, and a mere 25 per cent are funded by foreign investment.

funding of an average MFI.[11] Considering the costs of financing incurred, this structure hardly surprises. Equity, if not in the form of donations, is the most costly source of financing and is therefore rarely an option. It is followed by debt capital that usually prevails over the former as it incurs lower costs. Savings deposits are clearly favored as the most reasonable form of re-funding.

In an ideal world, and with respect to any future market development, MFIs should aim to increase their funding via local means. Adamantly so, because microfinance answers to underdeveloped markets in developing countries, and its main objective in the development of such markets is the mobilization of local means and the efficient utilization of these funds by way of local financial institutions.

Financial Orientation

Subsidies, donations and handouts create no incentives for sustainable economic activity, and they do not foster independence or freedom in micro entrepreneurs. Profit-oriented MFIs, however, ensure that financial means are implemented in a target-oriented, effective manner in order to promote business activities in their region. A lack of traditional banks that specifically align their commercial activity with poorer clients does not imply that low-income segments of the population are bad clients. On the contrary. The most notable accomplishment of microfinance lies in the fact that the poor can indeed be good and reliable clients for a bank. Informal lenders such as money lenders, neighbors and local traders may have client-specific information that traditional banks lack, but they are financially restricted. Microfinance thus is a problem-solving approach that strives to best link the means of a bank with the information and cost advantages of a local money lender. The advantage of microfinance therefore lies in its ability to attract external funds. Historically, microfinance is not the first concept to do this, albeit certainly the most successful to this day. It essentially owes its success to the systematic avoidance of mistakes and pitfalls of the recent past.

In the 1970s, it was generally accepted that there were considerable subsidies necessary to provide financial services to poorer segments of the population. Often, state banks took on this task and issued the majority of loans to agricultural enterprises. Yet, many of those banks were driven by political agendas and calculated interest rates that were below the current market interest rates. In addition to that, loan repayments were not monitored systematically and very often not claimed with ultimate consequence. The loan granting risks and the questionable incentives when it came to repayment frequency and payment morale spawned expensive and inefficient institutions that failed to reach particularly the destitute segments of the population.[12] Critics of the concept of subsidized banks argue that the poor are generally better off without these subsidies. They refer to the fact that subsidized banks force reliable informal money lenders out of the market, who in many places provide the poor with access to capital. On the other hand, the market interest rates of any given time are seen as a rationing mechanism. Only those with a project worthy of funding or a business idea with potential will be prepared to pay for a loan.

These subsidies pushed the interest rate for microloans well below the market interest rates. As a result, loans were no longer issued to the most committed and reliable borrowers, but in many cases, loans were granted on the basis of political agendas or social considerations. This severely undermined the basic concept of microfinance and was not by any measure economically sustainable. The steady flows of money from subsidies meant that banks had no incentives to offer savings services and poor households were left with unattractive and inefficient possibilities to invest their financial means. As banks were state-managed, they were under immeasurable political pressure to regularly cancel loan debts, which again led to dire mismanagement. Financial means that were destined for the poorer segments of the population flowed into the pockets of influential individuals. In other words, there were no incentives whatsoever for the foundation of efficient and sustainable institutions. Consequently, with a few exceptions, state-run loan programs suffered sizeable credit default rates, of 40 to 95 per cent in Africa, the Middle East, South America, South Asia and South East Asia. In such a system, the term "effective loans" hardly applies; they were rather government-funded subsidies.[13]

In the 1980s and 1990s, the microfinance sector was subjected to more substantial changes that thrust the profitability issues of these microfinance institutions into the limelight. It was decided that in the future, MFIs should be financially sustainable. The decision to aim for a profit-oriented type of microfinance can be put down to three arguments. First of all, the management of small credit volumes is more costly for banks. Yet, for want of a better option, poor households are prepared to pay higher interest rates. Annual interest rates of local money lenders regularly exceed the 100 per cent mark; anything less is therefore considered an acceptable option. Generally speaking, access to financial means is more important than the actual price. Secondly, subsidies do not only constitute the main problem in state-run banks, but they may have a detrimental effect on NGOs too, by weakening the incentive for cost-efficiency and innovation. Thirdly, is it assumed that volumes of existing and future subsidies will not suffice to sustainably promote growth in microfinance. Aligning its profitability and commercialization is therefore prerequisite to a speedy dissemination of the concept.

Figure 5.5 reveals the segmentation of the market into profit-oriented and charitable MFIs. The development of a profit-oriented microfinance sector is reflected in the relatively large proportion of profit-oriented MFIs. In 2013, 380 out of the 766 MFIs that were registered on the MIX Market (Microfinance Information Exchange) data platform were profit-oriented institutions. On top of this, these institutions collectively controlled more than 70 per cent of the total managed financial assets.[14]

Despite the fact that the choice of a profit-oriented legal form should put more emphasis on profitability, this does not necessarily reflect reality. The mere decision to operate as a profit-oriented institution is not the decisive factor. The form of enterprise does not imperatively determine

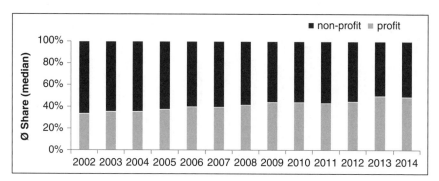

FIGURE 5.5   Profit-Oriented and Charitable MFIs
Data Source: MIX (2016)

The share of profit-oriented institutions has continually been on the rise in the recent past (median). In 2013 and 2014, half of all MFIs were profit-oriented. Charitable MFIs were mainly funded via subsidies and donations.

sustainable economic activity. In many cases, charitable organizations are also profitable, albeit they might not pay out their proceeds but instead reinvest them for the benefit of their clients.[15]

Microfinance, with its social mission, is sometimes criticized because of the fact that some MFIs are profit-oriented. Those in favor predict a stronger social impact in the future because high demands in terms of product efficiency and growing competition will stir up the traditionally rather less profit-oriented market. Clients will benefit from more affordable and efficient services. Critics, however, are adamant that profit orientation is utterly incompatible with their goal to alleviate poverty, or that it will severely compromise it at least. They argue that profit orientation will eventually lead to a departure from microfinance's original goal of financially integrating the poor. It will at the same time lead to a slump in services as well as higher interest rates meant to maximize profit. The commercialization of microfinance has been placed in a bad light in recent years, its main reproach being uncontrollable growth and high interest rates. The data evaluated by the MIX Markets information platform, however, shows a different picture altogether when it comes to profit orientation of the microfinance sector. Those institutions that accumulate high

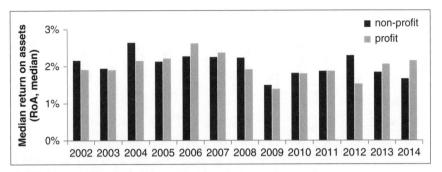

FIGURE 5.6   Profitability of Profit-Oriented and Charitable MFIs
Data Source: MIX (2016)

> This figure displays the return on assets (RoA, median). Profit-oriented
> and charitable organizations do not significantly differ in terms of
> return and costs. Profit orientation therefore does not necessarily lead
> to more profitability. And likewise, a charitable orientation does not
> necessarily signify lower costs.

proceeds, and that have aroused the general public's discontent, are statistical outliers and stand for a mere 10 per cent of all microfinance clients worldwide. The vast majority of clients use services from institutions where interest rates and return on equity (RoE) lie below 30 and 15 per cent respectively.

Historically, the returns on assets (RoAs) of profit-oriented institutions even lie below those of charitable MFIs. In addition to this, both profit-oriented and charitable MFIs have seen lower proceeds in recent years and are therefore hardly distinguishable in this respect. On the cost side too, there are not many differences. Profit orientation therefore does not mean profitable, and charitable does not inevitably lead to lower costs.[16] Figure 5.6 shows the RoA of profit- and non-profit-oriented microfinance institutions.

There seems to be a middle way when it comes to financing institutions. It is grounded in the belief that both profit-oriented and charitable MFIs are capable of fighting poverty long-term and generate sustainable business activities. They do not necessarily have to be in conflict with each other.

5.4 SERVICES

The transition of the microloan into comprehensive microfinance is predominantly a question of the range of services. In the past, emphasis was merely given to the supply of loans. However, it is becoming increasingly evident that the poor want to make use of a wider range of financial services such as savings deposit services or insurance products. Beyond that, there is a particularly high demand for non-financial services. The challenge for MFIs hence is to meet this demand with a suitable supply. They therefore need to supersede issues relating to market entry, most of all when it comes to informing the general public about their individual products.

Product information leads to a better understanding of the rights and obligations that come with the territory, which again leads to a higher demand. Nearly all MFIs supply loan services, while some institutions also offer additional financial and non-financial services. The range of services moreover depends on the goals of an MFI, the demand in its sales market and institutional structure. The most important aspect, however, is simply the supply of products that microfinance clients truly need and for which they are prepared to pay.

Financial Services

Beyond the microloan, MFIs also supply savings deposits, insurance and transaction services.

Loans are borrowed financial means with specific repayment conditions. It is sensible for microfinance clients to get a loan in situations where there is a lack of capital to fund a business and the proceeds of the borrowed capital exceed the interest rates of the loan. This prevents them from stalling their business activities until sufficient liquid funds for auto-financing have been found.[17] In many cases, MFIs also supply loans for healthcare, education and real estate as well as for other exceptional situations, as shown in Figure 5.7. MFIs aim to issue their loans in a sustainable, client-oriented manner. Transactional processes have to be as efficient and affordable as possible. The interest rate has to be economically viable and clients must have an incentive to repay their loans. Loans may be issued to individuals or groups. Individual loans are often issued to individuals with a minimal guarantee or collateral to secure the loan. Group loans are generally handed to individuals with a group affiliation or groups

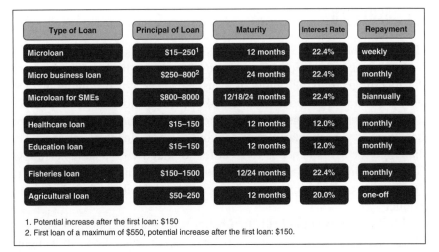

Type of Loan	Principal of Loan	Maturity	Interest Rate	Repayment
Microloan	$15–250[1]	12 months	22.4%	weekly
Micro business loan	$250–800[2]	24 months	22.4%	monthly
Microloan for SMEs	$800–8000	12/18/24 months	22.4%	biannually
Healthcare loan	$15–150	12 months	12.0%	monthly
Education loan	$15–150	12 months	12.0%	monthly
Fisheries loan	$150–1500	12/24 months	22.4%	monthly
Agricultural loan	$50–250	12 months	20.0%	one-off

1. Potential increase after the first loan: $150
2. First loan of a maximum of $550, potential increase after the first loan: $150.

FIGURE 5.7 Example of Types of Loans of an MFI in Pakistan
Data Source: BlueOrchard Research

MFIs issue various loans that are tailored to their clients' needs.

that organize the further allocation of those loans. The group members agree to joint guarantee for the redemption of the loans. Many MFIs do not require collateral since only successful repayment will secure access to further loans. More importantly, the fact that the different group members vouch for each other is a major incentive for timely repayment.[18]

By taking deposits in recent years, an array of informal MFIs and financial institutions have demonstrated that there is demand for these services in low-income groups. As the majority of poor segments of the population have no access to savings accounts with formal institutions, there is often no possibility for safe custody of their savings. Liquid assets are thus usually either "hidden" or entrusted to so-called money keepers, whose fees, however, factually equate to a negative interest rate on their assets. Although even formal MFIs are now offering their savings deposit services, there is a supply gap that is largely due to the regulatory framework. Non-regulated MFIs are not authorized to take deposits. MFIs that do collect them are therefore larger and most likely urban institutions. There are two types of product voluntary saving and mandatory saving. Voluntary saving happens at the client's own discretion. She or he has unrestricted access to their assets and receives an interest return. Mandatory saving means that the client is obliged to pay in order to be granted a particular loan. This may be a fixed amount or a percentage of the loan. This business model allows a client to benefit from institutionalized saving and an accumulation of wealth at the same time. Accumulated savings must, however, not be retired until maturity, and therefore act as a form of collateral. MFIs, on the other hand, profit from a stable source of funding to refinance loans and other services.

Insurance is a relatively recent and attractive addition to the range of products in microfinance. For poorer segments of the population in developing countries, the occurrence of daily hazards is significantly higher than in industrialized countries. Precarious living conditions increase the prevalence of illnesses and malnutrition. The quality of water and standards of hygiene are often poor. Inadequate safety precautions and the risk of environmental shocks greatly favor accidents of the poor. Micro insurance policies offer protection to a certain degree from these potential hazards. The supply of insurance products among other things includes life insurance, real estate insurance, health insurance and credit risk insurance, as well as some form of micro pensions.[19] Some MFIs, such as Grameen Bank, have introduced mandatory insurance and insist that a certain percentage of their credit volume should flow into an insurance fund. In the event of death, the insurance policy will both pay for the loan and the costs of the funeral. MFIs often serve as distribution channels for insurance services.

In combination with savings services or for a fee, transaction enterprises and certain MFIs also supply transaction services. As Chapter 5.2 has illustrated, these services are essentially the transmission of money, the backing of credit limits on bank cards of foreign relatives and money transfers. As a payment is usually issued before a check is cleared, MFIs carry the risk that a number of checks cannot be redeemed due to fraud or insufficient funds. For this reason, few MFIs currently supply these services. A continually rising demand, on the other hand, will certainly bring more service providers to this business segment and promote better conditions to allow for an economically viable supply of these services.[20]

Non-Financial Services

MFIs also supply non-financial services. These range from social intermediation – with the aim of accumulating social capital and fundamental skills – to business development services (see Figure 5.8).

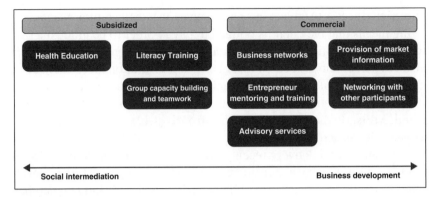

FIGURE 5.8   Non-Financial Services of MFIs
Data Source: Parker and Pearce (2002)

Figure 5.8 presents a purely illustrative example. The services shown may be both subsidized and commercial.

Social intermediation helps poorer segments of the population to reach a better understanding of various issues, for instance, healthcare services concerning vaccinations, drinking water, or pre- and postnatal care in women, or education services such as literacy programs. Business development services are meant for established but also potential business entrepreneurs. They include a range of training programs, the building of business networks and a general supply of market information.

5.5   REGULATION

The regulation of MFIs comprises many aspects and critical requirements MFIs have to fulfill in terms of capital resources, liquidity and their loan portfolio.

Why Should MFIs Be Regulated?

The degree of regulation and supervision of MFIs is one of the most pressing issues in microfinance. While a number of formal MFIs in certain countries are already regulated, most semi-formal and informal MFIs are not compulsorily subject to regulation. Deposit taking is, however. For this reason, many MFIs or NGOs fund their business models with deposits without authorization by simply renaming their services or by grace of the authorities, albeit at a considerable risk, as in the future even tighter rules and regulations may be implemented to counteract such cases, much to the disadvantage of all the protagonists in microfinance.[21] Financial supervision aims to audit and monitor MFIs with respect to compliance. Regulation seeks to avoid a financial crisis in the microfinance sector, maintains payment transactions, protects clients and their savings deposits, and promotes competition and efficiency. Ultimately, however, regulation has to be organized in a way that avoids a distortion of the market.

When Should MFIs Be Regulated?

Despite their extensive growth, MFIs still only reach a small part of their potential host of clients globally. The supply of financial services for the microfinance market will in the long run exceed the capacity of traditional sources of financing (donations and development organizations). For this reason, MFIs will in the future be constrained to increasingly resorting to commercial sources and savings deposits for the funding of their micro-loans. However, the funding of MFIs and loan portfolios via commercial funds and savings deposits calls for rigid regulation and supervision mechanisms; not least because of the organizational structure of MFIs that differs considerably from that of traditional banks.[22] The question, of course, is when MFIs should be regulated. Fundamentally, they should be regulated if they take deposits from clients, as microfinance clients are unable to correctly gauge an MFI's financial situation. They have to rely on an authority for this assessment. In addition to this, MFIs should also be regulated in the absence of minimum standards or in cases where they are disrespected, as often is the case when microfinance programs are launched prematurely and exclusively focus on loan granting. MFIs should also be regulated when they outgrow a critical size, and potential insolvency would have severe implications beyond the particular MFI and its clients.

What Are the Central Aspects of Regulation?

To do justice to the variety of MFI services, regulators distinguish between two types of MFIs: the non-deposit-taking MFIs, which only issue loans, and the deposit-taking MFIs, which both issue loans and take deposits.

MFIs that take deposits from the local population pose a higher risk from a regulatory point of view than non-deposit-taking MFIs, as savings deposits can be withdrawn at relatively short notice.

In the event of a bank run, MFIs with a high share of deposits would be likely to run into trouble financially due to the fact that in most cases they invest the money entrusted to them in loans that are issued to micro entrepreneurs on a long-term basis. Apart from these financial implications, there is a political dimension that must not be underestimated. A situation where clients are unable to withdraw their savings may easily lead to open rioting and social upheaval, and trigger a chain reaction that might have an adverse effect on other financial institutions. For this reason, deposit-taking institutions are usually subject to regulation that regularly monitors and assesses the financial situation of MFIs and takes the necessary measures wherever required.[23]

The regulatory framework for deposit-taking MFIs aims to protect depositors and the financial system alike with a number of instruments (see Figure 5.9). Most notably they regulate capital adequacy, minimum capital and liquidity.

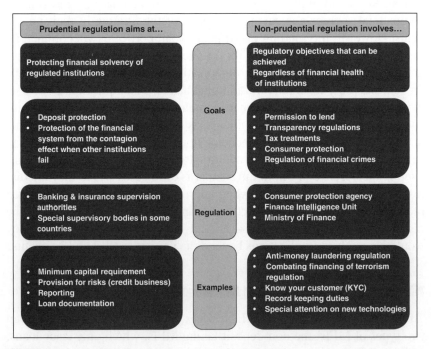

FIGURE 5.9 Regulation and Supervision Framework

MFIs with prudential regulation are subject to more rigid supervision than those with non-prudential regulation. Non-prudential regulation is based on goals that can also be reached without financial stability.

Regulation in terms of capital adequacy dictates the rules for the relationship between an institution's equity and (risk-based) assets. This ratio is called the capital adequacy ratio (CAR). A high CAR means less risk for savers and the financial system. At the same time, a high CAR limits the ways of funding, or external funding respectively, and lowers productivity. This may reduce the supply and therefore limit access to financial services. This contradicts the purpose of an MFI. Various characteristics of microfinance, on the other hand, require comparatively higher CARs than traditional banks, which is associated with several topics of the microfinance portfolio: high operating costs, aspects of diversity, management skills and a limited availability of monitoring instruments.

Although MFIs have lower default rates than commercial banks, these may in many cases deteriorate rapidly as microloans are often not secured and the access to further loans is a micro entrepreneur's main concern. If a micro entrepreneur therefore is alerted to the default of others, default in general rises with MFIs. Moreover, a micro entrepreneur may feel betrayed if he or she serves their loan and others do not. In the event of a rise in default payments, MFIs are at more risk than commercial banks, as most of these banks have a diversified portfolio that only devotes a fraction to microloans. High operating costs are another issue. A rise in defaults results in less capital for MFIs that might be used to cover current overheads.

In many cases, MFIs operate in one region, which is why they carry a higher risk than banks, which are geographically more diverse. MFIs also require higher capital buffers, because of their relatively short track record and their lack of experience of both management and employees. Also, many regulatory authorities in developing countries have neither the necessary experience nor the instruments to assess and supervise risks in microfinance.[24] In addition to this, MFIs often have limited means of funding in cases of emergency.[25]

Minimum capital requirements refer to the amount of equity that an institution must provide. Low capital requirements are synonymous with low market entry barriers and therefore more providers as a rule. On the good side, this promotes competition. However, a regulator only manages to supervise effectively a limited number of institutions, which in turn would speak for a higher entry barrier. The level of the minimum capital thus substantially depends on the size and structure of the market in question, and the rules and regulations vary from country to country.

Liquidity requirements refer to the provision of a minimal volume of liquid assets. Lower requirements allow for higher operative flexibility, but pose a higher risk at the same time. As loans that are issued by MFIs are usually short-term, MFIs may interrupt their loan granting in cases of emergency in order to improve their liquidity. This may have dire consequences for their clients and should at all costs be avoided. For this reason, the liquidity requirements for MFIs are in many cases rather stringent.

Apart from prudential regulation, there is also non-prudential regulation, which extends to deposit-taking MFIs as well as non-deposit-taking MFIs. Non-prudential regulation is also referred to as conduct of business and is mainly dedicated to client protection.

Client protection requires adequate and transparent information and may, for instance, mean that simple language is used to describe products, or that products are explained orally as many clients cannot read and write. To safeguard a fair conduct in client care, abusive loan practices have to be punished. Clients therefore must have a contact point where they can report cases of abuse free of charge. This is especially important because most microfinance clients cannot afford a lawsuit, be it for time or financial reasons.

Credit Bureaus

Alongside administrative regulation there has been a trend towards self-regulation in recent years. Increasing competition on the financial markets has exacerbated issues of insolvency and marred repayment incentives as well as causing the ensuing financial difficulties for MFIs. The lack of a common information system worsens the problem, because the growing number of MFIs increases the information asymmetry among the individual loan providers. The introduction of credit information systems (credit bureaus) can make amendments and increase the efficiency of the credit market and boost the number of loans issued to the poor. If individual MFIs on a market begin to share data about their clients, they inevitably

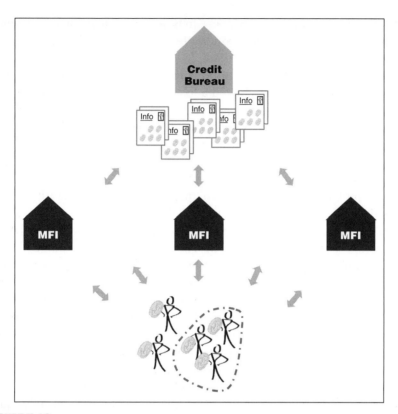

FIGURE 5.10 Credit Bureaus

Client data flows from clients via the MFI on to a credit bureau that collects all the data on a person and their loans and stores it for reference. This allows MFIs – and clients themselves – to assess their solvency and development.

encourage other MFIs to follow suit. It is only logical that the exchange of information within the framework of a credit information system will lead to a better risk assessment of potential clients and therefore encourage other creditworthy borrowers to join their ranks; loan default rates will drop and the quality of loan portfolios will rise (see Figure 5.10). Ultimately, borrowers will also benefit from this increase in efficiency.

The introduction of credit bureaus thus increases a financial system's efficiency and improves the position of each and every participant in the microfinance sector.

If there is no exchange of information among MFIs, a borrower will find it more difficult to be granted a loan, especially if there is no collateral. The lender, on the other hand, has no possibility to assess the risk of a loan to a new client. This raises the business risk substantially. However, if there is an exchange of information among these institutions, two types can be distinguished. First, only negative information about loan loss and payment default is shared. The compilation of a blacklist helps MFIs to exclude problematic borrowers from their loan portfolio. The filter effect mars the problem of negative selection. The fact that borrowers want to avoid their names appearing on this blacklist reduces the moral hazard in connection with the loan repayment. The second and more comprehensive form of information exchange features both positive and more negative data on the borrower. The whitelist with the positive data comprises data concerning all of the borrower's outstanding and past loans. This allows borrowers to create a flawless credit history for themselves – often in the form of a creditworthiness rating – and therefore facilitate access to further loans. MFIs on the other hand, can benefit from the fact that they can reduce their credit risk by a better assessment of their borrowers.[26]

The arrival of credit bureaus is generally regarded positively. The exchange of information among the different institutions not only mars the risk of over-indebtedness in borrowers but it also lowers the default rates, which in a competitive market environment inevitably leads to lower interest on loans. In the 1990s, many Asian and Latin American countries saw the launch of efficient and effective credit information systems that contributed substantially towards the stability of local financial systems. Africa has the least developed credit information systems. The swift growth of African financial markets in the recent past has, however, generated an enormous interest in a potential introduction of these systems.[27]

5.6 PRELIMINARY CONCLUSIONS

Microfinance institutions are crucial because they are responsible for the supply of services to micro entrepreneurs. Loan granting, deposit taking, and the wide range of non-financial services are not only the stepping

TAXI BUSINESS – ILOILO, THE PHILIPPINES

Jovel Panghari, 26, is married and has been running his own taxi business with a so-called motorized tricycle since 2012. This type of motorcycle with a sidecar is the typical means of transportation in the Philippines. To finance the purchase of the $400 tricycle, Mr. Panghari took a loan with the LiveBank foundation. He works long hours and earns the equivalent of $9 a day. A ride comes at a basic rate of 20 cents plus 3 cents per driven kilometer. Joel is planning to take out a second loan to purchase more tricycles and hire additional drivers.

Source: BlueOrchard

stones to financial integration of the world's most destitute, but they also contribute sustainably towards the fight against poverty worldwide.

Depending on their level of development and grade of commercialization, MFIs can be put into three categories (tiers 1, 2 and 3): Tier 1 contains established MFIs that have formal structures and that are predominantly state-regulated banks that are rated by rating agencies. Tier 2 MFIs are smaller and less established institutions undergoing a transformation up to regulated banks. Tier 3 institutions are either on the verge of profitability or are non-profit-oriented and pursue social goals. MFIs are largely funded via local means, but a sizable share of their funds comes from foreign investors – be it in the form of external capital or equity. Especially in the context of microfinance as a driving force in the development of local financial markets, the current trend towards raising capital locally is a much hailed development.

In the wake of the rather rapid development of the global microfinance sector, the aspect of regulation must not be neglected. MFIs should be subject to financial regulation and be supervised on a regular basis. In this way, crises can be averted and financial transactions upheld. More importantly, regulation of the microfinance sector promotes competition and efficiency in the finance sector and protects clients and their deposits in the long run. For this reason, the development of central loan offices as an industry standard is positive. Loan offices promote the exchange of information between the different MFIs and the authorities, mitigate the issue of client default and in a competitive environment lower default rates and interest rates in equal measure.

NOTES

1 Jeffrey Sachs, American economist and director of the Earth Institute at Columbia University in New York.
2 United Nations (2006), p. 5.
3 Ledgerwood (2000), p. 45.
4 United Nations (2006), pp. 10–13.
5 Reed, Marsden, Ortega, Rivera and Rogers (2015), p. 8.
6 Dieckmann (2007), p. 6.
7 Becker (2010), p. 54.
8 Dieckmann (2007), pp. 5–6.
9 In most cases, when it comes to the services that are provided, the balance sheet will only indicate deposits as liabilities. Albeit MFIs often provide a wide range of financial services that go beyond mere lending (and, increasingly, deposit taking), these services are normally provided in collaboration with specialized financial service providers. They are for this matter not listed as liabilities in the balance sheet of the respective MFI.
10 MIX (2015).
11 Becker (2010), p. 55.

12 Conning (1999), pp. 71, 74.
13 Braverman and Guasch (1986), p. 1256.
14 MIX (2011, 2015).
15 Cull, Asli and Morduch (2009), p. 174.
16 MIX (2011).
17 Rutherford (2001), pp. 6–7.
18 Ledgerwood (2000), p. 84.
19 MicroPensionLab (2014).
20 United Nations (2006), p. 114.
21 Ledgerwood (2000), p. 21.
22 Rock, Otero and Rosenberg (1996), p. 1.
23 Basel Committee on Banking Supervision (2006).
24 Christen, Lauer, Lyman and Rosenberg (2012), p. 17.
25 Standard & Poor's (2007).
26 Luoto, McIntosh and Wydick (2007), p. 318; Jappelli and Pagano (2000), p. 10.
27 McIntosh and Wydick (2005), p. 275.

CHAPTER 6

Lending Methodologies

The entire bank is built on trust.

Muhammad Yunus[1]

L ending in microfinance is based on trust.

Group loans, mutual monitoring and a progressive loan structure inspire trust among borrowers themselves on the one hand, and borrowers and MFIs on the other. Borrowers are prepared to redeem their loans to be able to have continuous access to capital.

Socio-economic factors such as location and gender also have an impact on the success of a micro entrepreneur's business activity.

6.1 TRADITIONAL CREDIT THEORY AND MICROFINANCE

Traditional credit theory is based on Stiglitz and Weiss's model of credit rationing.[2] They examined credit rationing in markets with imperfect information. Generally, high-risk borrowers pay higher interest rates and must provide higher collateral as their probability of default is higher than in low-risk borrowers. Credit rationing thus occurs when borrowers with a low degree of creditworthiness are willing to pay interest that is above the equilibrium interest rate at which banks issue loans. These borrowers, however, remain unserved because despite the elevated interest rate, the bank will refuse to take the higher risk of probability of default. Interest rate and collateral are in this case used as a means of selection to counteract issues with moral hazard, adverse selection and asymmetrical information. This issue is known as the principal–agent problem, as illustrated in Figure 6.1. It is mitigated by credit ratings that influence the two means of selection, i.e. interest rate and collateral. High creditworthiness is rewarded with low interest rates, borrowers with low creditworthiness will have to pay higher interest rates to compensate for their increased default risk; the

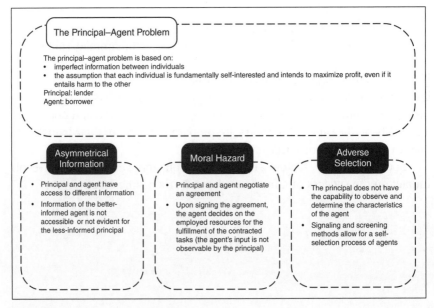

FIGURE 6.1   The Principal–Agent Problem

> The principal–agent problem describes the conflict that ensues when private information can only be accessed by the borrower, and not by the lender.

higher the default rate, the greater the demands on collateral. Financial collateral has two effects. It makes loans affordable for borrowers with a high default rate. For lenders, however, it offers compensation in cases of repayment issues.

Microfinance, however, is a concept that does not follow the traditional credit theory mentioned above. The principal–agent problem is not reduced by financial collateral, but rather with the help of a sense of security such as trust.[3] Financial resources are in this case lent to a network of trust consisting of families, friends and strangers, all supporting each other to have access to loans.[4] Let us not forget that micro entrepreneurs usually have one chance to access capital and therefore must proceed swiftly and carefully. If they default on one occasion, applying for another loan will be virtually impossible. In contrast, in industrial countries people are granted loans repeatedly by simply providing certain financial securities. Developing countries, however, often lack a reliable legal structure that settles property rights. In many cases, it is therefore impossible to establish ownership, let alone transform it into capital. In a country where no one can identify exactly what is owned by whom, property cannot simply be transformed into capital or be divided into stocks. As a result of this lack of framework, the value of property or ownership is impossible to determine. De Soto refers to this a "dead capital."[5] Lending methodology certainly plays an important part in the assessment of default risk, but so do socio-economic factors such as market proximity, the potential for activities that add value, and gender.

6.2 LENDING METHODOLOGIES

The microfinance sector knows several lending methodologies. Key elements in all of them are a collective duty of repayment for group loans, mutual monitoring, progressive lending and regular meetings with the MFI in charge.[6]

Group Loans

Lending in microfinance owes much of its success to group lending. Each individual subsidiarily vouches for the other members of the group and their repayments. Culturally, this means that Asian clients in particular lose face when they fail to repay their loans. As a result, borrowers support each other and share their knowledge and skills. This reduces the amount of private information that the lender has no access to. This mutual obligation to repay almost completely eliminates the risk of default.[7]

The characteristics of collective repayment can be described by means of a game theory scenario. Figure 6.2 displays the different moods of two borrowers who have taken out a group loan. The mood of player A is illustrated on the left, player B is seen on the right. The Nash equilibrium (NE) occurs if each player chooses the strategy from which he or she benefits the most, despite the fact that they know their opponents' best strategy and motivation.[8] It therefore takes into account the decisions of the other players, as long the other party's decisions remain unaltered, and describes the best possible reaction of both players, bearing this knowledge in mind. For our example, this means that the best option for both players A and B always is to repay the loan.

If player A repays the entire loan, player B had better redeem his or her loan as well. If player A slips into default, player B's best option definitely is to clear both of their debts. Repaying both of their debts still puts player B in a better position than without payment, as despite the fact that she or he has to bear the costs for player B's debts, player B will in all likelihood proceed with the repayment to secure access to financial resources in the long run, and not lose face. Non-repayments by both participants, therefore, are never an optimal solution. This game theory example shows that borrowers are determined to put their business ideas into action in a profitable manner and to manage their finances on their own accord, so as to repay their loans.

Mutual Monitoring

Mutual monitoring, with or without repayment liability, boosts the learning effect among borrowers, as they share their experiences and keep each other up to date. Their mutual support and monitoring secures timely payments and largely avoids default. Successful borrowers want to take out

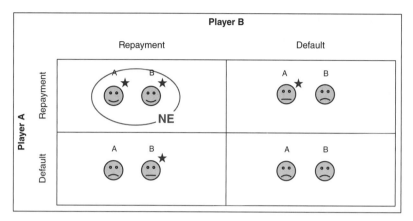

FIGURE 6.2 Group Loans and Game Theory

The Nash equilibrium (NE) is a solution concept in which each player in a game is making the best decision possible, thereby taking into account the decisions of the other player, as long the other party's decisions remain unaltered. For our example, this therefore means that the best option for both players A and B always is to repay the loan.

further loans and therefore educate and train other members of their group with potential repayment issues.[9]

Progressive Loans

In progressive lending, successful repayment allows for better terms in a borrower's subsequent loan. The progressive loan structure method reveals that learning effects have a positive influence on rates of repayment. Micro entrepreneurs who have successfully repaid their first, second and subsequent loan will ascend along the progressive loan structure. A higher level therefore means more stable and reliable repayment. In first loans the rate of repayment is generally more volatile, as default is more likely and borrowers are still in the process of acquiring new entrepreneurial and financial skills. Members who have advanced to a higher level in the progressive loan structure reveal a significantly more stable and notably better rate of repayment.[10]

Regular Meetings with MFIs

Frequent meetings with the MFI – which is also when interest is collected – allow for a more accurate assessment and monitoring of a borrower's business projects. MFIs can provide their clients with valuable information regarding the management of their assets, an improvement of the proceedings involved, and other useful skills. This enables loan officers to nip potential problems in the bud, before their clients' situation may even deteriorate.

6.3 SOCIO-ECONOMIC FACTORS

Socio-economic factors are decisive when it comes to lending in the microfinance sector, as they influence the generation of cash flows and with it the loan repayments. Particularly relevant are location and gender.

Urban vs. Rural Population

A look at the microfinance market globally reveals that about half of all loans are issued to clients in urban areas, 45 per cent to clients living in rural and 5 per cent to those living in semi-urban areas. Accessibility and market presence thereby play an important role.

As a rule, borrowers from urban areas have an advantage over rural clients. Information is more readily available and activities that add value find a wider clientele. This increases profitability in borrowers. Market proximity has a positive influence on the borrowers' cash flows that are used to redeem their interest and repay their loan. MFIs that grant loans in rural areas have much greater challenges to meet. For micro entrepreneurs in rural areas, going to market is considerably more difficult, as they will try to lower their transport costs per item sold. Consequently, they will only take their goods to market when they have produced sufficient quantities. Farmers, for instance, will only generate cash flows after their harvest. Interest cannot for this matter be paid on a regular basis, but payments are dictated by the maturity of their crops. Meeting these challenges and access to markets are highly influential when it comes to steadily increasing repayment rates in borrowers.[11]

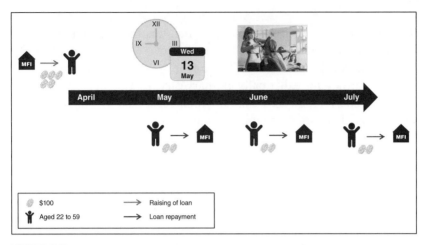

FIGURE 6.3 Example of a Micro Loan – Tameer Karobar Loan
Data Source: Tameer Bank

The Tameer Karobar Loan is a loan that predominantly serves micro entrepreneurs who generate a regular income from their business activities. The operator of a hair salon, for example, has borrowed $500 that he will redeem over the course of three months.

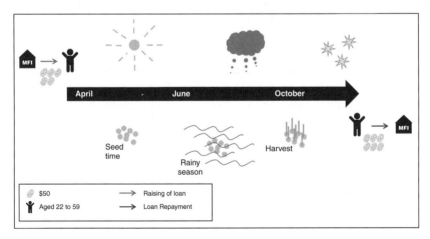

FIGURE 6.4 Example of an Agricultural Loan – Agri Group Loan
Data Source: Tameer Bank

Tameer Bank's Agri Group Loan is a loan that has been tailored to farmers in Pakistan. A Pakistani farmer borrows $250 for the cultivation of rice. Seedtime is in May. During the rainy season the crop will begin to grow and can finally be harvested in October. After the course of one year, the entire credit volume is repaid. During the life of the loan, there are no payments required.

MFIs also provide products to thwart the irregular cash flows of a market gardener, for example. Tameer Bank, an MFI in Pakistan, provides more than 20 different microloans, most notably the Tameer Karobar Loan (see Figure 6.3) and the Agri Group Loan (see Figure 6.4).

The Tameer Karobar Loan is a tailor-made loan for micro entrepreneurs, designed to fund circulating assets and make investments. The loan is repaid monthly, in equal installments. As this loan is based on monthly installments, it is only ever suitable for micro enterprises that manage to generate regular cash flows with their business model – for example, a micro entrepreneur who lives in the city and owns a hair salon, whose regular clientele will enable them to redeem their loan.

A vegetable farmer living in the hinterland of Pakistan would typically apply for a loan from Agri Group Loan. In Pakistan, this group loan is issued to farmers exclusively. Unlike with the Tameer Karobar Loan, the Agri Group Loan demands a one-off repayment of the entire loan including interest at the end of its term. The fact that no payments have to be made during the life of a loan is a concession to the farmers, as several months elapse between seedtime and harvest, and cash flows can only be generated when the goods are sold. With no savings on hand, grain growers are simply unable to repay their loans in weekly or monthly installments.[12]

These examples illustrate that MFIs have developed products that are made to measure for specific groups of clients by making allowances for irregular incomes. A client's creditworthiness should remain unaffected as a business model that only generates incomes every other month may well be as successful as a popular hair salon downtown.

Gender

More than two thirds of all loans are given to women, less than a third flows to men. Evidently there is a preference of female over male borrowers. This discrimination is more likely to be found on the supply side than on the demand side. Practice reveals that female borrowers carry less of a risk than men. What are the reasons for this?

There are many different reasons why women are preferable clients. Women exhibit certain characteristics that reduce the possibility of loan default. Their boundaries of shame are set much lower and they are more risk-averse than men.

Risk-averse properties in women are a sense of modesty, discretion and discipline. These properties root in cultural customs such as the fact that women are guardians of entire family clans and their ensuing roles as custodians of the family's funds. Women use their income to meet their children's needs, for their education, food and healthcare. Men, on the contrary, stretch their income to fund personal requirements such as their entertainment and status symbols.[13]

Against the cultural backdrop that borrowers lose face in their societies if they fail to repay their loans, women have been revealed to have a lower boundary of shame. For this reason, women are more susceptible to moral and social pressure than men and they more readily accept help. They share information, generally communicate more openly about their problems and regularly attend MFI meetings.

All in all, women who start their own business or seek financial resources are more risk-averse. They are thus more cooperative, and proceed more prudently and less opportunistically in dealing with their family's finances, which reduces information asymmetries and moral hazard adverse selection for their lender. Women are therefore less likely to seek a loan beyond their repayment capabilities.[14]

For these three reasons, loans given to women yield a lower rate of default than those given to men.[15] Higher risk aversion admittedly leads to an increase in repayment rate, but it may, however, not necessarily have a positive impact on an MFI's profitability. For one reason: albeit women reveal a lower average credit volume than men, an MFI will incur virtually the same operating costs for high and low volumes. MFIs therefore are challenged to bring the lower risk of default in women in line with their profitability in order to strike a balance between lending methodologies and socio-economic factors.[16]

6.4 LATE PAYMENTS AND OVER-INDEBTEDNESS OF CLIENTS

The portfolio at risk (PAR) is generally very low. It is a ratio that singles out the loans in the microfinance sector most at risk of default. Only 1–2 per cent of loans slip into default after as little as 90 days (see Figure 6.5). The repayment rate of micro entrepreneurs stands at more than 99 per cent. The following explains how many defaults may be "mended."

Over-indebtedness has become increasingly rare on account of credit bureaus, and MFIs are continuously monitoring their clients' situation to be able to react swiftly to any signs of trouble. One of the parameters, and an early warning system that MFIs employ, is the so-called over-indebtedness index, explained as follows (see Figure 6.6):

$$\frac{Monthly\ payments\ on\ business\ and\ household\ debt}{Monthly\ income\ net} \times 100$$

In practice, a factor below 76 per cent indicates that the borrower is solvent and therefore will be able to redeem his or her loan. A factor

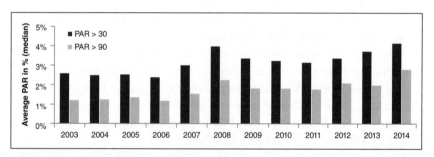

FIGURE 6.5 Portfolio at Risk (PAR) of MFIs
Data Source: MIX (2016)

The PAR denotes the number of outstanding loans after a period of 30 or 90 days respectively, compared to the total number of outstanding loans.

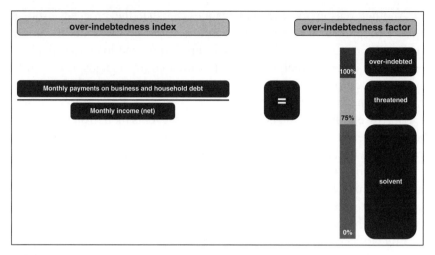

FIGURE 6.6 Over-Indebtedness Index and Over-Indebtedness Factor
Data Source: Schicks (2011); Liv (2013)

The over-indebtedness index assesses clients as either solvent, threatened or over-indebted.

between 76 and 100 per cent suggests that the borrower's repayments could be threatened. MFIs therefore often react when the index approaches the 76 per cent threshold. A factor of over 100 would imply over-indebtedness.

What are the triggers of over-indebtedness? The number one reason for over-indebtedness is repeated borrowing, followed by a lack of cash flows from a client's business activity, and their lack of financial knowledge or poor education.[17]

A survey of borrower behavior in Cambodia has revealed that a debt resulting from multiple loans with different MFIs severely decreases a borrower's likelihood of repayment.[18] An increase in loans that are taken out at the same time substantially raises repayment difficulties. Borrowers with more than four outstanding loans show a surge in repayment difficulties compared to those who have only one to three outstanding loans.

Another reason for over-indebtedness is that the proceeds from a micro entrepreneur's business are too low to cover the debts including interest. To avoid over-indebtedness of this nature, and to ensure that borrowers will adhere to their duties even if the market changes, it is vital to review and sculpt a particular business idea, as well as the cash flows generated by a potential project.

Borrowers' lack of financial knowledge prevents them from managing their finances sustainably and thereby repaying their debts. As a result, borrowers with an insufficient knowledge of the financial consequences are more prone to take multiple loans with different MFIs. MFIs in turn have recognized this and are now offering their clients training and upgrade courses that should make them more financially versatile. At the same time, credit bureaus put a halt to excessive and multiple borrowing.

Education in particular correlates positively with the rate of repayment, not least because educated borrowers more easily understand the relationship between finances and business.

Economic factors such as food inflation, diseases in plants, crop failure, as well as death and theft of livestock can lead to shocks in borrowers. This, however, need not necessarily be linked to over-indebtedness, as different borrowers follow different courses of action. Borrowers who invest in livestock and grain cultivation are more likely to meet their financial responsibilities than less diversified borrowers.

6.5 DEFAULT PREVENTION AND RESTRUCTURING

In the following, Peru will serve as an example for the prevention measures taken by regulators and MFIs to avoid possible over-indebtedness on the one hand and illustrate the procedures of MFIs in cases of default on the other.

Market Overview

Peru boasts a highly developed and well-regulated financial market serving more than 4.1 million micro entrepreneurs. A wide range of MFIs, small NGOs and commercial banks characterize the market. Consumer protection is enforced by SBS and INDECOPI,[19] the two regulators for financial service providers. SBS operates a central financial database that collects customer data concerning the debt charges of financial institutions on a monthly basis. This data is shared with a credit bureau that in turn supplies information to regulated and non-regulated MFIs. These collective efforts aim to combat over-indebtedness in microfinance enterprises by thwarting attempts to take out multiple loans with various MFIs at the same time. Borrowers with default issues in particular are targeted to keep them from taking out further loans to cover the costs of previous ones, as this strategy usually leads to a spiral of debt.[20]

Standard Measures in Case of Loan Default

If a borrower slips into default, an MFI will typically react after 7 to 15 days. It is common practice to contact the borrower by telephone, SMS or in an email as a first step. As a rule, the loan officer is in charge of the collection of outstanding payments for up to 30 days upon detection of default. Loan officers may sanction defaulted borrowers as they deem appropriate within a range of possible courses of action. Many MFIs have considerable leeway when it comes to collecting debts and they take different factors into consideration that may have led to a defaulted installment. In rural areas, for instance, borrowers may have experienced difficulties transporting their goods. As a result of their late arrival in the market, they suffer financial losses. Beyond that, there are manifold reasons for short-term default that do not suggest that a micro entrepreneur is unable or unwilling to repay a loan. In addition to this, a loan officer's visit to a client's home in order to assess their loan situation is costly and time-consuming, which explains why MFIs reluctantly resort to such measures straight away. Ultimately, the strong presence of credit bureaus is largely responsible for MFIs' delay in reaction to defaulted installments. Micro entrepreneurs are fully aware that defaulted payments lead to a negative credit rating and thus severely compromise their chances of any future loans.

If a late payment nevertheless is prolonged, after 30 days, the majority of MFIs will dispatch a loan officer to the client's home to assess the situation and attempt to address the problem on hand. In most cases, a chat will suffice for a mutual agreement. If not, and upon repeated default, the case will be transferred to a special internal department that is exclusively in charge of defaults. After a 60-day period of default, loans are often restructured and there will be a so-called haircut, or a reduction in interest rate. Micro entrepreneurs are closely involved in the restructuring process, which additionally strengthens the lender–borrower relationship. As a matter of fact, the vast majority of borrowers will adhere to the new terms

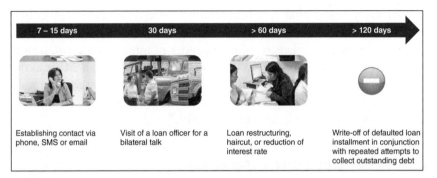

FIGURE 6.7   Measures upon Detection of Default
Data Source: Solli, Galindo, Rizzi, Rhyne and van de Walle (2015)

An MFI will only react 7 to 15 days after detection of late payment, as there may be innocuous reasons, such as a burst tire on the way to the market, that may have led to a loss of income. If the debt is not cleared upon contract, and should the bilateral talks yield no results, a loan is restructured and interest may be lowered. After 120 days, the MFI writes off the defaulted loan, but will continue to attempt to collect the outstanding debt.

and stay faithful clients of a particular MFI. Some MFIs, moreover, provide defaulted borrowers with special services such as comprehensive credit counseling. Such services – and the MFIs providing them – do recognize that many loan complications are a direct result of a borrower's domestic situation. If no solution can be found, defaulted installments are written off after 120 days, albeit the debts remain registered with the credit bureau – and in many cases MFIs will continue to attempt to collect them over a long period of time. Figure 6.7 is an overview of the measures taken by MFIs upon detection of default.[21]

It can be safely concluded that MFIs and their loan officers are more than anxious to avoid their clients' over-indebtedness, and for this reason supply a comprehensive package of measures that aims to find the best possible solution for both parties in the event of default. The role of a loan officer in the lending process is given further attention in the following.

6.6 OCCUPATION: LOAN OFFICER

The loan officer of an MFI embraces the entire process when micro entrepreneurs are granted loans. Business ideas, current business activities, as well as creditworthiness of potential clients are all assessed and rated.

Profile of a Loan Officer

Loan officers carry considerable responsibility and are therefore screened and scrutinized during their recruitment. They must have a well-balanced personal and skills profile. Loan officers must also be respected and responsible members of society, and display a particularly strong intrinsic motivation and act as role models at all times. Formally, their expected behavior is recorded in a code of conduct. Any offences will be sanctioned rapidly and rigorously.

Loan officers' skills typically involve technical and specialized knowledge of microfinance, but beyond that they are required to have a state-of-the-art knowledge of the entire range of legal and regulatory requirements and adamantly keep up to date. A profound knowledge of human nature and strong local ties are most beneficial too. In the cultural regions relevant to microfinance, personal contact is imperative in business relationships. Clients must therefore be able to trust their loan officer wholeheartedly for a solid and long-term relationship.[22]

Process

Figure 6.8 displays the screening and reviewing procedure of potential borrowers. In a first step of the loan granting procedure, a loan officer will advise their client: both transactions and mission of a chosen MFI are introduced and the MFI's credit policy is explained. Should a micro entrepreneur decide to apply for a loan, his or her application is registered with the MFI. The loan officer decides whether the MFI will support a potential client's enterprise based on this preliminary application form. In the case

FIGURE 6.8 Procedure to Assess Potential MFI Clients

Before the clients submit their application, they are instructed by the loan officer. Subsequently, all submitted documents are reviewed and an inspection of the premises is scheduled. If the comprehensive assessment results in a successful application, the credit contract can be signed.

of a decision in favor of the applicant, the loan officer assesses the client's business plan and financial statements with respect to the entrepreneurial and financial admission requirements. The assessment of a client's application takes seven days.

A further seven days are dedicated to assessing a client's creditworthiness. After a visit on the client's premises and an ensuing conversation, the loan officer decides if the client has a high or low credit risk profile. The client's information on the application form and his or her business plan, as well as the local framework, are taken into consideration. The local framework may include the implementation of the business plan, but also the micro entrepreneur's accommodation, geographical location, his or her relationships with neighbors and support from friends and family.

If the subsequent assessment leads to a positive decision, the loan contract can be prepared. This procedure takes another seven days. As many as 20 to 25 days may therefore elapse between a first advisory meeting and the actual signing of the contract.

Appendix A shows an example of a loan application form.

6.7 PRELIMINARY CONCLUSIONS

Classic credit theory by Stiglitz and Weiss (1981) investigates credit behavior in an environment of imperfect information. Via selection by means of financial collateral or the amount of an interest rate, asymmetrical information, moral hazard and adverse selection are reduced. Credit rationing occurs when borrowers are willing to pay a higher rate than the equilibrium interest rate at which banks offer loans. The reason for this is that with higher interest rates, banks also expect higher repayment default rates and the interest does not compensate for the losses incurred.

Lending in microfinance is based on a sense of security (i.e. trust), since micro entrepreneurs are unable to bring in financial collateral when

MUSICAL INSTRUMENTS – SANTIAGO DE CALI, COLOMBIA

In his workshop, Katanga Moreno and his family manufacture drums, marimbas, maracabas and other percussion instruments following an ancient African tradition. He collects wood on the Pacific coast and uses it for his production. He is a member of a music group and promotes the dissemination of Afro-Latin music in Colombia. The loans with WWB Colombia ($1700 and $5700) have allowed him to purchase the raw materials and tools for the manufacture of these instruments and to fund a steady expansion of his business.

Source: BlueOrchard

taking their first loan. Lending methodologies and socio-economic factors are decisive elements when it comes to credit contracts.

Any appropriate lending methodology relies on a micro entrepreneur's readiness and ability to repay their debts. Group loans, mutual monitoring, a progressive loan structure and regular meetings with the MFI of choice are indispensable in securing high repayment morale.

Location and market proximity are key elements too. In addition to this, it has become evident that women carry considerably more responsibility for their families than men. These two socio-economic factors have a positive influence on the repayment rate of micro entrepreneurs.

And yet there are occasionally cases of over-indebtedness of micro entrepreneurs, in developing as in industrialized countries. Credit bureaus and training programs in financial and business matters counteract over-indebtedness and lower default rates, therefore acting as a sustainable catalyst for the success of micro entrepreneurial endeavors. In general, the PAR is rather low, as only 1 to 2 per cent of all the granted loans are defaulted for longer than a period of 90 days.

NOTES

1 Muhammad Yunus, founder of modern microfinance and Nobel Peace Prize laureate.
2 Stiglitz and Weiss (1981), pp. 393–410.
3 Hartarska and Holtmann (2006), pp. 150–152; Kropp, Turvey, Just, Kong and Guo (2009), pp. 69–71, 83–84; Meyer and Nagarajan (2006), p. 168.
4 Barboza and Trejos (2009), p. 284; Zeller (2006), p. 197.
5 De Soto (2001), p. 6.
6 Armendáriz de Aghion (1999), pp. 80–81; Armendáriz de Aghion and Morduch (2005), pp. 119–122; Barboza and Barreto (2006), pp. 316–330; Barboza and Trejos (2009), p. 284; Besley and Coate (1995), pp. 2–3; Ghatak and Guinnane (1999), pp. 196–198; Kropp, Turvey, Just, Kong and Guo (2009), p. 70; Morduch (1999), pp. 1570, 1582–1583; Stiglitz (1990), pp. 351–353; Van Tassel (1999), pp. 3–25; Varian (1990), pp. 153–154.
7 Barboza and Trejos (2009), p. 287; Kropp, Turvey, Just, Kong and Guo (2009), pp. 69–70; Van Tassel (1999), pp. 3–25.
8 Nash (1951), pp. 286–295.
9 Armedáriz de Aghion (1999), pp. 80–81; Barboza and Trejos (2009), p. 284; Ghatak and Guinnane (1999), pp. 196–197, 225; Kropp, Turvey, Just, Kong and Guo (2009), p. 70; Stiglitz (1990), pp. 351–353; Varian (1990), pp. 153–154.
10 Barboza and Trejos (2009), pp. 294–295.
11 Barboza and Trejos (2009), pp. 289–297.
12 Tameer Bank (2015).
13 Armendáriz de Aghion and Morduch (2005), p. 183.
14 Armendáriz de Aghion and Morduch (2005), pp. 183–184; Hartmann-Wendels, Mählmann and Versen (2009), pp. 353, 358; Todd (1996), p. 182.
15 Remenyi (2000), p. 52.
16 D'Espallier, Guerin and Mersland (2013), p. 590.

17 Liv (2013), p. 16.
18 Ibidem, pp. 48–49.
19 Superintendencia de Bancos y Seguros and the Instituto Nacional de Defensa de la Competencia y de la Protección de la Propiedad Intelectual.
20 Solli, Galindo, Rizzi, Rhyne and van de Walle (2015), pp. 12–13.
21 Ibidem, p. 15.
22 The Collaboratory (2015).

CHAPTER 7

Loan Pricing

I firmly believe that giving people loans is to offer them an opportunity to get out of poverty by leveraging their own efforts.

Queen Máxima of the Netherlands[1]

The absolute costs for a loan of $100 are virtually the same as for a loan of $1000. However, with higher volumes of credit, these costs are much less significant than with microloans.

MFIs are economically sustainable and socially involved, provided they can cover their costs in the long run and fulfill their social mission at the same time. As the fixed costs (operating and capital costs) constitute more than 80 per cent of the overall costs of a microloan, loan pricing in the developmental regions that are accessed by MFIs has become rather inflexible. The higher operating costs compared to traditional loans in industrialized countries are compensated by means of income from interest.

Borrowers are willing to accept these less favorable conditions but in turn gain long-term access to capital. Their impressive profit margins from their business undertakings allow them to swiftly redeem their debts.

Increasing digitalization, and the use of new technology in developing countries, results in a bundling of efficiency in both lenders and borrowers, lowering the pool of costs.

7.1 INTEREST RATE COMPONENTS

The comparatively high interest rates are one of the most controversial and debated factors in the microfinance sector. Less favorable credit conditions in comparison with industrialized countries are often wrongly denounced as excessive or price gouging. They are justified even though they often figure in the double-digit range. The following will explain why.

Financial services in poor countries are costly, because revenue with MFIs is mostly only generated from their loan business proceeds, and because smaller credit volumes lead to higher costs per individual transaction. For this reason, banks and large providers of financial services do not issue microloans. A loan of $100 and a loan of $1000 require the same number of employees and amount of resources. The procedures involved for a single loan may easily amount to $25. In absolute figures this appears perfectly logical; relatively, however, in the case of a loan of $100, this may constitute a staggering 25 per cent of the credit volume. Consequently, the relative costs per transaction are considerably lower in larger credit volumes, which means that MFIs are forced to charge micro entrepreneurs rather high interest rates in order to cover their operating costs.

Figure 7.1 illustrates the financial determinants of the interest rates in microfinance and compares them to the relevant costs in industrialized

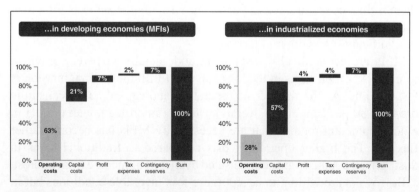

FIGURE 7.1 Determinants of Interest Rates
Adapted from: Bundesbank (2014) and Gonzalez (2011)

The comparison is based on data from Germany. Operating costs in connection with lending in developing countries amount to more than half of the total rate of interest. In industrialized countries, however, it is less than a third.

countries such as Germany or Switzerland. The graph displays the five financial determinants – operating costs, capital costs, profit, tax expenditures and contingency reserves – as well as their relevance when it comes to determining interest rates. Capital costs are another important cost factor, accounting for almost a quarter. Most MFIs are unable to fund themselves and therefore depend on banks or microfinance funds. The profit, the contingency reserves for loan defaults and the tax expenditures represent another 16 per cent of the overall credit costs.

In industrialized countries loans are less expensive, as the operating costs are lower. The capital costs (in this case, real interest rates), which also include a liquidity premium, constitute over half of the total volume of credit. The operating costs add up to about a quarter, and the contingency reserves, profit and tax expenditures amount to around 16 per cent.

This clearly shows that the share of operating costs in the interest rates of MFI loans is more than double those of loans in industrialized countries. The share of the contingency reserves for loan defaults is virtually the same in both MFIs and commercial banks. Microloans have a rather low default probability due to social collateral, and it is comparable to the loan default probabilities in industrialized countries. As the profits generated from lending are often the only source of income for MFIs, they are vital for any regional and national growth. For this reason, the proportion of the profit from microloans is more substantial than in a traditional loan. Commercial banks in industrialized countries are more diversified, as they can fall back onto other sources of income along with the credit business.

The following will explain why high costs are inevitable in an MFI's lending operations, and also focus on the parameters that will allow for cost efficiency which will eventually lead to lower interest rates for borrowers.[2]

Operating Costs

Microfinance is a business model that is rather labor-intensive. Moreover, the transactional costs for the client are higher than with other financial services providers, due to the smaller volumes of credit and the local credit rules and regulations.

Lending methodologies, the strategy of client acquisition and the collection of the usually weekly interest payments all influence the operating costs, which amount to nearly 63 per cent of the overall credit costs. The largest share of expenditures is consumed by staff and administration.

Whereas administration expenses such as stationery, rent and electricity are fixed and can therefore not be lowered substantially, the employment of staff in administration and with the micro entrepreneur locally may be structured more efficiently. All MFIs worldwide focus on effective and efficient deployment of personnel in an effort to continue to lower the credit costs for their clients. Efficiency does, however, have its limits, and mostly because of the all-important personal interaction between loan officers and their clients. Figure 7.2 illustrates the development of the average volume of credit and the share of employee expenditures. Between 2003 and 2014, the volume of credit per client increased steadily. The maturity of the market and progressive lending – which allows clients to take out more substantial loans based on successful repayment of any previous loans – are to be credited for this development. Higher volumes of credit lower personnel expenditures. Despite the fact that the same number of visits to a borrower's home will be required, they are less expensive in comparison.

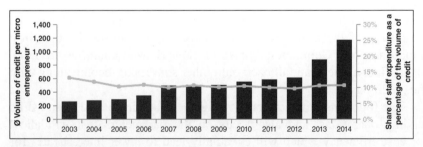

FIGURE 7.2   Volume of Credit Compared to Staff Expenditure
Data Source: MIX (2016)

Higher volumes of credit can lower staff expenditures, especially when borrowers have successfully repaid their first loan and decide to take out further loans (median).

Capital Costs

Apart from their own financial means, MFIs often borrow capital from commercial banks or funds that are specialized in microfinance. The costs of these means either correspond with the market interest rates of the banks or the revenue expected with investors. The capital costs are therefore fixed and cannot be lowered within today's financing structures.

Contingency Reserves

If micro entrepreneurs fail to repay their loans, the MFI will have to compensate for the defaulted interest rates and loan. This is referred to as a bad debt and is calculated on the basis of the defaulted obligations. In order to avoid such losses and be profitable at the same time, an MFI will have contingency reserves. This increase in interest rates must, however, be moderate enough, as higher interest rates usually result in a surge of micro entrepreneurs slipping into default or payment difficulties. This in turn will prompt an MFI to repeatedly increase their interest rates to be able to cover the defaults – a vicious circle and ultimately a downward spiral. As a consequence, contingency reserves are almost fixed and can hardly be lowered because of already low default rates.

Profit

An MFI will retain roughly 7 per cent of the interest rate as their profit, which is also the most substantial source of income of an MFI and needed to realize growth plans.

Tax Expenditures

Tax expenditures amount to roughly 2 per cent of the total interest rate and therefore are not considered decisive. The tax rate is determined by the respective national fiscal law.

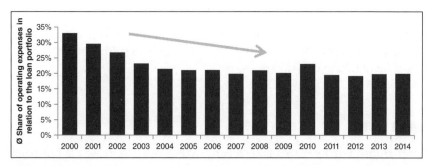

FIGURE 7.3 Operating Costs: Average Share of Operating Costs in Relation to the Total Loan Portfolio
Data Source: MIX (2016)

More efficient processes optimize procedures and therefore lower operating costs occur.

Boosting Efficiency

More efficient processes lead to lower operating costs. Figure 7.3 shows the operating costs as a share in percentage of the total loan portfolio of an MFI. It reveals an increase in efficiency in the microfinance sector worldwide.[3]

The components of interest rates largely are based on fixed parameters. Staff and digitalization are potentially the factors where a general decrease in interest rates seems feasible.[4] Employees on the whole are increasingly better trained to serve a larger client base. As a result, the turnover can be augmented while operating costs are reduced at the same time. Efficient planning of the local weekly loan installment collection trips reduces traveling expenses and with it the operating costs.

Increasing digitalization and the use of new technologies counteract unwanted expenditures. Mobile communication has greatly improved and made mobile phones the quickest and most widely used technology of all time.[5]

M-PESA – Mobile Money

According to estimates, 1.7 billion people worldwide do not have a bank account. Yet most of them have a mobile phone. Rural regions in emerging countries have evidently jumped the queue and skipped the landline option as a result of insufficient telecommunication infrastructure in favor of mobile phones and smart phones.

In Nairobi, the capital of Kenya, paying for a taxi fare with your mobile phone is easier than in Berlin or Zurich.

Launched in 2007 by the Kenyan mobile network operator Safaricom, M-Pesa allows users to deposit money into an M-Pesa account on their mobile devices to swiftly transfer money to other users all over the world without delay. The fast and reliable service is predominantly used by workers in cities to transfer money to their families living in more rural areas, and has given millions of people access to the formal financial system. Mobile transaction services are considerably less time-consuming and thus create time that can be spent more productively.

M-Pesa in Kenya is more successful than other service providers, for the following reasons:

- Lower transfer costs
- Clear and efficient marketing
- Dominant market position of Safaricom
- No formal governmental approval required, as the project was qualified an experiment by the government itself
- Instances of violence in the wake of the 2008 elections led Kenyans to have more faith in M-Pesa than their banks that were involved in ethical issues
- Network effect: an increase in users equals more benefit for all

Mobile phones can be integrated into the loan payment system.[6] M-Pesa is a branchless banking service that allows its customers to deposit and withdraw money from a network of agents. Kenya has been using this easy and reliable payment system since 2007. Borrowers may use their mobile devices to repay interest rates or loans. For borrowers and lenders alike this means more efficient business transactions and thus lower operating costs for MFIs and in turn a drop in costs for micro entrepreneurs. Loan officers' regular weekly visits to their clients' premises remain a must. Their presence locally allows them to monitor the implementation

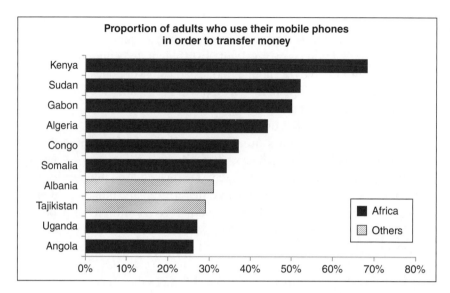

Availability of M-PESA in Africa

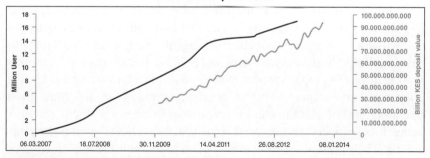

FIGURE 7.4 M-Pesa – Mobile Money
Data Source: Demombynes and Thegeya (2012); Mbiti and Weil (2011);
Pickens (2009); The Economist (2013); World Bank (2016), database 2012

M-Pesa (M stands for mobile and pesa means money in Swahili) is a leading mobile phone-based money transfer service in Kenya. (see Figure 7.4)

and success of business ideas and spot early warning signs in connection with repayment difficulties, which they try to tackle with the micro entrepreneurs.

7.2 SETTING SUSTAINABLE INTEREST RATES

MFIs establish their interest rates on the basis of their high lending costs. The following explains in a simplified manner how the effective interest rate can be calculated with the above mentioned determinants. The effective interest rate indicates how much profit an MFI must gain from a microloan in order to cover its costs and strengthen its business sustainably. The formula has been adapted from Rosenberg et al. and Ledgerwood and simplified.[7] The general assumption is that an MFI does not have an income generated from financial assets outside its loan portfolio. The effective interest rate (R) is determined by means of the following terms: the capital costs (C), the operating costs (O), the tax expenditures (T), the defaulted loans (D) and the profit (P)

$$R = \frac{C + O + T + D + P}{1 - D}$$

In the case of default, an MFI will lose both the loan and its interest payments. For this reason, the costs that an MFI must cover are divided by the share of repaid loans (1 − D), which consequently constitute the contingency reserves.

7.3 REGIONAL DIFFERENCES

There are regional differences when it comes to operating costs (see Figure 7.5). Whereas the average volume of credit influences the costs, sector-specific determinants as well as regional influences also play a role. Nevertheless, the following general conclusions can be drawn.

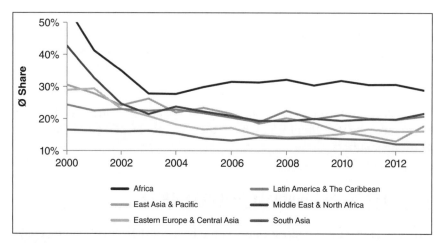

FIGURE 7.5 Operating Costs as a Percentage of the Loan Portfolio According to Region
Data Source: MIX (2016)

> Regions with a higher developed financial sector have a lower share in operating costs in the percentage of the loan portfolio than less developed regions such as Africa (median).

Operating costs of MFIs in South and South East Asia are generally lower than in other regions thanks to group lending, which usually results in a larger volume of credit.

The relatively low operating costs in South America may, however, not be explained through the prevalence of group lending, but are more likely to be the result of a comparatively mature financial system. In addition to this, the economic development in South America is more advanced than in other regions. MFIs can profit from an established infrastructure and boost their efficiency. Sub-Saharan Africa lacks both a developed economy and a developed financial system, which accounts for still comparatively high operating costs in this region.

7.4 LOAN RECIPIENTS' WILLINGNESS TO REPAY

Micro entrepreneurs are able to repay their loans largely because their cash flows are impressive, despite – or perhaps rather because of – their comparatively small businesses and therefore lower fixed operating costs, such as machinery or staff.

Selling Pineapples

The sale and resale of pineapples can generate an impressive profit margin per piece. In this example, the borrower can repay her monthly installments by selling five pineapples.

(Continued)

Selling price per pineapple   COP 2000*

Prime cost per pineapple   – COP 1600

= Profit margin per pineapple   = COP 400 (25%)

At an annual interest rate of 25 per cent, the principal of COP 100,000 would entail monthly interest liabilities of COP 2000. Selling five pineapples allows the borrower to repay her monthly installments.

*Colombian Pesos

Source: BlueOrchard

If a micro entrepreneur's retail business, agricultural harvest or the production of goods can generate a revenue of $5 a day – costs incurred of $2 – the result is a staggering gross profit margin of 60 per cent.

7.5 PRELIMINARY CONCLUSIONS

The absolute costs of a loan rarely depend on its amount. However, for a microloan of only $200 those are more significant than for larger volumes of credit.

The determination of sustainable interest rates allows MFIs to cover their lending costs, encourage growth based on their profits and acquire new clients. The interest rates for micro entrepreneurs are calculated on the basis of the MFI's operating and capital costs, profit, tax expenditures and contingency reserves for possible cases of default. In a more mature financial sector, efforts can be bundled and made more efficient with the help of larger volumes of credit (e.g. due to its progressive lending structure), as well as new technologies such as digitalization and mobile money transfer systems. All these measures reduce the operating costs of MFIs, which again will create more attractive loan terms for the client.

With their impressive cash flows, micro entrepreneurs in most cases manage to redeem their MFI loans in the course of a few days.

Generating an income to repay their loans is therefore not a micro entrepreneur's main challenge, but having access to capital is. Traditional banks do not issue loans in these regions as they are deemed to be inefficient and lack profitability. Instead local money lenders (e.g. loan sharks) provide loans that are not amortizable.

VEGETABLE STALL – BOGOTÀ, COLOMBIA

Nylsa Avendano, 39, runs a market stall that offers anything that grows in the Valle del Cauca: pineapples, bananas, tomatoes, beans, onions and more. Her working day begins at three o'clock in the morning. She used her first loan of $400 with WWB Colombia to set up her stall and steadily increase her range of products. She currently has a loan of $750. The steady increase in turnover and revenue has brought a tremendous change to her life, most notably that she can now finance a decent education for her children.

Source: BlueOrchard

Microfinance focuses on smaller volumes of credit and has success-fully filled this gap by developing a system to effectively support the pre-dominantly small enterprises.

NOTES

1 UN Secretary-General's Special Advocate for Inclusive Finance for Development (UNSGSA).
2 Nagarsekar (2012), pp. 9–14.
3 Rosenberg, Gaul, Ford and Tomilova (2013), pp. 13–14.
4 Chen and Faz (2015), p. 2.
5 Bezerra, Bock, Candelon, Chai, Choi, Corwin, DiGrande, Gulshan, Michael and Varas (2015).
6 Basel Committee on Banking Supervision (2015).
7 Ledgerwood (2000), p. 149; Rosenberg, Gaul, Ford and Tomilova (2013), p. 2.

CHAPTER 8

Social Performance Management

I've seen the power of micro-finance all over the world in the eyes of mothers and fathers. It's unmistakable – joy and deep satisfaction they feel from being able to work hard and provide for their children and their future.

Rich Stearns[1]

The microfinance sector distinguishes itself by means of its rapid growth and innovative potential. Profitability is an easily identifiable variable. However, new instruments are continuously being developed for the measurement of social performance and therefore the assessment of the social mission and outreach of MFIs as well as its impact. This is done to ensure that MFIs fulfill their social mission, contribute towards the fight against poverty and promote the financial inclusion of the poor.

Social performance is measured by MFIs and MIVs alike. There is no trade-off between social performance and profitability. Microfinance institutions do not have to decide on one or the other, as both goals can be met simultaneously. The double bottom line thus becomes even more significant.

8.1 SOCIAL PERFORMANCE

There is no doubt that the sustainable funding of MFIs has been instrumental in their success. Clearly, an MFI that is able to cover its costs, will in turn be able to fund growth and, as a result of that, supply an ever-increasing client base with loans. Despite the fact that a major part of the growth of the entire microfinance sector is based on sustainable profitability, investors, fund managers and MFIs insist on reaching the destitute and poor of this world, to provide them with useful financial services in order to improve their living conditions. Microfinance focuses on both financial and social aspects to reach these goals. They do not contradict but rather complement each other. In recent years, investors and financial institutions all over the world have been noted to seek ways of transparent assessment of social aspects to complement those of the profitability of investments.

Why does microfinance put so much emphasis on social performance? Microfinance's social aspect is a reservoir of the passion and commitment of all the investors and people involved in this line of business. People who identify with their clients witness and experience on a daily basis how microfinance helps their fellow beings to escape poverty. Governments, financial institutions, foundations, sponsors as well as private investors invest in microfinance from sheer conviction that their money will have a positive impact on societies locally. MFIs therefore must openly declare to their investors both the development of their social mission and how they intend to meet their goals. As a means of monitoring their services, customer satisfaction and the degree of improvement of living standards in their micro entrepreneurs, MFIs regularly publish their business reports.

Social performance is defined as the translation of a social mission into everyday actions of the institution in question. Social performance has to begin right at the core of the internal processes of an MFI, to define social determinants and variables and scale them.[2]

The Social Performance Task Force (SPTF), a global membership organization, has been working on a standard to advance social performance management in microfinance. Figure 8.1 illustrates the difference between social performance and social impact. Social performance denotes the number of poor and financially excluded who are reached by financial services (intent and design). The chart also displays the quality and usefulness of MFI services (internal systems and activities), as well as how borrowers profit from these services (output). Social impact, on the other hand, denotes the improvements on a micro entrepreneur's social

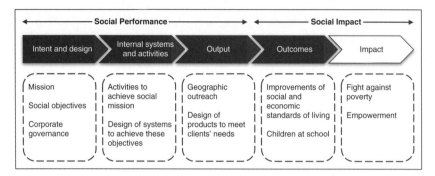

FIGURE 8.1 Social Performance and Social Impact
Data Source: Sinha (2006) and Social Performance Task Force (2014a)

Social performance measures an MFI's social responsibility. The mission of an MFI, as well as the quality and usefulness of suitable products and the ensuing improvement of a borrower's living standards, are thereby measured. Social impact, on the other hand, measures the improvements a loan has effectuated in a borrower's life as compared to people who have not taken a loan.

and economic standards of living as opposed to someone who has not received a loan (outcomes).[3] The changes effectuated by microfinance thus describe the impact on micro entrepreneurs. Microfinance and its idea to "do good" goes above and beyond the concept of any other socially responsible investment, where the main aim is "not to do damage."

8.2 MEASURING SOCIAL PERFORMANCE

Social performance can be measured by means of different methods. Figure 8.2 displays the different instruments often employed to measure social performance and social impact. The SPTF has devised six dimensions along which social performance can be measured, the so-called Universal Standards of Social Performance Measurement (USSPM). Today's practice often enough relies on these USSPMs, which include the CERISE Social Performance Indicators (SPI4) commonly used in the industry and designed in collaboration with the USSPM and Smart Campaign, an initiative promoting client protection.

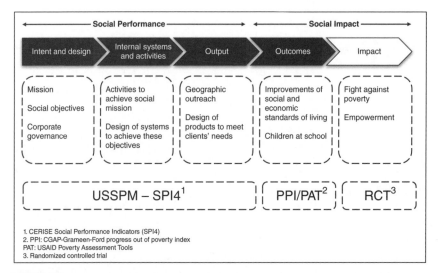

FIGURE 8.2   Measuring Social Performance

The USSPM and the SPI4 measure social performance, whereas the PPI and PAT instruments denote the result of social performance. Social impact is analyzed according to randomized controlled trials (RCTs).

Furthermore, the performance is evaluated in the individual regions where microfinance services are offered. CGAP, Grameen and the Ford Foundation have launched the Progress out of Poverty Index (PPI) that measures the results of social performance. The PPI investigates the degree of improvement in a client's social and financial situation, is available in 59 countries and is being applied by over 200 organizations.[4] The USAID poverty assessment tool (PAT), an initiative of the US Congress, also measures the level of poverty. All the partners that have assisted USAID in the development of microfinance and who borrow financial means from USAID must apply the PAT – if it is available for their country – and communicate their results. The tool is available in 37 countries and is being applied by 25 to 30 organizations. Both tools, PPI and PAT, are publicly accessible.

Universal Standards of Social Performance Management (USSPM)

The goal of the USSPM is to further illustrate the concept of social performance management and to standardize proven and tested practices. The USSPM are meant to assist MFIs to implement their social mission. The standards were devised seeing the demand in the sector for guidelines. They now combine the social performance initiatives of stakeholders all over the world in a single document (see Figure 8.3).

In addition to this, guidelines were defined alongside every standard. They will be further illustrated in this chapter by means of applying the SPI4.

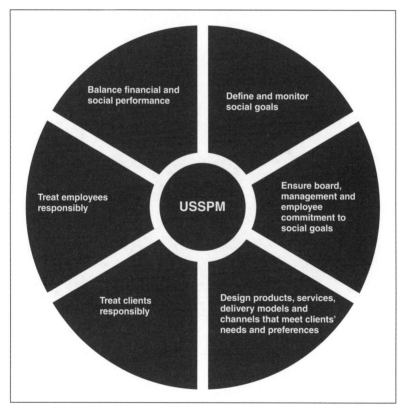

FIGURE 8.3 USSPM Overview
Adapted from: Social Performance Task Force (2014b)

Smart Campaign

The Smart Campaign certifies MFIs that commit to client protection. It was launched in 2013 and in April 2016 comprised more than 60 members worldwide (see Figure 8.4). The Smart Campaign's directive is the protection of clients: micro entrepreneurs should not borrow more funds than they will be able to repay, and not use products that they do not ultimately need. There is particular emphasis on a respectful treatment of the client and clients are given the chance to file a complaint, so that microloans can be issued even more effectively. The Smart Campaign has seven client protection principles that help MFIs to internalize an ethical mode of conduct with their clients. The following principles are the so-called essential practices i.e. basic conduct any client must expect on borrowing from an MFI.[5]

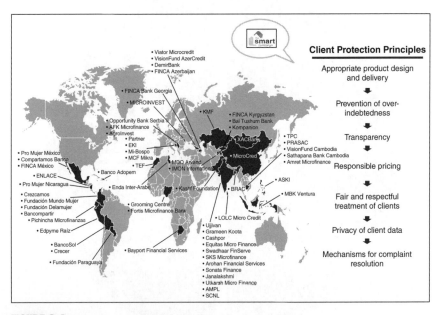

FIGURE 8.4   Smart Campaign
Adapted from: Smart Campaign (2016)

The Smart Campaign devised principles for client protection. In April 2016, there were 60 Smart Campaign-certified MFIs.

Appropriate product design and delivery

Providers will take adequate care to design products and delivery channels in such a way that they do not cause clients harm. Products and delivery channels will be designed with client characteristics taken into account.

Prevention of over-indebtedness

Providers will take adequate care in all phases of their credit process to determine that clients have the capacity to repay without becoming over-indebted. In addition, providers will implement and monitor internal systems that support prevention of over-indebtedness and will foster efforts to improve market-level credit risk management (such as credit information sharing).

Transparency

Providers will communicate clear, sufficient and timely information in a manner and language that clients can understand so that clients can make informed decisions. The need for transparent information on pricing, terms and conditions of products is highlighted.

Responsible pricing

Pricing, terms and conditions will be set in a way that is affordable to clients while allowing for financial institutions to be sustainable. Providers will strive to deliver positive real returns on deposits.

Fair and respectful treatment of clients

Financial service providers and their agents will treat their clients fairly and respectfully. They will not discriminate. Providers will ensure adequate safeguards to detect and correct corruption as well as aggressive or abusive treatment by their staff and agents, particularly during the loan sales and debt collection processes.

Privacy of client data

The privacy of individual client data will be respected in accordance with the laws and regulations of individual jurisdictions. Such data will only be used for the purposes specified at the time the information is collected or as permitted by law, unless otherwise agreed with the client.

Mechanisms for complaint resolution

Providers will have in place timely and responsive mechanisms for complaints and problem resolution for their clients, and will use these mechanisms both to resolve individual problems and to improve their products and services.

Smart Campaign certifies MFIs that have implemented adequate processes for client protection, ultimately not just for the profit of the client, but for the entire industry.

MFTransparency

Micro Finance Transparency (MFTransparency) is an NGO founded in 2008. It promotes pricing transparency in the microfinance industry.[6] MFTransparency allows for a transparent exchange of information concerning the prices of microfinance products among market participants. Information concerning loan products and their prices, for instance the effective annual interest rate, are presented in a clear and consistent manner so that they are comparable. The NGO collaborates with other institutions such as the SPTF, The Microfinance Index Exchange MIX and the Smart Campaign. By using MFTransparency, an array of market participants can contribute towards the development of transparency standards.[7]

Social Performance Indicators (SPI4)

CERISE is a research enterprise in the microfinance sector that has developed the SPI4 rating tool in collaboration with the Smart Campaign and the SPTF. The SPI4 measures social performance along the USSPM and targets and identifies the strengths and weaknesses of the MFI under scrutiny (see Figure 8.5). An evaluation of the internal systems and activities of an MFI on the basis of a questionnaire will establish whether the MFI has reached its social goals. The questionnaire examines to what extent low-income parts of the population and the financially excluded are being reached, whether products and services have been adapted to this target group, whether MFIs grant their clients not only social but also political capital, and whether they embrace the responsibilities of their organization altogether.[8] The SPI4 is publicly accessible and may be used for one's own assessment or for advisory services. The following examples will demonstrate the application of the SPI4 and illustrate the goals of the USSPM.

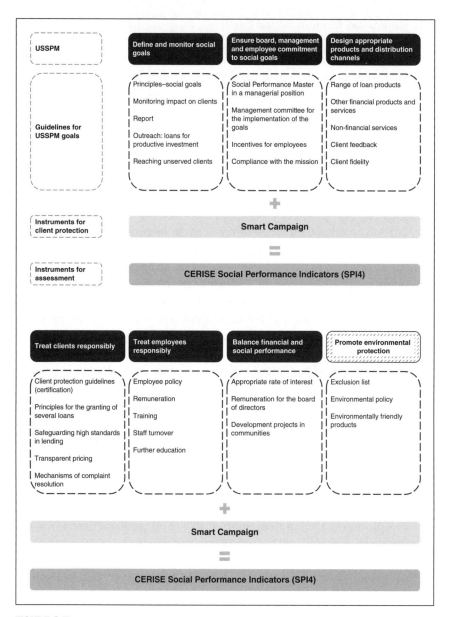

FIGURE 8.5 Measuring Social Performance by Means of USSPM
Data Source: Social Performance Task Force (2014b)

1. Define and Monitor Social Goals
   In a first step, both the mission of an MFI and its suitability for the target market are assessed. The focus thereby is on how the MFI measures those goals and achieves them, and how much attention it pays to monitoring its clients' performance as well as to client supervision during the entire lending process.

   Imon International, for example, is an MFI in Tajikistan that clearly stipulates its mission and means to achieve these goals, monitors them on a regular basis and measures their progress. Imon International manages to reach 82,000 people by mostly lending to the rural population and providing them with training and other non-financial services. They obtained their license to accept deposits in 2013 to broaden their range of services. In August 2014, Microfinanza Rating awarded Imon International an impressive A+ rating. The MFI's mission is "to promote sustainable economic development and improve quality of life in Tajikistan by ensuring reliable access to financial services for the economically active members of the population." Figure 8.6 displays the development of the social indicators that measure Imon International's social performance over the period of January to June 2014. It reveals that 10 of the 11 indicators are on target for their half-yearly goal and even exceeded it by up to 128 per cent.

2. Ensure Board, Management, and Employee Commitment to Social Performance
   Social goals can only be reached if an entire organization supports them wholeheartedly and commits to them on a daily basis.

   Ever since its foundation as an NGO in 1985, Banco Fie in Bolivia has subscribed itself to social performance (see Figure 8.7). Their efforts were awarded with a banking license in 2010. Banco Fie promotes the implementation of social performance throughout their company and therefore ensures that the supervisory board, management and all employees also contribute towards the success of this mission. The bank thereby reaches almost 25,000 borrowers and 800,000 depositors in their regional subsidiaries all over Bolivia.

3. Design Products, Services, Delivery Models and Channels that Respond to Clients' Needs and Preferences
   Product design is the be-all and end-all of microfinance. This indicator therefore investigates the range of financial and non-financial

Social Indicators	Dec 2015	% of target (6m)
"Get ahead!" business development training participants	2017	134%
Startup loans disbursed	627	78%
Financial education training participants	2050	256%
Education loans disbursed	1144	229%
Agricultural consultations provided	1980	371%
Technical assistance in construction and planning	1100	110%

FIGURE 8.6   Measuring Social Performance with Imon International
Data Source: BlueOrchard (2014)

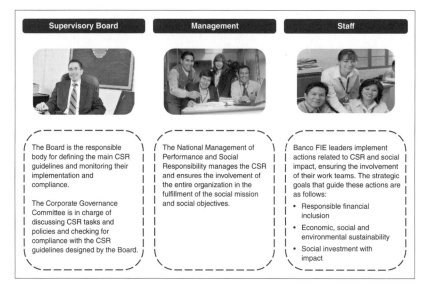

FIGURE 8.7   Banco Fie's Commitment to Social Performance
Data Source: BlueOrchard (2016)

Both upper management and employees are committed and dedicated to implementing the social mission.

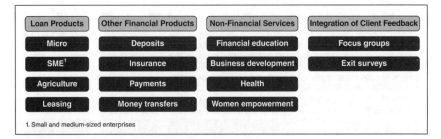

FIGURE 8.8   Products and Services of MFIs
Data Source: BlueOrchard (2014)

> Apart from financial and non-financial services, the products and
> services of an MFI also include the integration of client feedback
> resulting from focus groups and exit surveys.

products as well as how well these services manage to reach their
targeted clients (see Figure 8.8).

4. Treat Clients Responsibly

   The SPI4 promotes socially responsible lending. It engages MFIs in a
   transparent, sustainable and socially responsible mode of conduct.
   MFIs are to implement the Smart Campaign standards of client
   care or disclose their data with MFTransparency. Moreover, it investigates how MFIs can avoid over-indebtedness in their clients, protect
   their data and explain the mechanisms for complaint resolution. The
   example of Crezcamos in Columbia (see below) illustrates how an
   MFI can take responsibility for their clients by specifically enhancing
   their range of products.

5. Treat Employees Responsibly

   An MFI's interaction with its employees speaks volumes about its
   social responsibility. MFIs are role models for local enterprises and
   should therefore provide attractive employment opportunities. Among
   other things, staff turnover, staff assessment, compensation and
   opportunities for further training are all part of an MFI's assessment.
   The following box illustrates an MFI's responsibilities and how to
   assume them with respect to staff.

Crezcamos: Range of Products

Crezcamos is an MFI in Colombia that conducts a pilot project to devise an innovative crop insurance product for the benefit of micro entrepreneurs in agriculture.

Crezcamos currently provides loans to nearly 70,000 borrowers, predominantly in rural areas. In response to the specific risks faced by agricultural producers, the MFI's Rionegro branch is currently piloting an innovative crop insurance product that is meant to target an initial 6,000 agricultural borrowers. The MFI believes that more than 250,000 agricultural producers in the region could benefit from crop insurance.

In addition to this specific project, the MFI provides other products and services to meet their clients' needs:

- Client feedback is an integral part of the loan development
- Financing of 66 different types of agricultural activities, which generate cash flows
- All loan products are disbursed in local currency, in order to avoid currency risk
- Payment services (mobile phone top-ups, utility payments and international transfers) are provided to clients
- Affordable insurance policies are also provided and are being used by more than 85 per cent of borrowing clients
- Financial education courses are provided to clients to help them use their loans more effectively

Data Source: BlueOrchard Social Performance Report (2014)

6. Balance Social and Financial Performance

Successful MFIs all over the world demonstrate that profitability and social performance can exist side by side and may in many cases be increased simultaneously. A financially stable MFI can operate sustainably and extend its range of services to serve more clients. Thoughtful client care and client satisfaction prove its mindful conduct

---

Desirable Employer: Kenya Women Microfinance Bank

Founded as an NGO in 1981, Kenya Women Microfinance Bank Limited (KWFT) has now established itself as a licensed bank that reaches more than 240,000 borrowers and almost 400,000 savers. 70 per cent of its clients are located in rural areas.

To successfully maintain this vast nationwide network, the MFI relies on the dedication and hard work of its more than 2500 employees, including more than 1300 loan officers.

In an annual employment survey conducted by Deloitte, KWFT was awarded second and third place for the most desirable employer in Kenya in 2012 and 2013 respectively.

(Continued)

Annual staff turnover at KWFT is typically at 10 to 11 per cent and the management is targeting a reduction of 2 to 3 per cent. KWFT has also increased their range of non-monetary benefits for their employees.

Good performance is now being recognized by an employee stock ownership program, comprehensive health insurance, a group pension scheme and accessibility to an interest-free car loan. KWFT has an annual budget of approximately $225,000 to $340,000 to facilitate staff training.

Training is available to all members of staff, and new joiners undergo induction training.

KWFT underlines its responsibility as an employer. This commitment is reflected in minimal staff turnover, as well as its range of non-monetary benefits, insurance and access to interest-free loans for their employees.

Data Source: BlueOrchard (2014)

when it comes to society (see the example in the following box). This combination of profitability and social performance attracts investors' funds. The balance of profitability and social performance can be investigated with the following questions:

Does the MFI pass on any proceeds generated from bundled efficiency on to its clients?

Is the management adequately and reasonably rewarded for their efforts?

Does the MFI work in the interest of the community?

7. Promote Environmental Protection (not yet a USSPM)
   Other measuring tools such as the Social Performance Impact Reporting and Intelligence Tool (SPIRIT), which is based on the USSPM, also witness a proactive change in MFIs towards the development of the protection of the environment. SPIRIT investigates whether an MFI has included a comprehensive environmental policy into their standards and guidelines, and whether they also grant "green loans" to save energy and support environmentally friendly products. The Promotion of energy-saving models not only protects the environment, but also is cost-efficient and has a positive impact on the health of the local population. For example, the MFI HKL notably encompasses environmental protection by providing specific funding products for renewable energies as well as water and sanitary installations.

Alter Modus: Balancing Social Performance and Profitability

Alter Modus is a non-bank financial institution (NBFI) in Montenegro. It faces little competition in the market, and thus has strong pricing power. Alter Modus has made a commitment to pass efficiency gains on to its clients and has progressively reduced interest rates over the years.

Loan pricing is set based on the cost structure of the institution. As the MFI grows its portfolio and benefits from greater economies of scale, it is able to lower interest rates for loans.

Alter Modus has a transparent salary structure and compensation of management is reported to the Central Bank of Montenegro.

The MFI also provides financial support to community projects that promote education and entrepreneurship, including competitions for the best business ideas of local university students and, most recently, a project to rebuild and reopen kindergartens.

Alter Modus takes efficiency gains that have been generated by efficient cost structure and passes them on to their clients, a practice that has a positive effect on both clients and economies of scale.

Data Source: BlueOrchard Social Performance Report (2014)

Promoting Environmentally Friendly Products

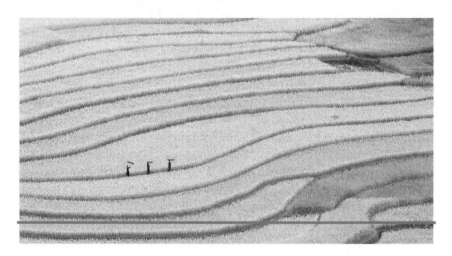

Hattha Kaksekar Ltd. (HKL) is an MFI in Cambodia that has a comprehensive environmental policy and an extensive and growing line of green product loans. Clients can benefit from the following products:

- Bio digesters
- Solar panels
- Wells and water distribution
- Water tanks and filters
- Latrines

After 18 months, HKL revealed a loan portfolio of nearly $500,000. Repayment rates are excellent, and HKL has partnered with the suppliers of the environmentally friendly products to ensure their high quality.

Data Source: BlueOrchard Social Performance Report (2014)

8.3 MEASURING THE OUTCOME OF MICROFINANCE

The PPI measures the economic development of MFI clients and the improvement of their living standards and makes them comparable on a global scale, leaving causality aside. A poverty scorecard was developed for this purpose (a points system in the fight against poverty) that relies on analyses of living standards measurement questionnaires in specific countries.[9] The indicators are simple, cost-efficient for detection, transparent and intuitive. The survey is based on ten easy questions, the answers to which indicate precisely whether borrowers live above or below the poverty line. Trials have revealed that these questionnaires yield precise results on both the rural and urban population of a country.

Figure 8.9 is an extract from the poverty scorecard of the Philippines. The points awarded for the answers were determined via econometric analysis based on a living standard measurement of the population of the Philippines. An MFI employee will question people locally and note down their answers. The subsequent evaluation will calculate the average answer and compare it with the data on a chart that displays the different stages of the likelihood of poverty. This determines the share of the population living below the poverty line. The scorecards of other countries rely on the

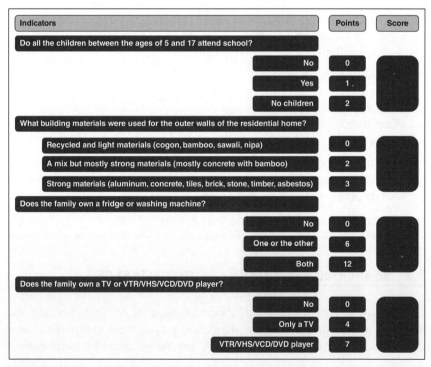

FIGURE 8.9 Poverty Scorecard of the Philippines (Extract)
Data Source: Grameen Foundation (2015)[11]

An extract from the poverty scorecard of the Philippines amply demonstrates the collection of data regarding the living standards of micro entrepreneurs.

same pattern, are equally simple and their aim is the same; the questions, however, are different.[10]

The USAID poverty assessment tool (PAT) works in a similar way and likewise collects household data.

8.4   SOCIAL RATING AGENCIES

Social rating predominantly aims to compare the social performance of all the MFIs in one sector. The rating report highlights the strengths of an institution and indicates the remaining potential in a poignant way.

The difference between a rating and a social performance assessment (which is mostly performed by asset managers and MFIs themselves) is mainly that reports of the institutions are not necessarily disclosed or published and are not compulsorily subject to a uniform process. Social performance can be measured in various ways.

In addition to their financial credit rating, rating agencies that are specialized in microfinance have introduced a social performance rating. These external ratings are based on USSPM, the Client Protection Principles (CPP) of the Smart Campaign, and the poverty assessment tools such as CGAP's PPI. The main aim of these ratings is client protection and to ensure that MFIs take care of their clients and their needs throughout the entire lending process. The four well-known rating agencies – M-CRIL, MicroFinanza, MicroRate and Planet Rating – generally distinguish between the standard methodology based on information from MFIs, and the comprehensive approach based on focus groups and client feedback.[12]

M-CRIL

The rating agency M-CRIL has played a pioneering global role in developing a systematic methodology for social rating. With its solid and fast approach to defining social performance in processes and investments, and to publishing the reports, M-CRIL has strengthened its commitment to supporting the microfinance sector.

Social ratings are conducted by means of a comprehensive and a standard methodology. M-CRIL uses the comprehensive rating to investigate all dimensions of the SPTF in the areas of social performance and impact (intent and design, internal systems and activities, output, outcomes, impact). This type of rating is more extensive than other methodologies. M-CRIL not only assesses the data of an MFI, but uses the results of a questionnaire to measure the impact the MFI has on a micro business. The standard rating methodology only comprises data on the level of an MFI, and therefore the impact on micro entrepreneurs cannot be measured adequately. Both rating methodologies rate an MFI with the Greek letters alpha, beta, and gamma. They are easily recognizable as they are preceded by a sigma as the following shows: $^{\Sigma}\alpha$, $^{\Sigma}\beta$ und $^{\Sigma}\gamma$ (see Figure 8.10).[13]

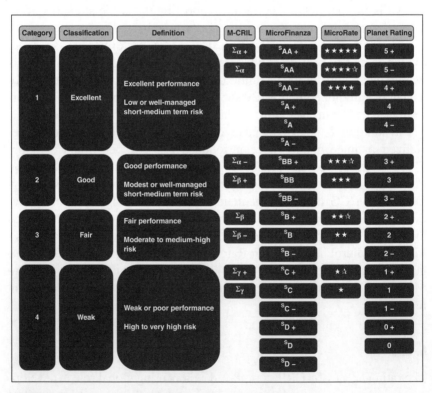

FIGURE 8.10 Rating Agencies for Social Performance
Data Source: The Rating Initiative (2013)

MicroFinanza Rating

To begin with, MicroFinanza exclusively used the standard methodology that corresponds with a simplified version of M-CRIL's rating. Nowadays, MicroFinanza and M-CRIL make use of both methodologies. MicroFinanza ratings are very similar in structure to those of the credit rating agencies Standard & Poor's and Fitch, recognizable by a preceding S, and range from ^{S}AA+ (excellent) to ^{S}D– (weak).

MicroRate

The rating methodology of MicroRate is similar to that of M-CRIL. In a first step, clients are questioned locally. Upon evaluation of the MFI in its headquarters and in selected branches, the final report that includes the rating will be written. The entire rating process takes an average of six to eight weeks, and the rating itself is evaluated by means of stars ranging from excellent to weak.[14]

Planet Rating

Planet Rating is the only one of the four rating agencies to evaluate social performance by means of the standard methodology only. Eventually, only data from the MFI will be taken into consideration when rating the MFI. The agency's rating is based on figures ranging from 5 (excellent) to 0 (weak).[15]

8.5 TECHNICAL ASSISTANCE

Managers of investment vehicles will base their assessment of an MFI's social performance on the instruments mentioned above. To further strengthen social values locally, to improve underlying processes or even build them, MIV managers also require technical assistance (TA). Besides that, TA promotes the implementation of new knowledge with the help of training and work groups. Standard TA projects provide tailored support services in areas such as strategy and business planning, quality of the lending process, product development, risk management and the reporting or measuring of social performance. TA therefore denotes advisory services that assist MFIs to implement their mission in a sustainable manner, as there is no doubt that only economically sustainable MFIs will receive investor funds.

Increase in MFI Capacity

TA can help to improve internal processes, strengthen IT systems and risk management, or introduce new products. The transformation process of an MFI into an official financial institution also makes part of the TA advisory services. Here is a list of the services that TA can provide:

- SWOT analysis[16]
- Developing new products, services and training thereof
- Planning of market strategies
- Conducting impact studies and market research
- Devising of business and improvement plans
- Introduction of IT systems
- Devising of social performance management

Strengthening the Financial Sector

To bolster the growth of the financial sector, TA applies not only to MFIs but to other protagonists at the same time: local microfinance networks, banks, governments, central banks and development banks.

TA is available with local microfinance networks in order to support regional businesses and establish specific local strategies. This includes the following services:

- Training programs for instructors
- Resource center
- Impact assessment and market research
- IT support
- Credit bureaus
- Development of internet portals

Banks and financial institutions support TA with the following activities:

- Impact assessment and market research
- Support of financial projects
- Training loan officers
- Assistance in the choice of business associates

Governments and central banks may profit by using TA to implement adequate standards and guidelines that will in turn boost growth in microfinance:

- Impact assessment and market research
- Definition of a national microfinance strategy
- Implementation of adequate guidelines and standards
- Improved supervision of MFIs

TA also works as a catalyst for development banks in their assistance of MFIs by means of the following:

- Impact assessment and market research
- Identification of sustainable and social MFIs
- Supervision of microfinance portfolios
- Employee training for successful evaluation of MFIs

TA therefore tackles an array of specific problems in microfinance. Social performance benefits society. The following will demonstrate the impact of social performance on micro entrepreneurs.

Impact on Micro Entrepreneurs

Measuring social performance in microfinance warrants that an investor's commitment always benefits the poor. This empowers the poor, because they are economically active, and achieve a better standard of living to allow them to provide for their families (see Figure 8.11). Successful

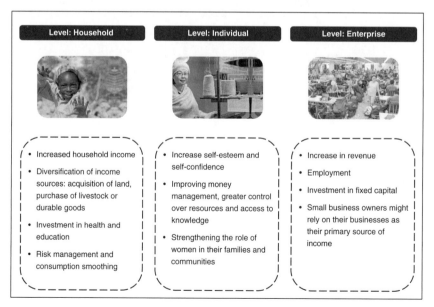

FIGURE 8.11 Impact of Microfinance

> Microfinance has a positive effect on various levels: on households, individuals and businesses.

micro enterprises on the other hand also boost the economy, employment and growth. As a result of the targeted social upswing, the respective region's experience improved and there were increased supplies of food and better health and education.

8.6 LINKING SOCIAL PERFORMANCE WITH PROFITABILITY

The double bottom line of the microfinance sector challenges MFIs to reach their social development goals. It is a common misconception that measures that have been implemented in order to achieve the social mission have a detrimental effect on an MFI's profitability. Figure 8.12 illustrates the empirical connection between social performance and profitability of the loans issued to MFIs.[17] It has become evident that there is no trade-off between the two goals. Loans with a high social performance are similarly profitable as loans with a lower social performance, which again supports the double bottom line theory.

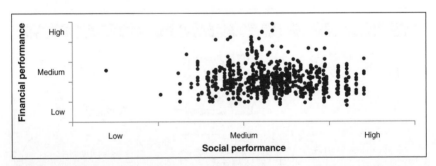

FIGURE 8.12 Social Performance and Profitability
Data Source: BlueOrchard, Mangold (2015)

> There is no indication of a trade-off between social performance and profitability when investing in MFIs. Both can be increased at the same time.

Systematic evaluation and an adequate investment process can boost social performance and profitability at the same time. This conclusion is all the more important as it means that MFIs do not have to choose between social performance and profitability. Both goals can be met simultaneously.

8.7 PRELIMINARY CONCLUSIONS

Measuring social performance ensures that all actions are performed in the interest of the fight against poverty and exclusively serve to meet the needs of the poor segments of the population. The SPTF devised six standards to measure social performance that in turn measure and evaluate the implementation of an MFI's social mission.

Measuring social performance in MFIs at the same time means a thorough investigation of their social impact. There are several issues under scrutiny: Is the client provided with a range of adequate products and services? Do these empower the micro entrepreneur to improve their living standards? Measuring social performance measures the impact on society at large, for instance the fight against poverty and the empowerment of women.

For MFIs, advisory services (TA) are provided that should help MFIs and other protagonists in the microfinance sector to operate successfully and sustainably and fulfill their social mission at the same time. TA on the other hand is also instrumental in introducing new products, as well as implementing efficient and innovative processes. Social performance is measured in addition to a credit rating. There are now a number of independent social rating agencies such as M-CRIL, MicroFinanza Rating, MicroRate and Planet Rating.

Empirical analysis has revealed that there is no trade-off between social performance and profitability, and MFIs therefore do not have to decide in favor of one or the other, as both can be met simultaneously. The double bottom line thus becomes even more significant.

Social performance is an integral part of microfinance. Only this way can we be sure that the poverty in this world is targeted so that micro entrepreneurs can create better lives for themselves and their families and thereby boost the economy of their region and their country.

MAKING FURNITURE – SOFIA, BULGARIA

Like many other micro entrepreneurs, Krassimir Petrov started off with a simple business idea. With the help of microloans he transformed his small furniture manufacture into a small enterprise and opened a furniture shop in Sofia. He currently employs a dozen people and is planning to construct a furniture factory and purchase more suitable production equipment. To put his plans into action, he has applied for a loan with a traditional bank. Krassimir entirely owes his transformation from underpaid worker to entrepreneur and employer to microfinance.

Source: BlueOrchard

NOTES

1 Rich Stearns, president of World Vision United States, one of the largest non-profit humanitarian Christian relief organizations.
2 Microfinance Centre (2007).
3 Hashemi (2007), p. 4.
4 Grameen Foundation (2015).
5 Smart Campaign (2016).
6 MFTransparency (2015).
7 Ibidem
8 Hashemi (2007), p. 5.
9 Schreiner (2010), pp. 118–137.
10 Hashemi (2007), p. 7.
11 http://www.progressoutofpoverty.org/country/philippines, (last visited 6 May 2015).
12 http://www.sptf.info/sp-tools/rating-tools, (last visited 6 May 2015).
13 http://www.m-cril.com/SocialRating.aspx, (last visited 6 May 2015).
14 http://www.microfinanzarating.com/index.php?option=com_content&view=article&id=144& Itemid=175&lang=en, (last visited 6 May 2015).
15 http://www.planetrating.com/EN/social-performance-rating-methodology.html, (last visited 6 May 2015).
16 Tool for strategic planning.
17 Based on 933 loans that BlueOrchard Finance S.A. has issued to various MFIs between 2001 and 2014; analyzed by Dr. Ruben Mangold, Research Fellow Harvard University 2014/15.

CHAPTER 9

Beyond the Reach of Microfinance?

Humanity's greatest advances are not in its discoveries, but in how those discoveries are applied to reduce inequity.

Bill Gates[1]

Prejudices and reservations, such as that the term "borrower" is synonymous with repayment difficulties and that extortionate interest rates exacerbate poverty rather than alleviate it, are deep-rooted.

Microfinance is a relatively young asset class, and detailed knowledge and research on it are yet to be made publicly accessible on a larger scale. It is therefore subject to widespread criticism that the microfinance industry has to account for.

9.1 PREJUDICES AND RESERVATIONS

Prejudices about the poor and how they handle money are deep-set. The consensus seems to be that low-income parts of the population should not borrow money, as they will fail to repay it anyway. Or that the poor, even on the verge of starvation, would rather squander the funds given to them to indulge themselves instead of investing them in a sustainable business activity. Practice, however, has shown a different picture altogether. As a rule, for the poor, long-term economic advancement clearly takes priority. Borrowers are fully aware of their unique investment opportunity, and there are loan officers who will ensure that a loan is used as specified. They will step in to monitor the situation more closely should it prove necessary. A partial use of a loan for food may in fact even be beneficial, as the example in Figure 9.1 reveals. A group of ceramicists in Siguatepeque in Honduras, for instance, used part of their loan for the purchase of food.

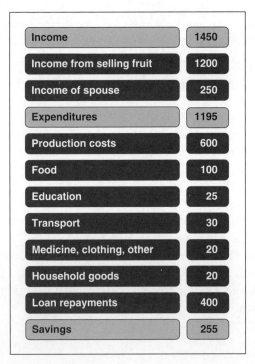

Income	1450
Income from selling fruit	1200
Income of spouse	250
Expenditures	1195
Production costs	600
Food	100
Education	25
Transport	30
Medicine, clothing, other	20
Household goods	20
Loan repayments	400
Savings	255

FIGURE 9.1 Exemplary Budget of a Female Borrower (in $)
Data Source: BlueOrchard Research

> The monthly budget of a female borrower in Peru discloses that she manages to save nearly 20 per cent of her income. Assuming that poor households are unable to save is therefore unfounded.

It allowed them to store their finished pots and wait for prices to rise instead of being forced to part with them less profitably.[2]

It is equally remarkable perhaps to note that the savings rate of micro borrowers is comparatively high. Deposits of the year 2014 accounted for an average of 30 per cent of the MFI loan portfolio.[3] To maintain that the poor do not save money is therefore utterly unfounded. What is true, however, is that they use their initial loan to generate their own income and then save a part of it.[4]

Why Are Microloan Interest Rates Seen as Excessive?

In microfinance, the share of the operating costs of the entire credit costs – i.e. the determinants of the interest rate – averages at 60 per cent. Chapter 7 has illustrated that this figure is largely the result of high resource intensity, the fact that micro entrepreneurs live in remote areas and the rather low amounts for which loans are issued, as shown in the example in Figure 9.2. Financial services for micro entrepreneurs are costly, hence the reluctance of commercial banks and financial service providers to supply them with loans. As a consequence, the operating costs that are incurred with a microloan are comparatively high.

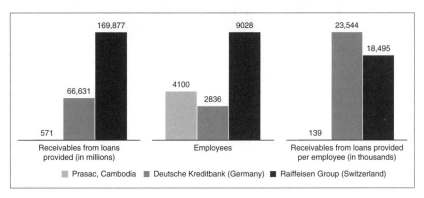

FIGURE 9.2 Receivables from Loans Provided Per Employee (in $)
Data: Deutsche Kreditbank (2015); Prasac (2015); Raiffeisen Group (2015)

Prasac, an MFI in Cambodia, reveals claims from lending operations of $571 million – which is a hundred times less than the Deutsche Kreditbank (DKB), where loans amount to 80 per cent of the total assets. This discrepancy is due to the size of these institutions and the credit amounts that are issued. Applying this volume to the number of employees, Prasac emerges with loan claims of around $140,000 per employee. The DKB is one of Germany's largest direct banks and with its 2836 employees in fact has fewer staff than the Cambodian MFI Prasac.[5]

Local rates of inflation, often two-digit, are another factor that distorts absolute interest rates. Figure 9.3 illustrates this phenomenon using Ghana as an example.

Transparency is a must, and costs are to be disclosed so that interest rates can be understood and corruption kept at bay. The ultimate proof that this model is successful in practice as well as in theory, however, lies with the fact that, except for a few, micro entrepreneurs manage to redeem their loans and interest on time.

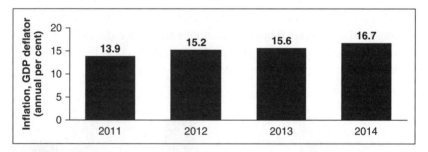

FIGURE 9.3 Inflation in Ghana
Data: World Bank (2016)

Over the last four years, the rate of inflation in Ghana has been fluctuating between 13 and 16.7 per cent. Compared to industrialized countries, this figure is rather high. The inflation-adjusted interest rates for micro entrepreneurs hence are considerably lower than the nominal rates would suggest.

What Are the Reasons for the Financial Crisis in India, the Suicides and Over-Indebtedness?

It is unclear how microloans may have been involved in some suicides in Andhra Pradesh in 2010 (see Chapter 11.2). The fact is that the country was savaged by a prolonged period of drought with devastating consequences for those working in agriculture. Loans were either only partly or not at all redeemed as crops had been lost. Borrowers were more than aware of the impending termination of all business activities of MFIs as a result of the weak political and legal framework, which in any case would have made any further loans virtually impossible.

At the same time, 82 per cent of all households in Andhra Pradesh had also taken out loans with informal money lenders, who would not only issue overpriced loans, but at the same time grant volumes that exceeded their borrowers' repayment capabilities. This illustrates the risks and size of the market of informal money lenders. A mere 11 per cent of the Andhra Pradesh households had borrowed from an MFI, and only 3 per cent of those borrowers were in debt with more than one MFI.[6]

To counteract similar situations, MFIs today also provide weather risk insurance. In collaboration with credit bureaus (see Chapter 5.5) an information system was devised that makes loan data and information accessible to MFIs and clients in an attempt to avoid over-indebtedness.[7]

With hindsight, it can now be safely established that the lack of regulation of informal money lenders was largely responsible for the destabilization of the entire microfinance industry in 2010. It is more than frustrating that not only borrowers from informal money lenders had to bear the brunt of it, but along with them millions of people who were consequently deprived of any chance of a loan.

Can Social Performance Be Measured at All?

Social performance measures to what degree MFIs implement their social mission and ensure that both management and employees contribute towards the same goal. It investigates whether an MFI tailors its products and services to its clients' needs, treats its clients and staff respectfully, and whether it manages to strike a balance between profitability and social performance.

The Social Performance Task Force, for instance, has devised global standards to measure social performance (see Chapter 8.2). The SPI4 is a tool that measures social performance by means of a points system.[8] The indicator also includes global standards of the Smart Campaign – an initiative devoted to client protection.

Rating agencies that assess an MFI as an institution (Microfinanza Rating) are joined by rating agencies that focus on social performance (M-CRIL, Microfinanza Rating, MicroRate, Planet Rating). Their aim is to disclose the results of their social performance ratings in order to achieve a uniform rating system for all MFIs.

In simple terms, social performance denotes to what degree MFIs assume their social responsibilities. Overall it is easily measurable, and there are various tools available to do so.

MFIs go to great lengths to implement their social mission, but how can their social endeavors be measured? Aforementioned tools such as the PPI and the PAT are easily applicable and reliable instruments. Research also uses sophisticated methods such as randomized controlled trials; however, they are less suitable in practice.[9]

On a macro level there is ample proof that poverty worldwide is decreasing (see Figure 9.4). Admittedly, not all the credit perhaps belongs to microfinance, but some undoubtedly does.

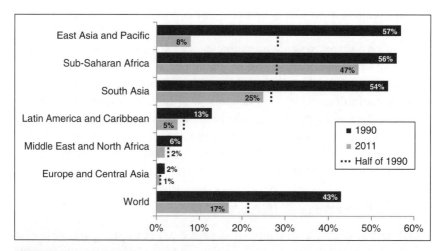

FIGURE 9.4   Comparison of Poverty Levels[10]
Data: World Bank (2016), database 2012

From 1990 to 2011, the level of poverty halved in all regions, except for Sub-Saharan Africa.

The countless success stories of micro entrepreneurs are the irrefutable proof of the efficacy and effectiveness of microfinance. Take Judith Martinez's story, for example. A microloan nine years ago allowed her to set up her own flower stall. With the proceeds she has been able to expand her business to meet the increasing demand for flower bouquets and pot plants. Today, she is renovating her house, can support her family financially and can increase the living standard of her entire family. Her second loan steeply increased to five times the amount of her first.

SELLING FLOWERS – BOGOTÀ, COLOMBIA

Judith Martinez's life revolves around flowers, her great passion. She has been running a flower stall at Galeria Alameda that she has been able to fund thanks to a loan with WWB Colombia. She was so overwhelmed by the impact that microfinance had had on her life that she decided to take out another loan to expand her business and renovate her house. Mrs. Martinez uses her additional income to financially support her relatives and particularly her parents.

Source: BlueOrchard

Does Microfinance Breed Corruption?

Many MFIs respond to a feeble legal system, and are amidst daily political conflicts and corruption. Corruption often takes the shape of bribery, fraud and blackmail.

In all honesty, it would be presumptuous to conclude that corruption is non-existent in MFIs, which are as a rule personnel-intensive. There are viable options, however, to keep corruption to a minimum. The most effective steps in the fight against corruption are an utmost degree of transparency in connection with the cash and interest rate flows of all the protagonists involved. But alongside transparency, supervision is key. Conventional and non-conventional control mechanisms can identify and fight systematic corruption and deceptive practices. In cases of fraudulent practices with a criminal energy, there are limits to what these control mechanisms can do, reminiscent of similar incidents in established

---

Examples of Corruption in Microfinance

(Continued)

- Grant fake loans and grant loans to fictitious borrowers
- Accept bribes from clients
- Manipulate financial data, give wrong or misleading information
- Steal money
- Get microloans to financially fund illegal activities
- Use revenues generated by businesses that are supported by an MFI in order to fund illegal activities

MFIs can be directly affected by corruption in microfinance by handing out fictitious loans, or indirectly by for instance accepting money from bogus transactions.

Source: Fanconi and Scheurle

financial institutions of the Western hemisphere. In microfinance, self-monitoring plays a much more important role than in Western institutions. There is considerable emphasis on social norms and honor, but most importantly, there is an awareness that human lives are at stake – fellow countrymen, neighbors, friends and family. To further counteract fraudulent practices, loan officers are usually well-paid, which makes them less prone to corruption.

MFIs may either be directly affected by corruption in microfinance by granting fictitious loans, or indirectly, for instance by accepting money from bogus transactions. Microfinance institutions may in fact take deposits from clients who are involved in corrupt affairs.[11] This is rather unlikely, however, as MFIs are in close contact with their clients and steadily monitor their business activities. Moreover, bogus transactions are more likely to be undertaken via larger financial institutions due to the fact that deposits or the transfer of larger sums of money usually attract attention in MFIs. Entrepreneurial activities of poor households usually leave little room for corruption.

Does Microfinance Actually Have an Effect on SME Growth?

Microloans mostly support small-scale activities. It is therefore wrong to maintain that microfinance does not promote the development of SMEs.

On the contrary, the support of activities on a small scale promotes financial and economic thinking right from the start and encourages and builds functioning, economic activity. If micro entrepreneurs are successful, they may turn their business venture into an SME with increasing local relevance. In fact, established SMEs are perhaps better served by banks than by MFIs, as they present collateral along with a successful business model and are able to take out a loan with more flexible maturities in the long run. Although a sound business development is significant for micro entrepreneurs, it is most relevant particularly for economic development on a national level.

Microfinance and Child Labor?

Small enterprises succeed or fail depending on their range of products and the diligence and determination of their founders. For this reason, they are usually supported by an entire family network, which naturally includes children. It would be mistaken, however, to refer to this as child labor. Child labor, according to the Oxford English Dictionary[12], refers to the employment of children in an industry or business, especially when illegal or considered exploitative. If children assist in their parents' business it does not primarily serve the purpose of generating financial revenue, but ensures the continuation of the business. Any additional income very often flows into the children's education at any rate. As women often generate an income for the benefit of their families (see Chapter 6.3), this strongly contradicts the assumption that the business aspect is in the foreground. Children's activities in their parents' business rather enhance the living standard of all the family members involved.

Impending Mission Drift?

The term "mission drift" refers to MFIs that stray from their social mission of providing poorer parts of the population with access to capital, but instead switch their attention to another target group, i.e. wealthy clients. In many cases MFIs deal with wealthy clients in a more profitable manner, as their higher collateral allows them to take out more substantial loans, which in turn lowers their risks and costs. Let us remind ourselves that the operating costs are mostly independent of the amount of a loan (see Chapter 7.1).

It is often incorrectly assumed that higher average loans are synonymous with mission drift.[13] Higher average loans may have perfectly positive aspects as well. On the one hand, it may well be that former micro entrepreneurs have expanded their business activities rather speedily and that their credit limits therefore have risen substantially over the years.

In such cases, severing all ties with a functioning business makes little sense for MFIs. On the other hand, macro-economic influences may also increase the amount of the loans. A country's increased welfare – undoubtedly also thanks to microfinance – automatically leads to higher loans. The existence of mission drift is widely disputed. Whatever the case may be, measuring social performance is the best way to keep it at bay.

Fund of Funds Diversification?

Although asset managers assess MFIs independently and with the help of different tools, investment into identical MFIs cannot be avoided. The reasons for this are as follows: firstly, the MFI universe in the different regions is limited, and secondly, MFIs are selected according to their financial and social performance. Sufficient diversification can therefore already be achieved by a single asset manager, provided that there are a high number of investments and the avoidance of correlation and country risks. Topical and sector-specific diversification, however, is a different and more individual issue.

9.2 PRELIMINARY CONCLUSIONS

The largest countries in the world, countless government funds as well as private initiatives and partnerships, increasingly commit themselves to development institutions, as the soaring growth rates of impact investing amply demonstrate.[14]

All the protagonists along the value chain of impact investing have to answer to the points of criticism that have been and are being raised in an attempt to find solutions to streamline processes for better efficacy and efficiency. In the first place, it is all about the micro entrepreneurs. In the past, over-indebtedness could be lowered by the launch of credit bureaus and the fact that they collect personal and loan-specific data on their clients, ultimately the reason for more transparency in the market. The data disclosed can be viewed by MFIs and borrowers alike, which enables the latter to self-monitor their borrowing over prolonged periods of time.

Impact investing is a relatively young financial sector, and processes are being streamlined on a daily basis. The two decisive factors thereby are digitalization and the implementation of new technologies.

MANUFACTURING THE MORINKHOR – ULAN-BATOR, MONGOLIA

Tumenulzi Zaya is 28 and married with two young children. In 2007, he began manufacturing the morinkhor, a traditional Mongolian musical instrument. He opened his own shop in 2011. His instruments are so popular that the most highly regarded Mongolian musicians and artists are among his clients. In 2015, his first loan with XacBank purchased him the materials required for the manufacture of the morinkhor. He is currently redeeming his fourth loan. The better tools and a computer that he was able to purchase with the help of his loans have been a boost to productivity, which now allows him to manufacture more than 50 instruments a month.

Source: BlueOrchard

NOTES

1 Bill Gates, Founder of Microsoft and the Bill & Melinda Gates Foundation.
2 Scofield (2015).
3 MIX (2016): MIX Database. Cross Market Analysis Tool, http://reports .mixmarket.org/crossmarket (last visited 20 November 2016).
4 Scofield (2015).

5 Direct banks are banks that provide financial services without relying on a branch network of their own.

6 *The Economist* (2010b).

7 *The Economist* (2010a).

8 CERISE Social Performance Indicators (SPIs).

9 Rosenberg (2010), p. 1.

10 Based on the purchasing power parity of 2005.

11 ResponsAbility (2010), p. 1.

12 http://www.oxforddictionaries.com/definition/english/child-labour?q= child+labour (last visited 22 February 2016).

13 Abrar and Javaid (2014), p. 122; Bethany (2013), p. 98; Mersland and Strom (2010), p. 28.

14 Forum Nachhaltige Geldanlagen (2015).

CHAPTER 10

Investing in Microfinance

And while the lack of financial services is a sign of poverty, today it is also understood as an untapped opportunity to create markets, bring people in from the margins and give them the tools with which to help themselves.

Kofi Annan[1]

Microfinance has grown into an established asset class. Private institutional investors in particular have considerably contributed towards its impressive growth in recent years.

The investment process is crucial for the quality of a microfinance portfolio, and a professional microfinance manager will always combine a top-down portfolio construction process with a bottom-up investment approach. Only a meticulous analysis of an MFI locally will allow for careful selection of investments.

Investments in microfinance have an attractive risk-return ratio, both individually and in the overall portfolio context. The outstanding characteristics of investments in microfinance act as diversifiers of an investor's total portfolio.

10.1 MARKET DEVELOPMENT

To begin with, predominantly development institutions such as the World Bank or the KfW Development Bank were investing in microfinance to employ their financial means sustainably in financial inclusion and the fight against poverty. Today, the asset class has established itself with institutional and private investors alike. Pension funds, foundations, fund of funds or insurances invest billions of dollars in microfinance. Typically, investors put their assets via funds into microfinance, ultimately to ensure a professional and efficient management of their assets. The bundling of assets in such MIVs has multiplied by ten in recent years to a staggering $11.6 billion at the end of 2015 (see Figure 10.1).

Albeit the volume of MIVs is rather small in comparison with international bond and stock markets, this asset class has well and truly outgrown its shoes. The fact that the share of institutional investors – who can document a rigorous and sophisticated selection process of their investment vehicles – has risen considerably over the years is a result of the professionalization of the microfinance sector. Microfinance no longer represents an exotic niche investment vehicle, but has become an integral part of asset allocation in general. Private investors have taken the place of development finance institutions (DFIs) as the main sponsors in microfinance (see Figure 10.2).

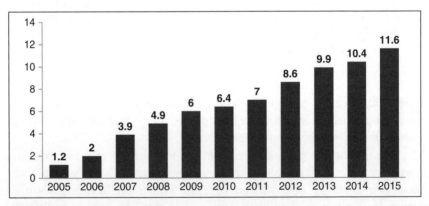

FIGURE 10.1   Assets in Microfinance Funds (in Billion $)
Data Source: Symbiotics (2016)

The assets managed by microfinance funds have risen ten times, from $1.2 billion in 2005 to over $11 billion in 2015.

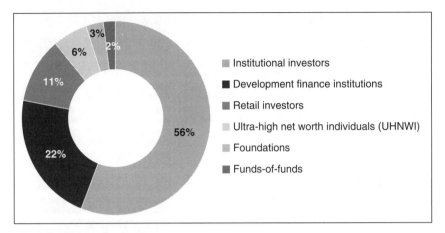

FIGURE 10.2 Microfinance Investors
Data Source: Microrate (2013b)

At 56 per cent, institutional investors constitute the majority of all investors, followed by development institutions and retail investors. Ultra-high net worth individuals, foundations and funds-of-funds combined amount to another 11 per cent.

10.2 MICROFINANCE INVESTMENT VEHICLES

Investing in microfinance institutions directly is a perfectly feasible option. Some DFIs and major pension funds are doing exactly that. In most cases, however, the lack of experience with this choice and the high costs incurred do not argue in favor of it. For this reason, professionally managed investment funds with efficient access to MIVs are an undoubtedly more effective choice.

Fixed-Interest Investments and Equity Commitment

Similar to traditional investment funds, investments in microfinance offer the option of fixed income investments or investments in stocks. For this reason, there are funds that exclusively invest in fixed income papers, or solely in equity capital. Other funds may prefer a mixed portfolio. Fixed income in this case refers to the fact that investments are only made in

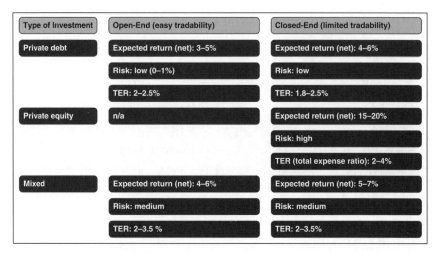

FIGURE 10.3   Fund Characteristics
Source: BlueOrchard Research

> The characteristics of funds reveal that investments in MFI equity yield the highest expected return, but at the same time also carry the highest risk. Debt capital funds yield a slightly lower return with a lower risk and a lower total expense ratio (TER).

loans that go to MFIs. On the other hand, funds with equity exposure lend equity capital to the MFIs. At 80 per cent, the global market for fixed income investments is considerably more substantial than the stock market with its roughly 20 per cent share.[2]

Thematic Funds

Microfinance investment funds may have a thematic focus, meaning that a fund is mainly used to promote and develop a particular topic such as agriculture, health, education or energy. Thematic funds issue loans and equity to MFIs that exclusively deal with the respective topics or engage in their funding (see Figure 10.3). Another possibility is to distribute funds to MFIs that commit to implementing the capital they receive in the name of these pre-defined goals, albeit they may additionally use the remaining funds to issue micro loans for other goals.

Public–Private Partnerships and Risk Sharing

The risk sharing between public and private investors is an appealing aspect of several microfinance funds. Several microfinance funds are set up as public–private partnerships, where public and private investors invest in the same funds. Very often, public investors provide a guarantee in the form of horizontal and vertical risk sharing. Horizontal risk sharing means that a public institution carries a certain share of potential risks. In the event of a 5 per cent loss, and in the case of horizontal risk sharing of 50 per cent, this public institution would carry half of the loss, and the private investors the other. With vertical risk sharing, public investors bear the brunt of the risk to a certain degree. This is also referred to as first-loss tranches. Vertical risk sharing of up to 20 per cent means that the public institution takes over losses of up to 20 per cent of the capital. Private investors are only affected by losses that exceed the 20 per cent mark.

Closed-End vs. Open-End Funds

As MIVs, i.e. investments in MFIs, predominantly feature in private markets with limited tradability, closed-end funds have several advantages over open-end structures.[3] Their fixed maturities manage to achieve a higher level of investment. Closed-end products at the same time are better suited for long-term loans, and can be managed more efficiently: no trading of shares needs to be assured, and their net asset value (NAV) needs to be assessed and published less frequently. Due to a limited circle of investors, the implementation of regulatory guidelines is usually easier than in open-end funds, and annual audits are less elaborate. For closed-end funds this results in lower costs and higher net returns.

Costs

At 2 to 4 per cent annually (TER), the management costs of microfinance funds are traditionally slightly higher than those of traditional investment funds, the reason being the labor-intensive analyses of MFIs. Professional microfinance fund managers are represented by their staff in the regions in question, which allows them to assess MFIs locally. This includes due diligence visits to MFIs that may take several days, during which interviews are conducted with the board of directors, the management, the MFI's employees and clients, and also loan documentations are reviewed.[4]

Microfinance Funds: Possible Pitfalls

As with any other financial investment, investing in microfinance funds is a question of diligence. Alongside the well-known factors, microfinance features additional characteristics that need to be taken into consideration.

Regardless of whether a microfinance fund provides MFIs with equity or debt capital, investments are largely conducted in private markets and are not traded on a stock exchange. Investments therefore have to be identified, reviewed, negotiated and structured locally. In many cases, critical information is only available locally and may be coded with local idiosyncrasies. Thus, the decisive factors in the choice of a fund manager are how well and in what regions the manager is represented by local staff, and in addition to that, how familiar the manager is with the local and regional setting and the economic and legal framework. Being proficient in the local language is mandatory, especially when conducting interviews with clients, reviewing and negotiating contracts. During the investment process, it is advisable to investigate whether the manager bases their decisions on their own research or whether they buy their data from third-party suppliers.

As mentioned earlier, the debt to equity ratio is around 80 to 20, i.e. 4 to 1. Apart from genuine private equity funds, therefore, in most cases a manager's loan experience is crucial. Investors are advised to carefully examine a fund manager's degree of experience. Among other factors, the investment team's specific wealth of experience, as well as the default rate of a loan portfolio, are clear reference points when it comes to assessing the quality of the loan process. It is equally relevant to establish the manager's experience in handling problematic loans. With private equity funds and mixed funds, a careful screening of the assessment methodologies and policies for equity investments is inevitable. Mixed funds additionally carry the risk of conflicts of interest, as in some cases the same MFIs are funded by means of debt capital and equity at the same time.

Microfinance funds are known to predominantly invest in developing countries, which are as a rule less politically and economically stable than industrialized countries. A microfinance manager therefore ought to have the skills to hedge the interest rate risks of local currency areas as well as exchange rate fluctuations. Country risks such as political crises and natural disasters are other well-known and monumental challenges that MIVs have to face. Diversification across different countries and regions is a crucial evaluation criterion when it comes to funds. Loans that have been

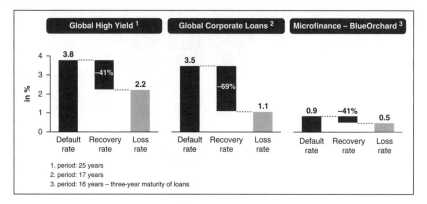

FIGURE 10.4 Default and Loss Rate[5]
Data Source: J.P. Morgan (2015); BlueOrchard

The default rate of the global high yield asset class is the highest at 2.2 per cent, followed by global corporate loans with a default rate of 1.1 per cent. Microfinance has a default rate of a mere 0.5 per cent.

granted or equity stakes are usually not traded on a stock market, which explains the relevance of the liquidity management.

If a fund can fall back on a bank line, potential funding gaps can be bridged. A bank line allows for flexibility on the investor's side and can be used to temporarily finance applications for and redemptions of shares in a fund.

10.3 THE INVESTMENT PROCESS

As the previous chapter has illustrated, microfinance funds invest in MFIs, and their analysis and selection processes are extensive and elaborate (see Figure 10.5). With respect to the portfolio, there are questions regarding its geographical diversification and extent and limits thereof, or regarding the nature of the risk-return profile. This profile is usually determined by means of a top-down process and determines the allocation of the assets. The analysis and selection of MFIs on the other hand follows a bottom-up process. A professional fund manager will combine both processes with a rigorous risk management.

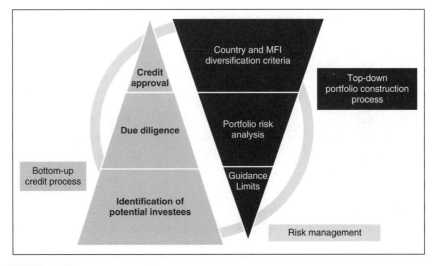

FIGURE 10.5 Microfinance Investment Process
Source: BlueOrchard

> The investment process consists of bottom-up and top-down components. The bottom-up approach analyzes and evaluates MFIs, the top-down approach leads to the portfolio composition and determines its degree of diversification.

The professionality of modern microfinance also manifests itself in its investment process. It is perfectly in line and up to date with what is considered best practice in other asset classes such as stocks, bonds or private equity.

Strategic and Tactical Asset Allocation

In simple terms: the result of the top-down process is a structure that defines the cornerstones of an investment strategy. It aims for optimal diversification across countries, regions and individual investments. Establishing this structure, however, is by no means trivial, as there are different dimensions that have to be considered and brought in line with one another. The following questions have to be addressed in this process:

- Which countries should be invested in?
- What (maximum) amount should be invested per country or region?
- What overall risk is acceptable?

- Which MFI segments (tiers 1, 2 or 3) should be invested in?
- How many MFIs should be included in the portfolio?
- What (maximum) amount should be invested per MFI?

Only a wealth of experience and in-depth knowledge of the global microfinance and financial markets will answer these questions. Successful fund managers adamantly have to know the risks involved with individual countries and regions and gauge them accordingly. They have to be able to pinpoint the MFI segments in each country and region that are attractive and ultimately investible for international investors.

The percentages for the strategic asset allocation are defined based on the country analysis (see Figure 10.6). Strategic asset allocation is rather rigid in its design and focuses on long-term goals. For this reason, tactical fluctuation bands are established that allow the fund manager a certain degree of flexibility in reacting to favorable and adverse conditions. This may be helpful especially when the political framework of a country takes a turn for the worse and emphasis on this particular country has to be tactically reduced. The contrary may be the case when a country becomes particularly attractive, which would lead to a temporary increase in portfolio weighting.

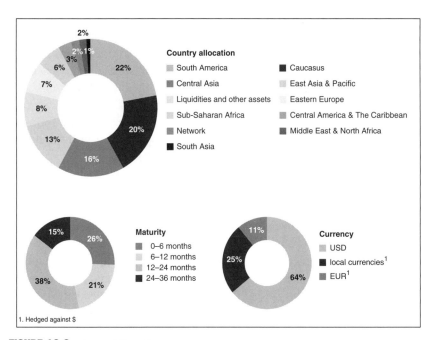

FIGURE 10.6 Asset Allocation
Data Source: BlueOrchard

Asset allocation can be split up into countries (top), maturities (bottom left) and currencies (bottom right). The fund managed by BlueOrchard as displayed in the chart mainly consists of investments in MFIs in South America, the Caucasus and Central Asia. The maturities of the loans to MFIs often are 12 to 24 months, and loans are in most cases issued in US dollars.

Analyzing and Selecting MFIs

There are around 4000 microfinance institutions. A single microfinance fund – depending on its size and geographical orientation – invests in about 50 to 200 institutions in this universe. Apart from the central risk-return considerations, several other factors influence the selection process.[6]

A microfinance fund manager's main task is to select the "right" MFI. The MFI analysis and selection process is crucial for the quality of a portfolio. The following illustrates the seven steps of this process (see Figure 10.7).

1. Define selection criteria
   Along with the benchmark figures defined by strategic asset allocation, further (quantitative or qualitative) basic selection criteria for investments may be either mandatory or supplementary, depending on the mandate. These additional conditions further reduce the investible universe.
2. Pre-DD committee review: screening and approval of due diligence
   Once the selection criteria have been defined, the screening follows. This means that MFIs are identified that appear to meet the criteria. Special databases and networks are used in this step.

   At this point, it will also be necessary to establish how much equity and debt capital these individual MFIs can or should raise.

   The information that has been gained so far is by no means sufficient to make an investment decision; however, it is usually substantial enough for a preliminary report on the choice of interesting MFIs. This report is typically compiled by an investment specialist. Due to possible conflicts of interest, she or he has no discretionary competence. Therefore, an investment committee will be needed to either terminate the process, seek more information or grant the investment specialist permission to continue with the process.

FIGURE 10.7   Process of Analyzing and Selecting MFIs

Until an investment into an MFI is ultimately effectuated, potential investments have to undergo a rigorous selection process.

If the fund manager pursues a hedging strategy with respect to currency and/or interest rate risks, it is further advisable to assess the hedging conditions early on in the process. The approach again depends on the individual fund manager. Some will hedge all transactions against interest rate and currency risks, others will only partly do so, and some investment managers will deliberately take a currency and interest rate gamble in the hope of an added profit alongside interest payments.

3. Conduct on-site due diligence

As soon as the investment committee has given the green light, an in-depth analysis will be conducted locally in order to gain a better understanding of the MFI and the essential risks on hand. Previous to that, an investment specialist will have gathered additional information from the MFI and prepared further steps accordingly. These preparatory operations will allow the investment specialist to travel to the resident country of the MFI under investigation.

What follows is the due diligence investigation of the MFI, which usually takes a few days. The information gathered locally will then be presented in a detailed report and handed over to the investment committee for further inspection.

4. Assign rating

The due diligence of the MFI informs the fund manager about the quality of an MFI. For an even more accurate assessment of an MFI, it can be assigned a rating, which pools all the relevant information. Quality is thereby defined as a probability of default, meaning that the rating should indicate the probability of an MFI sliding into financial difficulties.

Larger MFIs have already been rated by well-known rating agencies such as Fitch, Standard & Poor's or Moody's and may serve as a reference point for the fund manager's own judgment. Most MFIs, however, have not been rated yet – all the more reason why a fund manager's own evaluation may even be of vital importance to the MFI itself.

The rating methodology depends on the fund manager, though the calculation of a rating is highly complex and as a rule can only be performed by the most proficient service providers. The rating assignment process is ideally performed on several levels in a bid to avoid any conflicts of interest. Hence, although the investment specialist may well make suggestions for the rating, they will not be in a decision-making position. In many cases, a rating will therefore be confirmed by a committee consisting of investment specialists, portfolio managers and risk managers.

5. Internal investment committee review

Due to conflicts of interest, investment specialists do not decide single-handedly whether an investment in a particular MFI ought to be encouraged or not. They submit both their own proposal and the rating to the investment committee for approval.

There may be several investment committees along the fund hierarchy, which is why an investment proposal at times has to be approved by more than one committee. Combinations between internal investment committees at fund manager level and external committees for the fund, which is a separate legal entity, are quite common. The external thereby superordinates the internal committee.

6. Disbursement and hedging

The decision of the investment committee is followed by a series of operative steps to complete the transaction. First of all, the loan contract with the MFI is concluded and signed by both parties to be legally binding, then the contract is transferred to the custodian – usually a bank – for safe custody.[7]

What follows now are the hedging transactions, if at all provided. This encompasses additional tasks for the fund manager. They will begin to evaluate and select suitable hedging instruments and partners as well as structure contracts that are in line with the characteristics of the loan.

7. Monitoring

During its term, the investment is closely monitored, both virtually and locally. To enable the fund manager to monitor the investments from far, the MFI is obliged by the loan contract to disclose certain information to the manager in a predetermined frequency. Special occurrences are to be communicated immediately.

Ideally, these reports are evaluated by the investment specialists and risk managers involved. They assess the general situation of the MFI and check for breaches of the loan contract. In the event of negative developments or breaches of covenants, the risk management takes over the case and devises an adequate course of action.

10.4 LOAN AGREEMENTS AND PRICING POLICY

The result of any investment process is a contract between the fund and the MFI, or – in the case of equity investments – the fund and the shareholders of the MFI that sell the shares to the fund. A bilateral contract has to be negotiated that meets the requirements of both parties, unlike listed investments, which do not require contract negotiations, as only standardized contracts can be purchased.

Loan contracts contain a series of parameters that are negotiated between the fund manager and the MFI (see Figure 10.8). First of all, there is the loan amount as well as the maturity of the loan, the interest rate and its repayment frequency. Furthermore, there may be amortizations that have to be effectuated during the maturity. The loan has to be repaid in installments during its maturity, which mitigates the loan risk for the fund. The contract will also stipulate the seniority of the loan. This is relevant, should the MFI experience repayment difficulties, as loans with a high seniority are given precedence over others. The loan contract will further define the collateral that secures the loan, for example, buildings or inventory values. Ultimately, the contract also includes a number of sub-covenants that the MFI has to abide by (see Figure 10.9).

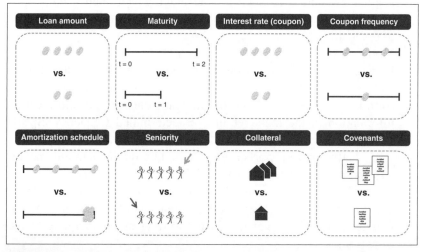

FIGURE 10.8 Negotiating Loan Details

Loan contract negotiations take into consideration the eight key figures as displayed: amount of loan, maturity, interest rate and coupon, coupon frequency, amortization schedule, seniority, collateral and covenants.

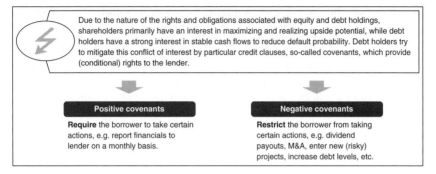

FIGURE 10.9 Positive and Negative Covenants

> A loan contract may feature positive and negative covenants to miti-gate conflicts of interest between shareholders and lenders.

Loan covenants are of utmost importance in avoiding, or at least miti-gating, any conflicts of interest between the owners of an MFI (the share-holders that are represented by the management) and the lenders of debt capital. Conflicts of interest between shareholders and lenders of debt capital are primarily the result of different expectations with respect to prospects of success. Shareholders may at worst suffer a loss of 100 per cent; their chances of profit, however, are potentially unlimited. Sponsors of debt capital, on the other hand, may equally suffer a total loss at worst, but they do not have any other chances of profit beyond the interest pay-ments. In the event of insolvency, debt investors will be served before equity holders. Shareholders therefore have a strong incentive to maxi-mize their chances of wealth by increasing their risk accordingly. Lenders of debt capital, however, prefer stable cash flows, predictability and mate-rial security.

To put it more simply, there are two types of covenants that may be employed by sponsors of debt capital: positive covenants, which largely cover reporting duties, and negative covenants, which oblige the MFI to refrain from certain actions.

Typically, these kinds of covenants apply to investment, payout or funding policy. Covenants may for instance restrict investments, prohibit dividend payouts or ban additional borrowing of debt capital.

The parameters mentioned above have a direct influence on the financial terms. The pricing of a loan largely depends on how secure its repayment is: the safer the repayment, the more favorable the terms that can be offered to the MFI.

Covenants thereby tend to have a favorable influence on a loan's default probability, as they are instrumental in stabilizing streams of cash flows. Shorter maturities also go hand in hand with a lower default probability, because longer maturities are synonymous with uncertainty. Collateral, amortization and high seniority, however, have no influence on default probability, yet they reduce a potential amount of loss. A fund manager's main goal therefore is to draft an optimal loan contract that will forge consensus of all parties.

DELICACIES FOR BUSY TRAVELERS – SANTIAGO DE CALI, COLOMBIA

Manjar Blanco is a Colombian specialty made from milk. Rubiela Sanchez and her husband have been producing this treat for over 13 years. At the beginning, most of the manufacturing processes were made by hand and with the help of basic equipment. Their loan with WWB Colombia enabled them to purchase modern equipment, increase productivity, revenue and profits. They sell their delicacies in various locations throughout the city, especially the central bus station, where they are incredibly popular with busy travelers.

Source: BlueOrchard

10.5 MICROFINANCE IN THE OVERALL INVESTMENT PORTFOLIO

Before the investment process is initiated, and before the most skilled fund managers and funds are evaluated and the microfinance portfolio is compiled, the weight of microfinance investments in the overall portfolio has to be determined. Investments in microfinance yield an attractive risk-return rate, both on their own and in the context of a portfolio, and they are a sensible course of action as they diversify the overall portfolio.

Microfinance correlates little or negatively with conventional asset classes such as bonds, shares or hedge funds. As a result, a portfolio with microfinance investments can yield higher returns than a portfolio that merely invests in conventional asset classes – at the same level of risk.

The economist and Nobel Prize Laureate Harry M. Markowitz proved by means of his modern portfolio theory (MPT) that a portfolio's risk can be reduced by adequate diversification. The risk of a diversified portfolio of assets is therefore considerably lower than that of a portfolio with a small number of assets (see Figure 10.10). Diversification lowers or mitigates the unsystematic risk so that the overall portfolio will only contain the market risk, i.e. the systematic, non-diversifiable risk. The diversification effect is based on the correlation (statistical interdependence) of the different assets in the portfolio. While positive correlations point to a parallel movement of return of both assets, negative correlation as a rule leads to counter movements, i.e. diversification.

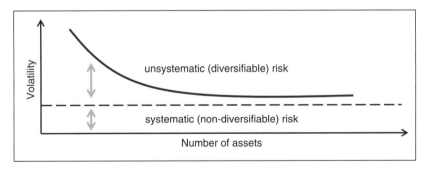

FIGURE 10.10   Diversification

There are unsystematic, diversifiable risks and systematic, non-diversifiable risks (market risk). The unsystematic risk can be mitigated by a higher number of diversified investments, whereas the market risk is not influenced by diversification.

Efficient Frontier

The efficient frontier concept was introduced by Markowitz in 1952 and is a cornerstone of MPT. It establishes the set of optimal portfolios that offer the highest expected return for a defined level of risk or the lowest risk for a specific level of expected return. Figure 10.11 displays two portfolios that carry an identical level of risk, but generate different returns. Therefore, only the portfolios on the solid line (efficient frontier) are efficient. They yield a higher return with the same risk (volatility) than the portfolios on the dotted line. The dot indicates the mean-variance portfolio, which is the portfolio that yields a specific return with the lowest risk.

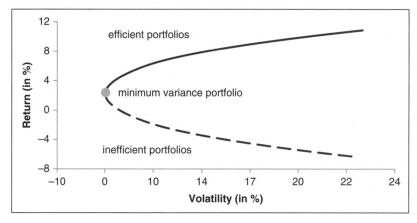

FIGURE 10.11   Efficient Frontier
Data Source: Markowitz (1952)

The efficient frontier concept was introduced by Harry Markowitz in 1952 and is a cornerstone of MPT. It establishes the set of optimal portfolios that offer the highest expected return for a defined level of risk or the lowest risk for a specific level of expected return. Inefficient portfolios (dotted line) are dominated by efficient portfolios (solid line), as they offer a higher return for the same level of risk (volatility). The dot denotes the mean-variance portfolio, i.e. the portfolio that yields a specific return with the lowest risk.

Correlations naturally follow suit when the values of the different investments change. Investors therefore reshuffle their portfolio based on these changes. However, the changes in correlations between the different asset classes are rarely significant enough to have a dramatic effect on risk minimization.

Sample Portfolio: Microfinance in the Portfolio Context (According to Markowitz)

A sample portfolio will serve to illustrate how the value added to a portfolio by microfinance is assessed, by means of six sample asset classes that create a portfolio:

- Microfinance
- Cash
- Government bonds
- Stocks
- Stocks – emerging markets (EM)
- Hedge funds

Figure 10.12 displays the key performance measures of asset classes i.e. their respective indices. Over the period of ten years, emerging market

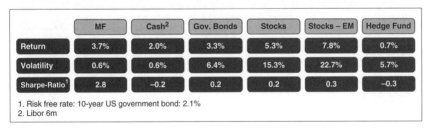

	MF	Cash[2]	Gov. Bonds	Stocks	Stocks – EM	Hedge Fund
Return	3.7%	2.0%	3.3%	5.3%	7.8%	0.7%
Volatility	0.6%	0.6%	6.4%	15.3%	22.7%	5.7%
Sharpe-Ratio[1]	2.8	−0.2	0.2	0.2	0.3	−0.3

1. Risk free rate: 10-year US government bond: 2.1%
2. Libor 6m

FIGURE 10.12 Key Performance Indicators of Asset Classes (1 January 2005 – 31 December 2015, Based on Monthly Returns in $)
Data Source: SMX, Bloomberg

This figure displays the key performance indicators of a sample portfolio. The following are the sample asset classes: microfinance, cash, government bonds, stocks, stocks – EM and hedge funds.

stocks (MSCI EM index) yield the highest return at almost 11 per cent annually, followed by stocks of industrialized countries (MSCI World) at 6 per cent. Government bonds (Morningstar government bond index) yielded a return of 3.3 per cent a year, MIVs (SMX – MIV Debt) yielded 3.7 per cent, cash investments (six-month US-Dollar LIBOR) 2 per cent, and hedge funds 0.7 per cent (global hedge fund index). While stock indices were particularly subject to turbulence during the financial crisis, microfinance and the money market managed to remain largely unscathed.

A look at the relation of the risk and the returns (Sharpe ratio) clearly reveals the appeal of MIVs. Taking account of the volatility, the return of 3.7 per cent p.a. yields a Sharp ratio – i.e. a risk-adjusted return – of 2.8 per cent and achieves the highest ratio of all the asset classes in the portfolio.

Figure 10.13 reveals that MIVs in fact correlate little with other assets. The value of the so-called correlation coefficient may figure anywhere between minus 1 and plus 1. A correlation of plus 1 indicates perfect positive linear correlation between the two asset classes, whereas a correlation of minus 1 indicates a perfect negative correlation. A correlation coefficient around zero indicates no linear correlation.

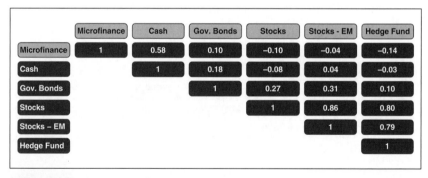

	Microfinance	Cash	Gov. Bonds	Stocks	Stocks - EM	Hedge Fund
Microfinance	1	0.58	0.10	–0.10	–0.04	–0.14
Cash		1	0.18	–0.08	0.04	–0.03
Gov. Bonds			1	0.27	0.31	0.10
Stocks				1	0.86	0.80
Stocks – EM					1	0.79
Hedge Fund						1

FIGURE 10.13 Correlations
Data Source: SMX, Bloomberg

The chart reveals the correlations of the sample asset classes. Microfinance correlates little or negatively with the other asset classes of the sample portfolio.

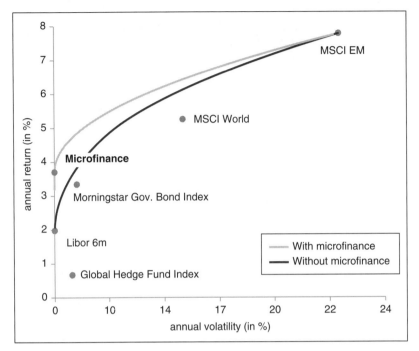

FIGURE 10.14 Microfinance in the Overall Portfolio
Data Source: SMX, Bloomberg

The efficient frontier is remarkably higher with microfinance in a portfolio than without it. This means that a portfolio with a higher share of microfinance yields a higher return with the same level of risk.

An efficient portfolio is one where the return of a portfolio cannot be increased with a given risk, or where the risk cannot be lowered with a given return. Figure 10.14 illustrates that microfinance boosts a portfolio's efficiency. This essentially means that including microfinance in a portfolio generates a higher return at the same level of risk than a portfolio that only consists of conventional asset classes.

10.6 INCENTIVES FOR INVESTING IN MICROFINANCE

What motivates public and private investors to invest in microfinance? The University of Zurich's Center for Microfinance and BlueOrchard thoroughly investigated this question in a joint comprehensive survey – the

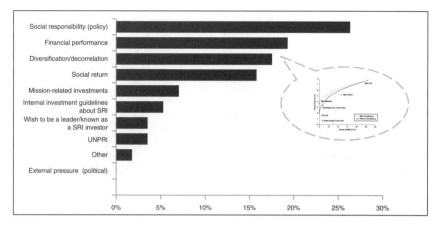

FIGURE 10.15   Incentives for Investors to Invest in Microfinance
Source: BlueOrchard and the University of Zurich (2014)

Social responsibility policies of institutions, followed by financial performance and diversification of a portfolio, are the main incentives for investors in microfinance. In the context of a portfolio, particular attention is paid to the financial performance and diversification of the mission-related investments.

'Swiss Institutional Investors Survey 2014' – among institutional investors. The answers of the respondents revealed that a great number of institutional investors invest in microfinance because of SRI guidelines imposed by corporate governance. The survey also disclosed that the stable financial performance of microfinance and its diversification are the key incentives for investments, followed by social return, as shown in Figure 10.15.

Institutional investors named risk and return as the decisive factors for their investment decisions (see Figure 10.16). The sample portfolio illustrates that microfinance has a more attractive risk-return ratio than conventional asset classes. At the same time, portfolios that have been diversified by microfinance become more efficient.

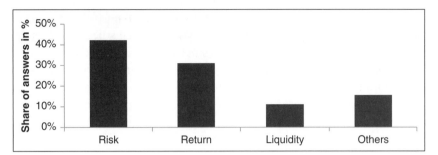

FIGURE 10.16 Criteria for Investment Decisions
Data Source: BlueOrchard and the University of Zurich (2014)

> Risk, return and liquidity are the three most important criteria for investment decisions of institutional investors.

10.7 PRELIMINARY CONCLUSIONS

Microfinance has grown into an established asset class. Private institutional investors such as pension funds, insurances or funds-of-funds in particular have considerably influenced this impressive growth in recent years. Investors appreciate the stable returns and outstanding diversification properties of this asset class. Investments are predominantly made via investment funds to ensure that they are managed professionally and efficiently. This also offers investors the opportunity to make their investments alongside development banks, benefiting from their experience and partly also from their risk-sharing mechanisms.

The investment process is crucial for the quality of a microfinance portfolio, and a professional microfinance manager will always combine a top-down with a bottom-up approach. The top-down process determines the basic parameters of a portfolio, such as geographical allocation or the risk-return profile. The bottom-up approach includes the identification, analysis and ultimately the selection of individual investments. Only a meticulous analysis of an MFI locally will allow for careful selection of investments.

The investment process terminates with the actual loan contract negotiations between the fund manager and the MFI. The aim is a contract stipulating the amount of loan, maturity, interest rate, collateral and particularly covenants that are acceptable for both parties involved. Covenants are vital aspects of a loan contract, as they mitigate conflicts of interest between shareholders and lenders of debt capital.

MPT is instrumental in the search for the optimal portfolio that maximizes returns with a given level of risk. Microfinance's negative correlation with cyclical asset classes such as stocks and hedge funds over recent years amply shows that a portfolio including microfinance yields a higher return with the same risk factors (volatility and economic cycle).

Institutional investors base their decision to settle for microfinance on an internal strategy that promotes socially responsible investing, followed

FISHING – ILOILO, THE PHILIPPINES

Christina und Wilmer Barba live in a small fishing village near Iloilo, on the Western Islands of the Philippines. They have four children between the ages of 2 and 22. Every morning, Mr. Barba and his elder sons set out to sea to catch the fish his wife then sells in the regional market. In 2002, the family took out their first loan with the LiveBank foundation in order to purchase fishing nets that would allow them to start their business. Currently, the Barba family – now owners of two fishing boats and employers of several people from the region – are repaying their thirteenth loan.

Source: BlueOrchard

by the attractive financial returns and outstanding diversification opportunities of microfinance.

In conclusion, microfinance is not only attractive as an investment opportunity, but its outstanding diversification properties in a portfolio truly make it one of a kind.

NOTES

1 Kofi Annan, former United Nations Secretary-General.
2 Microrate (2013b).
3 Closed-end funds have a limited circle of investors who acquire shares in a fund through an initial public offering. Their maturity is fixed beforehand. In the meantime, the purchased shares cannot be handed back. Open-end funds have an open circle of investors and trading of the shares is periodically possible. For this reason, open-end funds usually do not have a maturity that is fixed in advance.
4 For details concerning the investment process see Chapter 10.3.
5 Default: annual, technical (acceleration based on covenant defaults) and payment defaults loss: based on annual default rate.
6 Based on the process of BlueOrchard Finance SA.
7 The process in the case of equity capital is similar; however, the other party to the agreement need not definitely be an MFI, but can be a third party from which the shares have been purchased. The underlying contract is therefore a share purchase agreement rather than a loan or credit agreement. Moreover, further agreements may apply, such as a shareholder pooling agreement.

CHAPTER 11

Real and Financial Economy

The man (real economy) walks down a street. The dog (financial economy) sometimes falls behind and sometimes runs on ahead. However, both man and dog ultimately reach their destination together.

Joseph Schumpeter[1]

The real economy – the part of the economy that deals with the production of goods and services, unlike the financial markets – is where borrowers are active. It is hardly influenced by the global economic cycle. Borrowers of microfinance institutions hence generate their incomes on local markets, and the local real economy's infrastructure to connect it to the rest of the world is either rudimentary or simply non-existent.

The financial economy, on the contrary, can influence large microfinance institutions, as they are partly funded by international capital markets. The financial means of microfinance have not faltered despite the global financial crisis.

11.1 MICROFINANCE IS CRISIS-PROOF

Microfinance's two-digit growth rates even during the financial crisis amply demonstrate its resilience in the face of changes in the global economic cycle (see Figure 11.1), the reason being that in microfinance, borrowers generate their income in a largely independent, closed economy. They mostly engage in very local markets, which depend more on regional politics, the regional economy and local natural disasters than on the cycles of other economically dominant countries.

Microfinance is fundamentally influenced by aspects of the real economy. Its integration in the financial system may result in local markets being affected by global macro-economic influences. Investors may choose to refrain from further investments in the capital market, which would eventually lead to a drop in the financial means that MFIs can employ for lending. So far, MFIs have been able to collect means from international

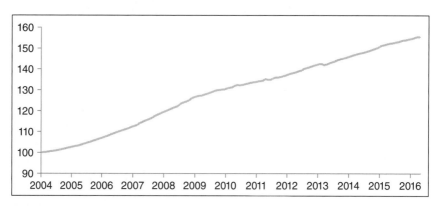

FIGURE 11.1 SMX
Data Source: SMX

Figure 11.1 shows the development of the microfinance debt index (SMX – Symbiotics Microfinance Index) since 2004. It is evident that microfinance yields positive returns even during crises. The highest growth rates in microfinance were generated until 2009, but they continue to figure in the two-digit bracket after that.

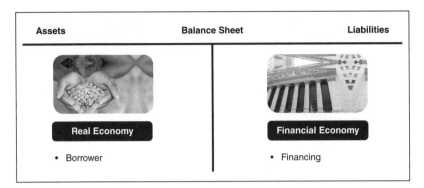

FIGURE 11.2 Balance Sheet of an MFI

The assets consist of borrowers, who are largely influenced by the real economy of their region. The liabilities contain the financing, which is influenced by the global financial economy, as far as means of international capital markets are concerned.

capital markets even during times of crises. They have remained unaffected by investor withdrawal.

Figure 11.2 displays the balance sheet of an MFI. The assets depend on the real economy and therefore on lending to micro entrepreneurs. The liabilities represent the funding side. To prevent risks presented by the real economy, recent years have seen the introduction of stability mechanisms, such as credit bureaus, micro insurance and enabling MFIs to take deposits.

11.2 REAL ECONOMY AND LOCAL INFLUENCING FACTORS

Figure 11.3 compares the trade balances of selected countries that are active in microfinance with those of Germany and Switzerland. These two countries, along with Azerbaijan, Vietnam and Mongolia are the only ones to reveal a trade surplus. All the other countries that are displayed import more than they export.[2] Markedly, their volumes of imports and exports are considerably smaller than those of industrialized countries. Germany's export volume is almost five times that of India, despite the fact that the population of India is 15 times that of Germany. A high foreign trade volume indicates that the countries depend on each other. A drop in demand

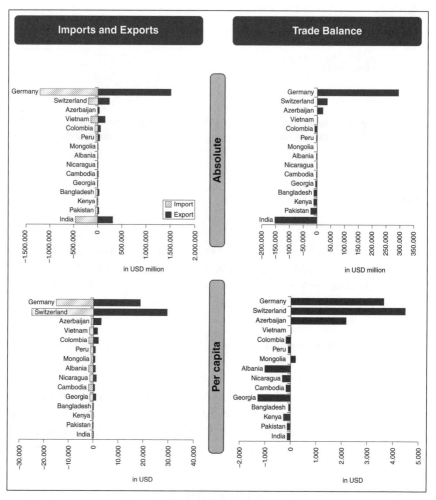

FIGURE 11.3 Trade Balances of Selected Countries
Data Source: World Trade Organization (2015)

This table displays the imports and exports of the year 2014, the top right shows the respective trade balance. Below are the per capita figures for each selected country.

in the regions of destination for Germany's exports will naturally result in a decrease of the German trade surplus and hence lower its GDP. Germany, as an industrial nation, therefore depends on global economic cycles.

The repayment rate of micro entrepreneurs, however, is largely independent of either a global boom or a global recession, as their business model is based on their local economy. Chapter 4 has revealed that about a third of the volume of loans is handed out to borrowers in the local trade, followed by agriculture at 28 per cent and services at 21 per cent. Local purchasing power does react to regional parameters; however, it remains unaffected by interest rate cuts and economic crises in other countries and on other continents. Moreover, microfinance regions lack the infrastructure to make them an integral part of the global network. The repayment rate of micro entrepreneurs therefore depends on aspects of the real economy and the local framework in particular. Micro entrepreneurs operate locally, and this entails a key advantage: diversification is particularly effective. Events such as the catastrophic drought in Andhra Pradesh remain geographically isolated. Any economic activity a mere few kilometers away remains unfazed. A diversified portfolio is therefore the best option to avert losses.

11.3 FINANCIAL ECONOMY

Micro entrepreneurs, and MFIs indirectly also, remain virtually unaffected by global developments of the real economy. Global financial integration has increased over the last few decades, and emerging countries have matured into participants of the global capital market. What is the situation of MFIs with respect to the financial economy?

Influencing Factors

The key factors relating to the financial economy are the liquidity trap, inflation and currency devaluation. The lack of availability of refinancing funds for an MFI may lead to liquidity problems. This can be observed in a decrease in international investment flows or local funding.

Depending on the type of funding, some MFIs may be more strongly affected by capital decrease at times of international tensions than others. Most MFIs in India, for example, fund themselves by means of local capital, i.e. via local banks, whereas MFIs in Nicaragua are mainly funded by capital from international markets.

Inflation, on the other hand, can also influence an MFI's liquidity situation, albeit indirectly. Soaring prices result in rising wages, as the labor market adjusts to inflation. This means that in addition to the rising

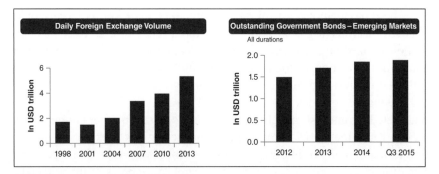

FIGURE 11.4 Foreign Exchange Volume and Outstanding Government Bonds
Data Source: BIS (2013) and BIS (2015)

Figure 11.4 illustrates the integration of the international financial markets based on the rising daily foreign exchange volumes and outstanding government bonds of all maturities of emerging economies.

costs for production materials, micro entrepreneurs will incur higher operating costs with respect to employees and administration. Inflation will, however, also boost turnover, for the simple reason that goods may now be sold at higher prices. The temporal delay in price adjustments between the purchase and distribution of goods and services may affect the liquidity of micro entrepreneurs, which may in turn lead to loan repayment delays.

Local currencies may be devalued because of slow economic growth or rising inflation. Any devaluation changes the exchange rate and may thus have an impact on the profitability and the management of the assets and liabilities of MFIs, should they be funded in foreign currency.

Prevention and Hedging Against Risks from the Financial Economy

Risks posed by the financial economy are particularly relevant with respect to the liquidity management and the asset liability management of a microfinance institution. In order to prevent and hedge risks from the financial economy, regulators and investors have imposed a series of measures.

In most countries regulators define, for example, strict minimum liquidity requirements. In addition to this, the analysis of the liquidity situation of an MFI is an integral part of the rating and investment processes, which explains why MFIs are eager to maintain sufficient liquidity reserves. Today, there are various instruments available even for exotic currencies that will allow a fund manager to hand out loans in local currencies and hedge the currency risk at the same time. Neither MFI nor investor will thus be subjected to currency risks.

The successful development of many emerging economies and the ensuing increased local funding of MFIs additionally reduce the liquidity squeeze and credit crunch risk. Even during the financial crisis of 2008, microfinance managed to attract new funds and was one of the few asset classes to yield a positive return during these arduous times.

11.4 STABILITY MECHANISMS

With the aim of supporting the rising returns and further strengthening an already stable microfinance sector, numerous credit bureaus have been launched and the regulatory framework has been pushed on.

Credit bureaus record data of micro entrepreneurs and the terms of their loans with their responsible MFI in order to monitor multiple loans. Institutions such as the Central Bank regulate MFI business activities and structures. The World Bank has further increased its commitment locally to exert more influence on the local microfinance markets in the short and the long run.

Micro insurance is another financial service that further enhances the stability of the system. It covers both micro entrepreneurs and MFIs against loan default. In many cases, the premium of this mandatory insurance makes part of the loan terms and conditions.

Further, regulation enables MFIs to take deposits, much to the benefit of the entire industry. Figure 11.5 reveals that the proportion of deposits in comparison with outstanding loans has been on a steady increase since 2004. This means that MFIs have more financial means at their disposal for lending, and the currency risk can be averted. Most micro entrepreneurs are reliable savers in any case, putting money aside for times of hardship and to support the business they have launched. Saving and borrowing are not by any means a contradiction in terms.

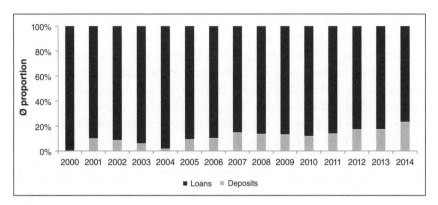

FIGURE 11.5 Deposits Compared to Loans
Data Source: MIX (2016)

The average proportion of deposits of the transaction volume of MFIs steadily increased from 2000 to 2014.

11.5 PRELIMINARY CONCLUSIONS

Microfinance is an overwhelming success story and has unfailingly sustained its two-digit growth rates all the way through global economic and financial crises, and turbulence in emerging markets.

From a real economy point of view, microfinance most of all benefits from the locally-bound activities of micro entrepreneurs, which amplify the effects and impact of diversification. From a financial economy perspective, both the intense focus of MFIs on their liquidity situation and appropriate hedging instruments provide a reliable shield against losses.

Credit bureaus and other stability mechanisms have been introduced to prevent crises, and regulation has been tightened. Today, beyond all these measures, specially designed insurance policies additionally protect borrowers and lenders alike.

BEEKEEPING – VISOKO, BOSNIA-HERZEGOVINA

Ahmo Culov, 72, and his wife are beekeepers. Beekeeping is an ancient tradition in this region, and Mr. Culov's father was a beekeeper too. With his first loan of $3000 in 2006, Mr. Culov purchased additional beehives and colonies. He now has more than 80 colonies of bees that produce over two tons of honey a year. The largest share of his production is sold in local markets in the region and to occasional customers. His income enables him to continue to expand his business.

Source: BlueOrchard

NOTES

1 Joseph Schumpeter, economist and politician: dog and master simile.
2 World Trade Organization (2015).

CHAPTER 12

Discussion of Results
and Conclusions

*Microfinance is not charity. This is business: business with a
social objective, which is to help people get out of poverty.*

Muhammad Yunus[1]

Microfinance perfectly synchronizes the interests of borrowers, investors and society. This is an outstanding achievement – and unprecedented in the world of asset management.

New technologies, such as mobile money transfer systems or the use of satellite data, will only serve to further boost the productivity of an already effective operative business.

In the years to come, an increasing number of people will be able to benefit from an even more efficient microfinance sector. At the same time, microfinance will become an important part of professional investment portfolios, thanks to its attractive risk-return patterns.

12.1 WIN-WIN-WIN

The significant decrease in global poverty since the creation of the MDGs in 2000 can undoubtedly also be credited to microfinance, a powerful and effective tool for the financial integration of the poor segments of the population and households. Society in general and investors in microfinance in particular also benefit from it, for the simple fact that social and financial return are not mutually exclusive, but can evidently be met simultaneously.

Another of microfinance's convincing aspects is that it respects and trusts its micro entrepreneurs. They are appreciated as equal partners on their way out of poverty and in all their unwavering endeavors to improve their economic situation. They can use their skills to the best of their abilities and exploit their potential. At the same time they are keen not to undermine the trust that has been placed in them. The default rate of micro loans is insignificantly low.

Society benefits from micro entrepreneurs in many ways. On the one hand, they create employment, which multiplies its economic impact. On the other, women in particular use the income that is generated via micro loans very prudently. They use it for their children's education or to improve their family's healthcare, which in turn sustainably strengthens social development.

Investors can achieve a sense of satisfaction by making a social contribution, but they also gain financially. The attractive returns of microfinance go hand in hand with outstanding diversification properties. Microfinance investment vehicles, therefore, are particularly valuable in the context of a portfolio. Its stable financial return has established microfinance as an asset class that is being used by institutional and increasingly by private investors alike.

One of microfinance's feats – unprecedented in the world of asset management – is that it perfectly synchronizes and lines up the interests of borrowers, investors and society.

12.2 ONWARDS AND UPWARDS

New technologies such as mobile money transfer systems or the use of satellite data will influence the world of microfinance and boost its efficiency. Data and services will be available around the clock, electronically, free of charge and in a respectful way. The value chain will continue to be optimized, costs will be lowered and competition will increase. It would come as no surprise to find that most of these future developments will have been instigated by MFIs and smaller banks. New technologies, rapid progress and innovations will be the brainchildren of those enterprises that are not bogged down by burdens of the past. Micro entrepreneurs will undoubtedly profit from this development too, as it will facilitate and accelerate the way loans can be accessed.

As a result of the attractive risk-return ratio, more and more private and institutional investors will provide capital. Demand will surge and emphasize the importance of microfinance as an asset class in its own right.

The range of microfinance services will be widened quite substantially to adapt to the rising demand. Stronger diversification and specialization of investment opportunities will be the natural consequence of this development. Lending facilities as such and increasingly also savings products, insurance services, training and medical care – but also questions concerning renewable energies – will gain center stage. Global enterprises from sectors such as healthcare, insurance, the food industry, agriculture, technology and telecommunication will recognize that micro entrepreneurs are their clients of the future. Their care will be of the utmost importance.

The number of people who are excluded from the financial system will drop significantly and the number of people living in poverty will continue to decrease. However, poverty will not simply vanish off the face of the earth, but instead transfer to countries and regions of slow growth that profit only marginally from technological advances. In the years to come, microfinance will therefore assume two main tasks: firstly, to support those who have been neglected, and secondly, to pave the way for innovation – in a new world order in which financial institutions are becoming key protagonists, while classic banking will become less important.

All in all the following developments are to be expected:

- Absolute poverty will decline distinctly.
- Large parts of the population will have access to financial services.
- The geopolitical relevance of impact investing will continue to rise and exert a stabilizing effect on entire regions and countries.
- The level of education and medical care in developing countries will be improved.
- Innovative financial products will serve to mitigate the negative effects of climate change.

- MFIs will develop into efficient and effective financial service providers.
- For banks and companies, takeovers and joint ventures will be instrumental in securing the last mile.
- Financial service providers in developing countries will act as drivers of innovation for technological development.
- Microfinance and impact investing will assume a key role in the world of investment.

CASHMERE WEAVING – ULAN BATOR, MONGOLIA

Tsetsgee Batush, 46, is the founder and owner of Edelweiss Cashmere. She lives in Ulan Bator and has two children studying abroad. Mrs. Batush's plans to export jumpers and other items of clothing to Russia made her team up with two employees to start her own company in 2004. Her collection was an immediate success and prompted her to take out a loan to meet the rising demand in Russia. She used her loan of EUR 9000 to purchase additional production equipment and employ more workers. Today, she sells more than 1200 cashmere jumpers in Mongolia and Russia a year.

Source: BlueOrchard

In all that microfinance has achieved, its core idea remains that it is based on trust. Trust creates performance, not the other way around. It is this trust that people in need have to be awarded to empower themselves to progress economically and live a life of dignity. For this reason, further explanatory efforts are imperative to continue to raise awareness of the enormous potential of microfinance.

Small Money – Big Impact!

NOTES

1 Muhammad Yunus, founder of modern microfinance and Nobel Peace Prize laureate.

APPENDIX A

Example of a Loan Application

LOAN APPLICATION					MFI 'XYZ'

LOAN REQUEST

Loan officer name: *Augusto Villena Riccardi*	Date of application:	dd 13	mm 02	yyyy 2015

Branch: *Cumbayá*

☒ BORROWER   ☐ CO-BORROWER

Requested Amount

Amount	Term	What is your monthly payment capacity?	Type of loan:	☒ Microcredit ☐ Education ☐ Health
USD 5,500	*24 months*	*USD 300*		

Borrower's personal information

Last name (father): *Zambrano*	How are you known in the neighborhood?
Last name (mother): *Sanchez*	*Rafael*
First name: *Rafael*	☒ ID ☐ Passport N° *1702345670*
Middle name: *Jose*	Gender ☒ Male ☐ Female

Birth place (country, city): *Ecuador, Quito*	Profession: *Manufacturing*
Age: *24 years-old* Birth Date: dd mm yyyy	Economic activity: *Manufacturing and sale of shoes and other leather products.*
Nationality: *Ecuadorean* 23 07 1990	

Marital status	Premarital agreement on division of property?	Occupation	Education
☐ Single ☐ Widow	☐ Yes ☒ No	☐ Employee ☒ Micro-entrepreneur	☐ Elementary
☒ Married ☐ Divorced		☐ Student ☐ Independent professional	☐ College
☐ Cohabitant		☐ Housewife ☐ Retired	☐ High School
		☐ Other	☒ Technical
		Specify Other	

Borrower's spouse personal information

Last name (father): *Torres*	☒ ID ☐ Passport N° *1719876543*
Last name (mother): *Correa*	Gender: ☒ Male ☐ Female
First name: *Maria*	Age: 25 Date of Birth dd mm yyyy
Middle name: ––––	Nationality: *Ecuadorean* 08 09 1989

Place of birth (country, city): *Ecuador, Quito*	Education
Profession: *Administrator*	☐ Elementary ☐ High School
Economic activity: *Employee in local company*	☒ College ☐ Technical

Phone	Operator	Occupation
Tel. 1: *990 099 887*	Telcel:	☒ Employee ☐ Micro-entrepreneur
Tel. 2: ––––	––––	☐ Student ☐ Independent professional
		☐ Housewife ☐ Retired
		☐ Other
		Specify other ....

Domicile information

Province: *Pichincha* Canton: *Quito*	Phone number 1: *289 4567*
Neighborhood: *Quito*	Phone number 2: *————*
Address: *Cuero y Caicedo, cruce con Mariana de Jesús*	Cellphone number: *991 987 654*
Address (reference): *————*	Email: *rafaza@gmail.com*

Current address since / month *02* / year *2010*	**Type of residence**		Name of the house owner/landlord: *Manuel Costa*
	▣ Own house ✕ Rented ▣ Family house	Is the house mortgaged? ▣ Yes ▣ No	Phone number of the house owner/landlord: *976 098 543*

Business Information

Name of the business: *Zapatería El Rafa* Position: *Owner*	Phone number 1: *289 0987*
Province: *Pichincha* Canton: *Quito*	Phone number 2: *————*
Neighborhood: *Cumbayá* Point of sale: Commercial premises ✕ Street ▣ Vendor	Cellphone number: *991 987 654*
Address of the business: *Francisco de Orellana, cruce con Acacias*	Type of location: ✕ Urban ▣ Rural
Current business since: /month *06* /year *2010*	Name of landlord: *Jose Mujica*
Commercial premises: ▣ Own ✕ Rented ▣ Other	Phone numer of landlord: *909 888 765*

Job information (only if applicant is an employee)

Occupation / Position in business:		Monthly net salary:	Currently working since	dd	mm	yyyy
Name of workplace:		Phone 1:				
Main economic activity:		Phone 2:	Type of location:			
Address of workplace:			✕ Urban ▣ Rural			

References from individuals not living in your same home address

First name: *Carlos*	Phone number: *289 9094*
Last name: *Perez*	Workplace address: *Corea, cruce con Amazonas*
Home address: *Corea, cruce con 8 de Diciembre*	Workplace phone number: *289 3456*
	Relationship with applicant: *Supplier*
First name: *Patricia*	Phone number: *289 5432*
Last name: *Correa*	Workplace address: *————*
Home address: *Isla Pinzon y Floreana*	Workplace phone number: *————*
	Relationship with applicant: *Sister-in-law*

Sketch house map

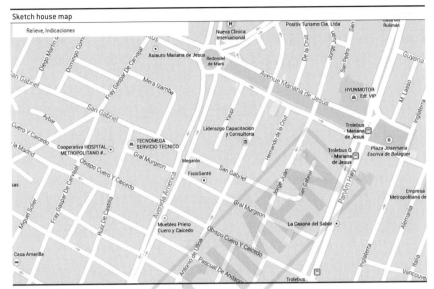

Representations and authorization

I declare under oath that the origin of the funds given to the MFI XYZ are lawful, and I declare under oath that the funds that I receive from the MFI XYZ will not be used to developing or financing of any illegal activity, therefore I release the MFI XYZ of all responsibility, including liability towards third parties if this statement is false or incorrect. I am aware of the provisions of the «Law on Prevention, Detection and Eradication of the Crime of Money Laundering and Financing of Crime» and expressly authorize the MFI XYZ to perform analyzes and verifications it deems necessary, as well as other competent authorities in case the existence of transactions and / or unusual and unwarranted transactions is determined.

In virtue of the above-stated, I renounce to hold any civil or legal action against MFI XYZ I authorize expressly and irrevocably to MFI XYZ to get, whenever it deems necessary, and from any source available including credit bureau reports, information related to my credit history, savings or checking accounts, credit cards, etc. Likewise, I expressly authorize MFI XYZ to provide information on the performance of my duties, whether direct or indirect, whenever it deems necessary to the Credit Bureaus legally authorized to operate in Ecuador in accordance with Ecuadorean Law.

I certify that the information provided is correct and authorize the verification of personal data provided for the purposes of making a pre-evaluation of the credit application and I agree to provide further documents as necessary. I agree that the documentation submitted with this application will not be returned.

I acknowledge that MFI XYZ may approve, deny or suspend the credit application depending on compliance with some policies of the Bank.

To my best knowledge, as of this date I do not keep any connection with the Bank, either by property or by administration or management; however, I agree to immediately inform the Bank in case that this situation changes.

Signature ....

Name ....

ID ....

Place and date ....

APPENDIX B

Due Diligence of Socio-Economic Impact Factors

SOCIO-ECONOMIC INFORMATION					MFI 'XYZ'

MICRO-ENTREPRENEUR

☒ BORROWER　　　☐ CO-BORROWER

Socio-economic information				
Name of loan officer: *Augusto Villena Riccardi*	Date of on-site visit	dd *15*	mm *02*	yyyy *2015*
Name of borrower: *Rafael Zambrano Sanchez*	On-site visit duration (in minutes)			
Branch: *Cumbayá*	Visit started at: *9:30am*			
	Visit ended at: *10:00am*			
	Total time *30 minutes*			

Evaluation of qualitative factors

Character

Personal references 1	☒ Positive	☐ Negative
Personal references 2	☒ Positive	☐ Negative

Business management capacity

Start of business	☒ > = 3 months	☐ = < 3 months
Knowledge of the business activity	The applicant has 'good' knowledge of the business and he is fairly aware of the related costs of the business and the need of the clientele it serves. Otherwise, rate this section 'bad'.	
	☒ Good	☐ Bad

Collateral

Collateral required based on requested amount:	☒ Unsecured	☐ Chattel	☐ Real Estate
Do the borrower and co-borrower have the same domicile?	☒ No ☐ Yes, but he/she is financially independent ☐ Yes, and he/she is financially dependent		

Fill-in only if the requested amount equals or exceeds USD 5,000

Character

References from provider 1	☒ Positive	☐ Negative
References from provider 2	☒ Positive	☐ Negative

Business conditions

Geographic location	Applicable to trade and services only. Assess as 'good location' if business premise is easily accessible and noticeable to clients, and if it is well-known in the neighborhood. Otherwise, assess 'Needs improvement'. ☒ Good location　☐ Needs improvement
Competitive advantages	Assess as 'good level of competitiveness' if the business has a strong differentiating factor related to the quality of its service/product or of its customer service. Otherwise, assess as 'Needs improvement'. ☐ Good level of competitiveness　☒ Needs improvement

221

Ongoing operations seen on-site	Confirm if you observed that actual operations took place during your on-site visit (e.g. people working in factory, goods being delivered, presence of clients and/or providers, etc.) ▢ Yes ▢ No

Business management capacity

Layout of the business' premises and products	Layout is orderly organized and adequately implemented. ☒ Yes ▢ No
Record of acquisitions and sales. Check 'yes' if at least 20% of acquisitions or 20% of sales during the most recent month are supported by proper documentation (invoices).	▢ Yes ☒ No

Collateral

Do the borrower and co-borrower have the same domicile?	▢ Yes ☒ No

Evaluation of quantitative factors

Current assets	USD	Fixed assets	USD	Other assets	USD
Cash	500	Land and buildings	----	Specify (other)	
Savings	1,800	Machinery and equipments	8,000		
Accounts receivable	----	Vehicles	----		
Inventory	1,120	Other	----		
Total current assets	3,420	Total fixed assets	8,000	Total other assets	----
Total assets	11,420				

Breakdown of fixed assets

Items	Description	In domicile?	In business?	State of conservation
Furniture and fixtures	2 counters with exhibitor		Yes	Good
	1 desk and 4 chairs		Yes	Good
Machinery and equipment	2 sewing machines for leather		Yes	Regular (4 years old)
	2 cutter machines		Yes	Good
	1 skiving machine		Yes	Regular (4 years old)
	2 leather polishing machines		Yes	Good
Vehicles	----			
Lands	----			
Buildings	----			

Breakdown of liabilities					
Items	Description	USD	Total # of installments	Amount of installments	# of pending installments
Providers	Purchase of raw materials	800	1	800	1
	Purchase of other accessories	300	1	300	1
Banks	Loan with Bank ABC	1,914	18	319	6
Retail	Purchase of TV	159	6	53	3
Total liabilities		3,173			
Equity		8,247			
Total liabilities and equity		11,420			

Inventory of goods (for trade-related businesses)				
List of best-selling products	Price USD	Cost of sales	Current inventory	Share in total sales (%)

Inventory of goods (for industry-related business)			
List of main raw materials	# of units of raw material needed to make one item of finished good	Current inventory	Cost per unit
1. Leather sheets	2 meters (dress shoes)	50 meters	USD 19 / meter
2. Rubber soles	2 units	50 units	USD 3 / pair
3. Colors and dyes	½ bottle	10 bottles	USD 2 / bottle
4.			
5.			
6.			
7.			
8.			
9.			
10.			

List of best-selling finished goods	Current inventory	Price (USD)	Cost per unit (USD)	Share in total sales (%)
1. Men dress shoes (black) – model 1	10 pairs	75	30	20
2. Men dress shoes (brown) – model 2	8 pairs	75	30	15
3. Men sandals – model 1	8 pairs	45	18	15
4. Children dress shoes (black) – model 1	10 pairs	45	18	15
5.				
6.				
7.				
8.				
9.				
10.				

Analysis of sales

Seasonality of sales. Daily sales.

Daily sales	Cash	Credit	Month	Cash	Credit
Monday			January	2,600	
Tuesday			February	2,600	
Wednesday			March	2,600	
Thursday			April	2,600	
Friday			May	2,000	
Saturday			June	2,000	
Sunday			July	3,200	
Weekly sales	**Cash (USD)**	**Credit**	August	3,200	
First week	600		September	2,600	
Second week	600		Oktober	2,600	
Third week	700		November	2,600	
Fourth week	700		December	3,000	
Bi-weekly sales	**Cash (USD)**	**Credit**	Average	2,633	
1st half	1,200		If total annual sales equal or exceed USD 100,000 or total		
2nd half	1,400		costs and expenses equal or exceed USD 80,000 the borrower		
Monthly sales	**Cash (USD)**	**Credit**	must have a valid tax ID number.		
Monthly sales	2,600				

Comments (mention credit history and overall assessment of the business):

The client is a current client of MFI XYZ and this would be his second loan. He has made all its payment punctually under the current loan.

The credit bureau report shows that the client has debts with only one additional lender besides MFI XYZ and has no payment default in those other debts. The months of July and August are of high demand due to the beginning of the scholar season. Sales also increase in December due to festivities of year-end.

Breakdown of income / expenses (monthly)			
Business income	USD	**Other sources of income**	USD
Sales	2,600	Other businesses	–
COGS	650	Spouse's salary	700
Gross margin	1,950	Rental	–
Operating expenses	USD	Retirement payout	–
Salaries	400	Remittances	–
Rental	400	Other (specify)	–
Water supply	25	Total family income	700
Electricity supply	100	**Family expenses**	USD
Phone service	50	House rental	200
Maintenance and repairs	30	Food	180
Transportation	20	Education	25
Financial expenses	415	Water supply	30
Taxes	20	Electricity supply	30
Other	52	Phone service	40
Total business expense	1,512	Health care	20
Business net income	438	Transportation	50
Disposable income	USD	Apparel	20
Business net income	438	Leisure and entertainment	20
Family net income	22	Insurances	10
Total disposable income	460	Other debts	53
Monthly payment capacity (60 %)	276	Total family expenses	678
Monthly payment capacity requested (65 %)	300	Family net income	22
Number of dependents	2	Number of students (school or college)	2

Name of dependents: spouse and children (up to 18 years old)				
Last name (father)	**Last name (mother)**	**Given names**	**Date of birth (dd/mm/yyyy)**	**Relationship**
Zambrano	Torres	Agustín	21/04/2008	Son
Zambrano	Torres	Natasha	15/03/2010	Daughter

1.	**Client application**		2.	**Loan officer recommendation**	
	Requested loan amount	*USD 5,500*		Recommended loan amount	*USD 5,500*
	Requested loan term	*24 months*		Recommended loan term	*24 months*
	Requested monthly payment	*USD 300*		Recommended monthly payment	*USD 300*
	Date (dd/mm/yyyy)	*13/02/2015*		Date (dd/mm/yyyy)	*15/02/2015*

Notes:

Notes: Recommend to approve an exception to the monthly payment equal to 65% of net disposable income, instead of 60%.

3.	**Credit committee approval**	
	Approved loan amount	*USD 5,100*
	Approved loan term	*24 months*
	Approved monthly payment	*USD 275*
	Date (dd/mm/yyyy)	*17/02/2015*

Notes: The loan amount was reduced to comply with the 60% limit over the net disposable income. Requested exception was not approved.

Signed by Loan Officer ....

Signed by Credit Committee ....

....

....

List of Abbreviations

ADB	Asian Development Bank
AUM	Assets under management
CAR	Capital adequacy ratio
CGAP	Consultative Group to Assist the Poor
CPP	Client protection principles
DFI	Development finance institution
DJSI	Dow Jones Sustainability Index
EBRD	European Bank for Reconstruction and Development
ECB	European Central Bank
ESG	Environmental, social and governance
FINMA	Swiss Financial Market Supervisory Authority (Eidgenössische Finanzmarktaufsicht)
FMO	Dutch Development Bank
GDP	Gross domestic product
GPFI	Global Partnership for Financial Inclusion
IFC	International Finance Corporation
ILO	International Labour Organization
IMF	International Monetary Fund
INDECOPI	Instituto Nacional de Defensa de la Competencia y de la Protección de la Propiedad Intelectual (Peru)
KfW	Kreditanstalt für Wiederaufbau (German Development Bank)
MDG	Millennium development goal
MFI	Microfinance financial institution
MIV	Microfinance investment vehicle
MPT	Modern portfolio theory
MSME	Micro-, small- and medium-sized enterprise
NBFI	Non-bank financial institution
NE	Nash equilibrium
NGO	Non-governmental organization
OECD	Organization for Economic Co-operation and Development
OeEB	Oesterreichische Entwicklungsbank (Austrian Development Bank)

OPEC	Organization of the Petroleum Exporting Countries
PAR	Portfolio at risk
PAT	Poverty assessment tool
PPI	Progress out of Poverty Index
PRI	Principles for Responsible Investment
RoA	Return on asset
RoE	Return on equity
SBS	Superintendencia de Bancos y Seguros (prudential authority for banks and insurances in Ecuador)
SDG	Sustainable development goals
SFG	Sustainable Finance Geneva
SI	Sustainable investment
SME	Small- and medium-sized enterprise
SMX	Symbiotics Microfinance Index (comprises listed global bond funds that mainly invest in microfinance)
SNI	Socially neutral investing
SPIRIT	Social Performance Impact Reporting and Intelligence Tool
SPTF	Social Performance Task Force
SRI	Socially responsible investment
SSF	Swiss Sustainable Finance (platform promoting Switzerland as a leading center for sustainable finance)
TA	Technical Assistance
TER	Total Expense Ratio
UN	United Nations
UNCTAD	United Nations Conference on Trade and Development
UNDP	United Nations Development Programme
UNEP	United Nations Environment Programme
USD	US dollar
USSPM	Universal Standards of Social Performance Management
WEF	World Economic Forum
WTO	World Trade Organization

Glossary

Assets under management (AUM)   AUM refers to the volume of assets that are managed by a financial institution (banks, asset managers, fund managers etc.) on behalf of their investors.

Conventional investment   Conventional investment exclusively focuses on generating a financial return.

Credit bureau   A credit bureau collects data about outstanding or previous loans of borrowers and makes this information available for microfinance institutions and other loan service providers. Credit bureaus boost the efficiency of lending, and at the same time effectively prevent over-indebtedness.

Double bottom line (DBL)   The term "double bottom line" refers to a new way of extending the conventional bottom line that solely measures financial performance. It adds a second bottom line to the aspect of performance in terms of positive social impact. An increasing number of companies now opt for a means of measuring performance that includes social aspects.

Development finance institution (DFI)   DFIs are financial institutions that occupy the space between public aid and private investment. Very often they provide funds for investments in developing countries, for which there are not enough private funds available. Examples of development institutions are the German Development Bank (KfW), the Dutch FMO or the Asian Development Bank (ADB).

Economically active poverty   Economically active poverty refers to persons who have some form of employment and reliable income and who are not in food deficit or destitute. The distinction between extreme, moderate and economically active poverty is based on whether a stable and secure income can be generated that averts existence-threatening over-indebtedness, secures a certain degree of healthcare and permits the accumulation of assets.

Extreme poverty   Extreme poverty refers to living conditions where a person has to get by on less than $1.25 a day, the minimum subsistence level. According to estimates, at least 1 billion people are afflicted by extreme poverty.

Grameen Bank   Grameen Bank was the first ever microfinance institution worldwide, and was founded in 1983 by Muhammad Yunus, in Bangladesh. Grameen is still operating successfully in the microfinance industry today.

The truly outstanding character of this bank is that 90 per cent of it is owned
by its borrowers, while the remaining 10 per cent is in the hands of the
Bangladeshi government. The enterprise and its founder Yunus were awarded
the Nobel Peace Prize in 2006.

Group loan   The term "group loan" refers to a number of people who join forces
in order to take out a loan. The members of the group vouch for each other
and ensure timely loan repayments. The key element with this type of loan is
the sense of mutual trust among all the borrowers involved.

Impact investing   Impact investing is a form of investment that generates both
financial and social returns.

Microfinance investment vehicle (MIV)   MIVs are the link between investors
and microfinance institutions. MIVs include funds that provide private and
public investors with an efficient and diversified investment in microfinance.

Microfinance   Microfinance was called into life by Muhammad Yunus and his
Grameen Bank in a bid to combat poverty in India and Bangladesh.
Microfinance provides commercial financial services to those afflicted
by poverty.

Microfinance institution (MFI)   MFIs are the contacts in the field for micro
entrepreneurs. It is their responsibility to assess a borrower's creditworthiness, grant and monitor loans, and they are in charge of the customer care
management.

Microloan   The term "microloan" refers to a loan, usually between a hundred
and a few thousand dollars, that is commonly handed out without collateral.
Microloans are given to impoverished people that have no access to the
financial system.

Micro entrepreneur   A micro entrepreneur is a person who operates a micro
enterprise. The term generally refers to people who operate their business
either single-handedly or together with other members of the family in order
to make a living. Occasionally, a handful of other workers may also be
involved. Within the context of microfinance, a microloan enables micro
entrepreneurs to either establish or expand their business.

Moderate poverty   Moderate poverty refers to segments of the population with
an income that only just covers the basic necessities in life such as minimal
calorific intake, water, clothing, accommodation and basic healthcare.

Non-governmental organization (NGO)   A non-governmental organization is
a private, independent and non-profit-oriented organization formed to pursue
a social and socio-political objective. The issues addressed by NGOs run the
gamut of human concerns: environmental protection, human rights, development assistance, anti-discrimination, migration and refugee issues, homelessness charity, drug-counseling services etc.

OECD   The Organization for Economic Co-operation and Development is an
institution that comprises 34 member countries. The OECD's main objective
is to promote higher economic and social wealth globally.

Philanthropy   Philanthropy denotes sponsoring or the charitable donation of financial means – with the aim of creating a positive social and environmental impact on society. Financial performance is thereby considered to be irrelevant.

Poverty   The term "poverty" denotes living conditions where a person has to manage on less than $2 a day. According to estimates, about 2 billion people live in poverty.

Social performance   Social performance measures the sustainable social impact that a borrower's financial commitment achieves (e.g. with respect to food, healthcare, education, etc.). Social performance and financial performance (profitability) are the cornerstones of microfinance. While profitability can be easily monitored, the measuring of social performance requires a range of sophisticated tools that manage to identify the nature and degree of social impact.

Technical assistance (TA)   TA denotes a particular type of consulting service provided to MFIs and their borrowers. Its goal is to promote social and economic advancement. TA fosters the efficacy and improvements of e.g. internal processes, or the strengthening of IT systems or risk management.

Triple bottom line (TBL)   Instead of focusing solely on its finances, the triple bottom line gives consideration to a company's social, economic and environmental impact. It therefore describes the separate financial, social and environmental "bottom lines" of companies that commit to it in a bid to make their contribution towards a sustainable development.

References

Abrar, A. and A.Y. Javaid (2014): 'Commercialization and Mission Drift – A Cross Country Evidence on Transformation of Microfinance Industry', *International Journal of Trade, Economics and Finance*, 5(1), pp. 122–125.

Annan, K. (2005): Microfinance, now important factor in poverty eradication, should be expanded, Secretary-General tells Geneva Symposium, www.un.org/press/en/2005/sgsm10151.doc.htm (Last visited 27.7.2015).

Armendáriz de Aghion, B. (1999): 'On the Design of a Credit Agreement with Peer Monitoring', *Journal of Development Economics*, 60(1), pp. 79–104.

Armendáriz de Aghion, B. and J. Morduch (2005): *The Economics of Microfinance*, MIT Press, Cambridge.

Barboza, G. and H. Barreto (2006): 'Learning by Association, Micro Credit in Chiapas, Mexico', *Contemporary Economic Policy*, 24(2), pp. 316–331.

Barboza, G. and S. Trejos (2009): 'Micro Credit in Chiapas, Mexico: Poverty Reduction Through Group Lending', *Journal of Business Ethics*, 88(2), pp. 283–299.

Basel Committee on Banking Supervision (2010): Microfinance activities and the Core Principle for Effective Banking Supervision, Basel, August.

Basel Committee on Banking Supervision (2015): Range of practice in the regulation and supervision of institutions relevant to financial inclusion, Basel, January.

Becker, P.M. (2010): *Investing in Microfinance. Integrating New Asset Classes into an Asset Allocation Framework Applying Scenario Methodology*, Gabler Research, Wiesbaden.

Berg, C. and M. Shahe Emran (2011): Does Microfinance Help the Ultrapoor Cope with Seasonal Shocks? Evidence from Seasonal Famine (Monga) in Bangladesh, papers.ssrn.com/sol3/papers.cfm?abstract_id=1802073 (Last visited 10.1.2015).

Besley, T. and S. Coate (1995): 'Group Lending, Repayment Incentives and Social Collateral', *Journal of Development Economics*, 46(1), pp. 1–18.

Bethany, L.P. (2013): 'Institutional Lending Models, Mission Drift, and Microfinance Institutions', University of Kentucky: Doktorarbeit.

Bezerra, J., W. Bock, F. Candelon, S. Chai, E. Choi, J. Corwin, S. DiGrande, R. Gulshan, D.C. Michael and A. Varas (2015): The Mobile Revolution: How Mobile Technologies Drive a Trillion-Dollar Impact, https://www.bcgperspectives.com (Last visited 5.2.2015).

BIS (2013): Triennial Central Bank Survey, www.bis.org/publ//bl//rpfx (Last visited 2.12.2014).

BIS (2015): Quarterly Review: Debt securities statistics, www.bis.org/statistics/secstats.htm (Last visited 12.5.2015).

BlueOrchard (2014): Raising our SPIRIT: Social Performance Report 2014, Genf, December.

BlueOrchard and the University of Zurich (2014): Swiss Institutional Investors Survey 2014, Zurich, June.

Braverman, A. and J.L. Guasch (1986): 'Rural credit markets and institutions in developing countries: Lessons for policy analysis from practice and modern theory', *World Development*, 14(1), pp. 1253–1267.

Bundesbank (2014): https://www.bundesbank.de/Navigation/EN/Publications/Reports/Monthly_reports/monthly_reports.html?https=1 (Last visited 20.11.16)

CGAP (2014): Microfinance FAQs, www.microfinancegateway.org/(2014-is-microfinance (Last visited 18.11.2014).

Chen, G. and X. Faz (2015): 'The Potential of Digital Data: How Far Can It Advance Financial Inclusion?' *CGAP Focus Note*, 100(1), pp. 1–12.

Christen, R.P., K. Lauer, T. Lyman and R. Rosenberg (2012): *A Guide to Regulation and Supervision of Microfinance, CGAP*, Washington D.C., October.

CIA World Factbook (2008): https://www.cia.gov/(2008): publications/the-world-factbookactb (Last visited 5.1.2015).

Collaboratory, The (2015): Microfinance Loan Officer: Learners Guide, www.thecollaboratoryonline.org/w/images/CMF_GSM_UP_Microfinance_Loan_Officer.pdf (Last visited 26.6.2015).

Collins, D.J., J. Morduch, S. Rutherford and O. Ruthven (2009): *Portfolios of the poor: How the World's Poor Live on $2 a Day*. Princeton University Press, Princeton.

Conning, J. (1999): 'Outreach, sustainability and leverage in monitored and peer-monitored lending', *Journal of Development Economics*, 60(1), pp. 51–77.

Cull, R., D.-K. Asli and J. Morduch (2009): 'Microfinance Meets the Market', *Journal of Economic Perspectives*, 23(1), pp. 167–192.

De Soto, H. (2001): *The Mystery of Capital: Why Capitalism Triumphs in the West and Fails Everywhere Else*, Black Swan, London.

D'Espallier, B., I. Guerin, and R. Mersland (2013): 'Focus on Women in Microfinance Institutions', *Journal of Development Studies*, 49(5), pp. 589–608.

Demirguc-Kunt, A., L. Klapper, D. Singer and P. Van Oudheusden (2015): *The Global Findex Database 2014, Measuring Financial Inclusion around the World*, The World Bank Development Research Group, Working Paper, Washington D.C.

Demombynes, G. and A. Thegeya (2012): *Kenya's Mobile Revolution and the Promise of Mobile Savings*, The World Bank Development Research Group, Working Paper, Washington D.C.

Desai, J., K. Johnson and A. Tarozzi (2015): 'The Impacts of Microcredit: Evidence from Ethiopia', *American Economic Journal: Applied Economics*, 7 (1), pp. 54–89.

Deutsche Kreditbank (2015): Geschäftsbericht 2014, Deutsche Kreditbank AG, Berlin.

Dickinson, T. (2012): Development Finance Institutions: Profitability Promoting Development, www.oecd.org/dev/41302068.pdf (Last visited 14.12.2014).

Dieckmann, R. (2007): 'Microfinance: An emerging investment opportunity – Uniting social investment and financial returns', *Deutsche Bank Research*, pp. 1–20.

Economist, The (2010a): Microfinance: Leave Well Alone, 20.11.2010.

Economist, The (2010b): Microfinance under scrutiny: Overcharging, 20.11.2010.

Economist, The (2013): The Economist explains: Why does Kenya lead the world in mobile money?, http://www.economist.com/blogs/economist-explains/2013/05/economist-explains-18 (Last visited 9.2.2015).

Economist Intelligence Unit, The (2014): Global Microscope 2014: The enabling environment for financial inclusion, London, November.

Fairbourne, J., S. Gibson and W. Dyer (2007): *MicroFranchising: Creating Wealth at the Bottom of the Pyramid*, Edward Elgar Publishing, Cheltenham.

Forum Nachhaltige Geldanlagen (2015): Marktbericht: Nachhaltige Geldanlagen 2015 Deutschland, Österreichund die Schweiz, Berlin, May.

Geczy, C., R.F. Stambaugh and D. Levin (2005): Investing in Socially Responsible Mutual Funds, papers.ssrn.com/sol3/papers. cfm?abstract_id=416380 (Last visited 1.5.2015).

Ghatak, M. and T. Guinnane (1999): 'The Economics of Lending with Joint Liability: Theory and Practice', *Journal of Development Economics*, 60(1), pp. 195–228.

Gonzalez, A. (2011): Publication Update: Analyzing Microcredit Interest Rates A Review of the Methodology Proposed by Mohamed Yunus, MIX Data Brief No. 4., www.themix.org/sites/default/files/MBB%20Publication%20Update% 20data%20brief%204.pdf (Last visited 18.10.2014).

Grameen Foundation (2015): Progress out of Poverty Index (PPI), www .progressoutofpoverty.org/Fo (Last visited 22.5.2015).

Griffith, R. and M. Evans (2012): Development Finance Institutions, Advocates for International Development, London, July.

Gurley, J. and E. Shaw (1955): 'Financial Aspects of Economic Development', *American Economic Review*, 45(4), pp. 515–538.

Hartarska, V. and M. Holtmann (2006): 'An overview of recent developments in the microfinance literature', *Agricultural Finance Review*, 66(2), pp. 147–165.

Hartmann-Wendels, T., T. Mählmann and T. Versen (2009): 'Determinants of banks' risk exposure to new account fraud. Evidence from Germany', *Journal of Banking and Finance*, 33(2), pp. 347–357.

Hashemi, S. (2007): 'Beyond Good Intentions: Measuring the Social Performance of Microfinance Institutions', *CGAP Focus Note*, 41(1), pp. 1–12.

Hofmann, M. (2015): Nachhaltige Entwicklung: Die Welt gibt sich neue Ziele, www.nzz.ch/schweiz/die-welt-gibt-sich-neue-ziele-1.18466894 (Last visited 7.5.2015).

Hollis, A. and A. Sweetman (2004): 'Microfinance and Famine: The Irish Loan and Funds during the Great Famine', *World Development*, 32(9), pp. 1509–1523.

Holvoet, N. (2004): 'Impact of Microfinance Programs on Children's Education: Do the Gender of the Borrower and the Delivery Model Matter?', *Journal of Microfinance*, 6(2), pp. 27–49.

Impactspace (2014): Social, Environmental and Financial Impact, impact-space. com/public/ (Last visited 23.2.2015).

Jappelli, T. and M. Pagano (2000): *Information sharing in Credit Markets: A Survey*, CSEF Working Paper No. 36, University of Salerno.

J.P. Morgan (2015): J.P. Morgan Institutional Library, am.jpmorgan.com/ca/institutional/library.

Khandker, S. (1998): *Fighting Poverty with Microcredit: Experience in Bangladesh*, Oxford University Press, New York.

Kropp, J., C.G. Turvey, D.R. Just, R. Kong, P. Guo (2009): 'Are the poor really more trustworthy? A micro-lending experiment', *Agricultural Finance Review*, 69(1), pp. 67–87.

Leatherman, S., K. Geissler, B. Gray and M. Gash (2012): 'Health Financing: A New Role for Microfinance Institutions?', *Journal of International Development*, 25(7), pp. 881–896.

Ledgerwood, J. (2000): *Microfinance Handbook: An Institutional and Financial Perspective*, World Bank Publications, Washington D.C.

Ledgerwood, J. (2013): *The New Microfinance Handbook: A Financial Market System Perspective*, World Bank Publications, Washington D.C.

Leive, A. and K. Xu (2008): 'Coping with Out-of-Pocket Health Payments: Empirical Evidence from 15 African Countries', *Bulletin of the World Health Organization*, 86(11), pp. 849–856.

Littlefield, E., J. Morduch and S. Hashemi (2003): 'Is Microfinance an Effective Strategy to Reach the Millennium Development Goals?', *CGAP FocusNote*, 24(1), pp. 1–12.

Liv, D. (2013): Study on the Drivers of Over-Indebtedness of Microfinance Borrowers in Cambodia: An In-depth Investigation of Saturated Areas, Cambodia Institute of Development, Phnom Penh, March.

Luoto, J., C. McIntosh and B. Wydick (2007): 'Credit Information Systems in Less-Developed Countries: Recent History and a Test with Microfinance in Guatemala', *Economic Development and Cultural Change*, 55(2), pp. 313–334.

Mangold, R. (2015): *Do Microfinance Investment Managers Add Value, and How?* Working Paper, pp. 1–29.

Markowitz, H. (1952): 'Portfolio Selection', *Journal of Finance*, 7(1), pp. 71–91.

Maslow, A. (1943): 'A theory of human motivation', *Psychological Review*, 50(4), pp. 370–396.

Massa, I. and D. Willem te Velde (2011): 'The role of development finance institutions in tackling global challenges', *Overseas Development Institute Project Briefing*, 65(1), pp. 1–4.

Mbiti, I. and D.N. Weil (2011): *Mobile Banking: The Impact of M-Pesa in Kenya*, *The National Bureau of Economic Research*, Working Paper, Cambridge.

McIntosh, C. and B. Wydick (2005): 'Competition and Microfinance', *Journal of Development Economics*, 78(2), pp. 271–298.

Menning, C.B. (1992): 'The Monte's Monte: The Early Supporters of Florence's Monte di Pieta', *The Sixteenth Century Journal*, 23(4), pp. 661–667.

Mersland, R. and R. Oystein Strom (2010): 'Microfinance Mission Drift?', *World Development*, 38(1), pp. 28–36.

Meyer, J. (2013): 'Investing in Microfinance: An Analysis of Financial and Social Returns', University of Zurich: PhD thesis.

Meyer, R. and G. Nagarajan (2006): 'Microfinance in developing countries: accomplishments, debates and future directions', *Agricultural Finance Review*, 67(1), pp. 167–194.

MFTransparency (2015): What We Do, www.mftransparency.org/what-we-do/ (Last visited 26.5.2015).

Microcredit Summit Campaign (2014): The State of the Microcredit Summit Campaign Report, Microcredit Summit Campaign, Washington D.C., June.

Microfinance Centre (2007): MFC, From Mission to Action – Management Series for Microfinance Institutions, www.microfinancegateway.org/sites/ default dfiles/ mfg-en-toolkit-from-mission-to-action-management-series-for-microfinance-institution-strategic-management-toolkit-handbook-2007.pdf (Last visited 28.11.2014).

Micro Finance Institutions (Development and Regulation) Bill (2012): Arrangement of Clauses, Bill No. 62, www.prsindia.org/uploads/media/Micro%20Finance%20Institutions/Micro%20FiFinan%20Institutions%20%28Development%20and%20Regulation%29%20Bill,%202020.pdf (Last visited 4.10.2014).

MicroPensionLab (2014): What we do, www.micropensions.com (Last visited 9.1.2015).

Microrate (2013a): Microfinance Institution Tier Definitions, www.micro-rate.com (Last visited 25.1.2015).

Microrate (2013b): The State of Microfinance Investment 2013: Survey and Analysis of MIVs – 8th Edition, Washington D.C., November.

MIX (2011): Myths and Reality: Cost and Profitability of Microfinance, www.themix.org/publications/microbanking-bulletin/2011/03/myths-and-reality-cost-and-profitability-microfinance (Last visited 12.1.2015).

MIX (2015): MIX Database. Cross Market Analysis Tool, reports.mixmarket.org/crossmarket (Last visited 21.5.2015).

MkNelly, B. and C. Dunford (1998): Impact of Credit with Education on Mothers and Their Young Children's Nutrition: Lower Pra Rural Bank Credit with Education Program in Ghana, Freedom from Hunger, Davis, March.

Morduch, J. (1999): 'The Microfinance Promise', *Journal of Economic Literature*, 37(4), pp. 1569–1614.

Nagarsekar, G. (2012): A Report on the Interest of Microfinance Institutions, Birla Institute of Technology and Science, Pilani, December.

Nash, J.F. (1951): 'Non-Cooperative Games', *Annals of Mathematics*, 54(2), pp. 286–295.

Panjaitan-Drioadisuryo, R.D.M. and K. Cloud (1999): 'Gender Self-Employment and Microcredit Programs: An Indonesian Case Study', *Quarterly Review of Economics and Finance*, 39(5), pp. 769–779.

Parker, J. and D. Pearce (2002): 'Microfinance, Grants, and Non-Financial Responses to Poverty Reduction', *CGAP Focus Note*, 20, pp. 1–20.

Pickens, M. (2009): Window on the Unbanked: Mobile Money in the Philippines, CGAP Brief, Washington D.C., December.

Prahalad, C.K. and S.L. Hart (2002): The Fortune at the Bottom of the Pyramid, Strategy + Business, first quarter, 2002.

Prasac (2015): Annual Report 2014, Prasac, Phnom Penh.

Raiffeisen Group (2015): Geschäftsbericht 2014, Raiffeisen Gruppe, St. Gallen.

Rating Initiative, The (2013): Social Rating Guide, www.sptf.info/images/he (201%20rating%20guide_english_nov%202014.pdf (Last visited 27.9.2014).

Ravallion, M., S. Chen and P. Sangraula (2008): *Dollar a Day Revisited*, The World Bank Development Research Group, Working Paper, Washington D.C.

Reed, L.R., J. Marsden, A. Ortega, C. Rivera and S. Rogers (2015): The State of the Microcredit Summit Campaign Report 2014, Washington D.C., June.

Remenyi, J. (2000): *Microfinance and Poverty Alleviation: Case Studies from Asia and the Pacific*, Taylor & Francis Group, New York.

Renneboog, L., T. Jenke and C. Zhang (2008): 'Socially responsible investments: Institutional aspects, performance, and investor behavior', *Journal of Banking and Finance*, 32(9), pp. 1723–1742.

ResponsAbility (2010): Korruption und Finanzkriminalität – ein Problem in Mikrofinanz?, Zurich.

Robinson, M.S. (2001): *The Microfinance Revolution: Sustainable Finance for the Poor*, The World Bank Publications, Washington D.C.

Rock, R., M. Otero and R. Rosenberg (1996): 'Regulation and Supervision of Microfinance Institutions: Stabilizing a New Financial Market', *CGAP Focus Note*, 4, pp. 1–4.

Rosenberg, R. (2010): 'Does Microcredit Really Help Poor People?', *CGAP Focus Note*, 59, pp. 1–8.

Rosenberg, R., S. Gaul, W. Ford and O. Tomilova (2013): Microcredit Interest Rates and Their Determinants 2004–2011, CGAP, Washington D.C., June.

Rutherford, S. (2001): *The Poor and Their Money*, Oxford University Press, New Delhi.

Sachs, J. (2006): *The End of Poverty: Economic Possibilities for Our Time*, Penguin Group, New York.

Schicks, J. (2011): Over-Indebtedness of Microborrowers in Ghana: An Empirical Study from a Customer Protection Perspective, Center for Financial Inclusion, Brussels, November.

Schreiner, M. (2010): 'Seven Extremely Simple Poverty Scorecards', *Enterprise Development and Microfinance*, 21(2), S. 118–137.

Schumpeter, J. (1926): *Theorie der wirtschaftlichen Entwicklung*, 2. Auflage, München, Leipzig.

Scofield, R. (2015): The evolving microfinance revolution has yet to run its full course, https://www.devex.com/news/the-evolving-microfinance-revolution-has-yet-to-run-its-full-course-86017 (Last visited 1.5.2015).

Seibel, H.D. (2003): 'History matters in microfinance', *Small Enterprise Development*, 14(2), pp. 10–12.

Sen, A.K. (1999): *Development as Freedom*, Knopf, New York.

Simanowitz, A. and A. Waters (2002): 'Ensuring Impact: Reaching the Poorest while Building Financially Self-Sufficient Institutions and Showing Improvement in the Lives of the Poorest Women and Their Families', in: S. Daley-Harris (ed.), *Pathways out of Poverty: Innovations in Microfinance for the Poorest Families*, Kumarian Press, Bloomfield.

Sinha, F. (2006): Social Rating and Social Performance Reporting in Microfinance: Towards a Common Framework, Argidius Foundation, Washington D.C., January.

Smart Campaign (2016): The Smart Campaign: Certified Organizations, www.smartcampaign.org/certification/certified-organizations (Last visited 26.5.2015).

Social Performance Task Force (2014a): Social Performance Task Force, sptf. info/sp-task-force (Last visited 28.10.2014).

Social Performance Task Force (2014b): Social Performance Task Force: Universal Standards for Social Performance Management, www.sptf.info/ images/ usspm %20englishmanual%202014%201.pdf (Last visited 18.10.2014).

Solli, J., L. Galindo, A. Rizzi, E. Rhyne and N. van de Walle (2015): What Happens to Microfinance Clients who Default? An Exploratory Study of Microfinance Practices, The Smart Campaign, Washington D.C., January.

Standard & Poor's (2007): Microfinance: Taking Root in the Global Capital Markets, New York, June.

Staub-Bisang, M. (2011): *Nachhaltige Anlagen für institutionelle Investoren*, Verlag Neue Zürcher Zeitung, Zürich.

Stiglitz, J. (1990): 'Peer Monitoring and Credit Markets', *The World Bank Economic Review*, 4(2), pp. 351–366.

Stiglitz, J. and A. Weiss (1981): 'Credit rationing with imperfect information', *American Economic Review*, 71(3), pp. 393–410.

Sustainable Finance Geneva (2014): 10 Finance Innovations: Geneva, the Sustainable Finance Laboratory, Geneva, September.

Symbiotics (2016): 2016 Symbiotics MIV Survey, Geneva, September.

Tameer Bank (2015): www.tameerbank.com/agri-group-loans.html (Last visited 19.11.2016)

Todd, H. (1996): *Women at the Centre: Grameen Bank Borrowers after One Decade*, Dhaka University Press, Dhaka.

UN News Centre (2015): Climate change and sustainability key to future development agenda, www.un.org/apps/news/story.asp?NewsID=50165#.VUuEjGeJ iUm (Last visited 7.5.2015).

United Nations (2001): Die UN-Millenniums-Entwicklungsziele, un-kampagne. de/index.php?id=90 (Last visited 16.10.2015).

United Nations (2006): *Blue Book: Building Inclusive Finanical Sectors for Development*, The United Nations Department of Public Information, New York.

United Nations (2014): The World We Want – A Future For All, Website https://sustainabledevelopment.un.org/sdgsproposal (Last visited 7.5.2015).

UNCTAD (2014): World Investment Report 2014: Investing in the SDGs, unctad.org/en/PublicationsLibraryublicationsLibraryLast visited 21.5.2015).

UNDP (2014): Millennium Development Goals, www.undp.org/ (Last visited 12.12.2014).

Van Tassel, E. (1999): 'Group Lending Under Asymmetric Information', *Journal of Development Economics*, 60(1), pp. 3–25.

Varian, H. (1990): 'Monitoring Agents with Other Agents', *Journal of Institutional and Theoretical Economics*, 146(1), pp. 153–174.

VisionFund (2015): Average Loan Size, www.visionfund.org/1501/(2015)wwhe (Last visited 28.5.2015).

World Bank (2001): *World Development Report 2000/2001: Attacking Poverty*, Oxford University Press, New York.

World Bank (2014): *Global Financial Development Report: Financial Inclusion*, World Bank Publications, Washington D.C.

World Bank (2015a): Financial Inclusion Data/Global Findex, datatopics.world-bank.org/financialinclusion (Last visited 17.6.2015).

World Bank (2015b): Inflation, GDP deflator (annual %), data.worldbank.org/ indicator/NY.GDP.DEFL.KD.ZG (Last visited 18.6.2015).

World Bank (2016): PovcalNet Database, iresearch.worldbank.org/ PovcalNet PovcalNetorld (Last visited 20.2.2015).

World Trade Organization (2015): Balance of Trade, www.wto.org (Last visited 16.6.2015).

Xu, K., D.B. Evans, G. Carrin, A.M. Aquilar-Rivera, P. Musgrove and T. Evans (2007): 'Protecting Households from Catastrophic Health Spending', *Health Affairs*, 26(4), pp. 972–983.

Xu, K., D.B. Evans, K. Kawabata, R. Zeramdini, J. Klavus and C.J. Murray (2003): 'Household Catastrophic Health Expenditure: A Multicountry Analysis', *The Lancet*, 363, pp. 111–117.

Zeller, M. (2006): 'A comparative review of major types of rural microfinance institutions in developing countries', *Agricultural Finance Review*, 66(2), pp. 195–213.

Photo Credits

Alter Modus	105; 148
Andrea Staudacher for BlueOrchard	53; 203
Banco Fie	133; 143
iStock.com/AfricaImages	203
iStock.com/Audioslave	155
iStock.com/Bartosz Hadyniak	1; 19; 49; 211
iStock.com/CapturedNuance	168
iStock.com/chinese_elements	68
iStock.com/JuergenBosse	11
iStock.com/narvikk	33
iStock.com/tbradford	119
Johann Sauty for BlueOrchard	8; 30; 47; 50; 53; 58; 60; 71; 95; 112; 115; 129; 131; 145; 155; 158; 167; 172; 190; 198; 209; 214
LOLC Micro Credit	175
Peter Fanconi for BlueOrchard	66
Pictureguy/Shutterstock.com	161
Piter HaSon/Shutterstock.com	149
Richard Lord for BlueOrchard	99; 146
Samara.com/Shutterstock.com	201
Vision Banco	155

Index

abbreviations' list, 227–8
abusive loan practices, 92
ACCION, 14
accountabilities, 6, 27–8
accounts receivable, 222
ACLEDA Bank Plc, 68
adverse selection, 100–1, 107, 114
Afghanistan, 2–3
Africa, 1, 2–3, 21, 38, 59–64, 82, 94, 115, 125–8, 166, 183
African Development Bank, 38
Agri Group Loan, 105–6
agriculture, 6, 28, 49–51, 60–1, 64–8, 75, 86, 104–6, 110, 129–30, 143, 144, 145–6, 165, 178, 205, 213
    loan types, 104–8
    shocks, 110, 165, 181, 205
Albania, 126, 204
alcohol, 27
Algeria, 126
Alter Modus, 148
amortization, 188–90
Andhra Pradesh, 165, 205
Angola, 126
animal protection, 27
animal testing, 27
Annan, Kofi, 175
appendices, 114, 217–19, 221–6
Argidius Foundation, 31
Asia Pacific, 49, 61–4, 67, 94, 102, 128, 166, 183, 203–5
Asian Development Bank (ADB), 38, 227
asset liability management, 206
asset managers, 36–7, 39–41, 43, 44–6, 151, 171, 176–98, 211–15, 227
assets under management (AUM), 39–41, 46–7, 171, 176–98
    see also microfinance investment vehicles

definition, 40–1
statistics, 40–1, 176–7
asymmetrical information, 92–6, 100–1, 107, 114, 180
audits, 89, 179
Austria, 29, 38
Austrian Development Bank (OeFB), 38
Azerbaijan, 203–5

balance sheets, 65, 67, 78–9, 203, 222–3
Banco Fie, 142–3
Bangladesh, 14, 61, 65–6, 204–5
bank accounts, statistics, 21–3, 124–5
bank lines, 181
Bank Rakyat, 14
banking licenses, 78, 142, 146
banks, 5–6, 7, 12–14, 15–16, 21–4, 34–47, 72–3, 74–6, 78–9, 81–2, 90–6, 154–6, 163–4, 213–14, 223
    see also loans
    historical background, 12–14, 42–6
    politics, 81–2, 180–3
    runs on banks, 90
    types, 74–6, 78–9, 81–2, 154, 163–4
Belgium, 41
beyond the reach of microfinance, 161–72
bilateral contracts, investments, 187–90, 197–8
bilateral DFIs, 37–9
biodiversity, 6
BIS, 206
black lists, 94
Bloomberg, 193–4
BlueOrchard, xv, 34, 40–1, 44, 47, 51, 59, 61, 64–6, 68, 95, 115, 130, 131, 143, 144, 145, 148, 149, 156, 158, 162, 167, 181, 183–4, 190, 195–6, 198, 209, 243
boards, 137–58, 179
Bolivia, 17, 142

bonds, 182, 191, 193–5, 205–6
Bono, 33
Bosnia-Herzegovina, 209
bottom-up/top-down selection processes,
  investments, 181–7, 191–5, 197–8
Brazil, 4, 14
bribes, 169
budgets, 162–3
Bulgaria, 158
business ideas, 17, 43–6, 81–2, 113–14, 127,
  158, 213–15
business management capacity, 221–2
business networks, 57–9, 88, 125–7, 154–6, 183
business reports, microfinance institutions
  (MFIs), 134–5, 140–51

Cambodia, 66, 68, 109, 138, 149, 163–4, 204–5
capital, 4–5, 7, 11–12, 14–15, 16–17, 20–5,
  29–30, 34–48, 49–52, 56, 67, 71–2, 78–9,
  85–8, 96, 101, 119–21, 123, 127, 130–2,
  134–5, 155–6, 167, 211–15
  see also financial services; loans
  costs, 119–21, 123, 127, 130–2
capital adequacy requirements, 37, 90–6, 207
Caribbean, 21, 38, 61–4, 67, 128, 166, 183
Caribbean Development Bank, 38
cash, 193–5, 222
cattle, 60–1
Central Asia, 2–3, 21, 59–64, 94, 102, 128, 166,
  183–4, 203–5
Central Bank of Bangladesh, 14
central banks, 14, 34, 154, 206–7
ceramics, 162–3
CERISE Social Performance Indicators (SPI4),
  135–6, 140–9, 165–6
charities, 26, 29, 73, 75–7, 82–4, 211
child labor, 170
child mortality rates, 4
Chile, 2–3
China, 59–63
CIA World Factbook, 3
civilian law, 73
client protection, 90–1, 92, 110–12, 135,
  138–58, 165
climate change, xi, 6–7, 38–9, 213–14
closed-end funds, 178, 179
clothing needs, 52–5
collateral, 7, 14, 36, 74–6, 86–7, 94, 100–1,
  114–15, 121–2, 170, 188–90, 197–8,
  221, 222
  see also repayments

Colombia, 115, 129–30, 131, 145–6, 167,
  190, 204–5
commercial banks, 74, 75, 76, 78–9, 91,
  110–12, 121–3, 163–4
commercial law, 73–6, 89, 101, 123
competitive advantages, 92, 96, 221–2
complaint resolution mechanisms, 138–49
Congo, 61, 126
Consultative Group to Assist the Poor (CGAP),
  23–4, 31, 136, 151–3
  see also Progress Out of Poverty Index
consumer loans, 57–8
contagion, 90
contingency reserves, 121–2, 123, 130–2
  see also default rates
conventional investments, 5, 9, 15–16, 25–7,
  31, 91, 100–1
Cooperative Rural Bank of Bulacan
  (CRBB), 8–9
corporate governance, 27, 44–5, 135–6, 143,
  196
corporate social responsibility, ix, 26,
  135, 195–7
corruption, 4, 90, 139, 164, 168–9
costs, 37, 84, 119–32, 163–4, 179, 206, 225
  see also capital. . .; expenses; fixed. . .;
  operating. . .
country risk, 171, 180–4
coupons, 188–90
covenants, investments, 188–90, 197–8
craftwork, 49–50, 64, 67
Crecer, 17
credit bureaus, 34–48, 92–6, 108, 110, 111–12,
  116, 154–6, 165, 171, 203, 207–8,
  224
  see also creditworthiness; loan officers
  definition, 37, 92–3, 96, 207, 224
  reports, 92–4, 224
credit committees, due diligence, 184–7, 226
credit cooperative system, 12–14, 72–3, 74, 75
credit funds, historical background, 12–13
credit rating agencies, 77–9, 95–6, 151–3,
  157, 186
credit ratings, 77–9, 95–6, 100–1, 111–12,
  151–3, 157, 186
credit rationing, 100–1, 114
credit risk, 76, 82, 87, 90–2, 100–1, 114, 139,
  165, 203, 207–9
credit risk insurance, 76, 87, 165, 203, 207–8
credit theory, traditional credit theory, 100–1
credit unions, historical background, 12–14

creditworthiness, 35, 37, 92–6, 100–1, 106–7, 113–16, 123
  see also credit bureaus
  interest rates, 100–1, 114–16, 123
Crezcamos, 145–6
currencies, 35, 180, 183, 185–7, 205–7
currency hedging, 35, 185–7
currency risks, 181, 183, 185–7, 207
current assets, 65–7, 78–9, 203, 222–3
customer care, 35, 85–8, 90–4, 110, 133–58
Cyrano, 40

De Soto's notion of 'dead capital' 101
'dead capital' 101
debt capital, 77–84, 96, 177–81, 184–90, 201–9
  see also investments; loans
debt to equity ratios, 180–1
default rates, 20, 37, 82, 91–4, 96, 101, 102–3, 107, 110–12, 116, 121–2, 123, 127, 130–2, 180–1, 189–90, 207–8, 212
  see also contingency reserves; creditworthiness; restructured loans
  asset classes, 180–1
  reasons, 110, 111, 112
Deloitte, 146
democratization, 4
deposit-taking MFIs, 89–92, 203
deposits, 12–14, 16–17, 22, 24–5, 29–30, 65–7, 68, 71–3, 74–6, 77–9, 85–96, 125–7, 142, 203, 207–8, 222
desertification, 6
Deutsche Kreditbank (DKB), 163, 164
Developing World Markets, 40
Development Bank of Latin America, 38
development banks, xi, 7, 34–36, 44, 154–5, 176–7, 197–8
  see also development finance institutions
development finance institutions (DFIs), 37–9, 73, 176–7
  see also bilateral. . .; development banks; microfinance institutions; multilateral. . .; regional. . .
  definition, 37–9
Dexia Microcredit Fund, 44
disbursements185, 187, 196–7
disposable income, 17, 225
  see also income
diversification, 9, 16–17, 35, 72–3, 91–2, 110, 121–2, 171, 175–6, 180, 182–7, 191–8, 205, 208, 212

donations, 12–14, 18, 26, 29, 71, 73, 76, 78–9, 80–3, 89
double bottom line (DBL), xi, 18–21, 28, 30–1, 73–4, 133–4, 156–8
  see also financial performance; impact investments; social performance; triple. . .
  definition, 18–19, 28, 156
  statistics, 20–1
Dow Jones Sustainability Index (DJSI), 43, 227
due diligence, 37–8, 179, 182, 184–7, 221–6
Dutch Development Bank (FMO), 37–8, 227

East Asia, 21, 49–50, 59–64, 82, 94, 102, 128, 166, 183, 203–5
Eastern Europe, 21, 62–4, 128, 158, 166, 183, 203–5
economic growth factors, 4–5, 6, 16–17, 21–2, 24–5, 73, 155–7, 206, 208, 212–15
economic pyramid, 2–3, 23–4, 31, 54–5
  see also poverty
economically active poverty, 52–5, 67
ecosystems, 6
education, xi, 3–4, 6–7, 9, 11–12, 15–17, 24, 28, 30, 47, 49, 51–2, 56–9, 67, 73–4, 85–6, 103, 110, 131, 135, 141–9, 150–1, 162–3, 178, 212, 213–14
  see also training
  goals, 16, 17, 24, 30, 49, 56–7, 144–6, 150–1, 155–7, 212, 213–14
Edyficar, 58
effective interest rate, definition, 127
efficiencies, operating costs, 124–7, 148, 171, 211
efficient frontiers, portfolios, 192–5, 197–8
employment, 6, 7, 22, 42–4, 52–5, 122–3, 124, 137–58, 163–4, 170, 206, 212
energy resources, 6, 27, 147, 178, 213
environmental impacts, ix, 4, 5, 6–7, 26–9, 46, 141, 147–9, 213
  see also sustainable development
environmental, social and governance (ESG), 46
equity, 34–5, 67, 77–84, 91–2, 96, 177–98, 201–9
  see also investments
ethical investments, 26–8, 44–5
Ethiopia, 61
European Bank for Reconstruction and Development (EBRD), 38, 227
European Investment Bank, 38
expenses, 119–32, 162–3, 178–81, 225
  see also costs
exports, statistics, 203–5, 214

family expenses, 162–3, 225
famines, 14, 205
Fanconi, Peter, ix, xii, xv, 243
feedback, 141, 144–51
filters, investments, 26–7, 94
Finance in Motion, 40
financial cooperatives, 74, 75
financial economy, 9, 201–3, 205–9
  definition, 201–3, 205–6
  influencing factors, 205–6
  stability mechanisms, 207–8
financial inclusion, 21–4, 29–30, 133–5,
    213–15
  see also inequalities
financial infrastructure, 4–5, 6–7, 11–12, 128
  see also microfinance. . .
financial orientation, microfinance institutions
    (MFIs), 80–4
financial performance, ix, x, xi, 7, 9, 11–12,
    15–16, 18–21, 26–9, 30–1, 72, 80–4,
    133–4, 137, 146–9, 156–8, 195–7, 212
  see also profits
  statistics, 20–1, 84, 156–8
financial services, 4–5, 7, 11–12, 14–18, 19–22,
    23–5, 29–30, 34–5, 49–52, 56, 65, 71–2,
    85–8, 111–12, 131, 134–5, 155–6,
    167, 211–15
  see also capital; microfinance
  definition, 15–17
finished goods, 224
First MicroFinanceBank (FMFB), 30
Fitch credit rating agency, 153, 186
fixed assets, 78–9, 203, 222–3
fixed costs, 119–20
fixed-interest investments, 177–8
focus groups, 144, 151–2
food, 3–4, 6–7, 14, 16, 28, 49, 52–5, 56, 67,
    110, 156, 162–3, 164, 213, 225
food inflation, 110
Ford Foundation, 31, 136
forests, 6
foundations, 5, 31, 35, 51, 95, 134–5,
    136, 176–7
fraud, 87, 90, 168–9
fridges, 150
fund of funds, 171, 176–7, 197
fund managers, 34–48, 64–5, 153–4, 171,
    177–98
  see also investments; microfinance invest-
    ment vehicles
  regulations, 36–7, 207–9
  roles, 184–7

funding, microfinance institutions (MFIs)
    76–84, 96, 121–2, 180–98, 201, 203,
    206
furniture manufacturers, 158
future prospects, microfinance, 211–15

G-20, 23
Gabon, 126
gambling, 27
game theory, 102–3
Gates, Bill, 161
GDP, 24
gender issues, 3–9, 16, 18, 24, 30, 33–4, 47, 49,
    50–1, 54, 58–9, 63–4, 66–8, 73, 99–101,
    107–8, 116, 129–30, 131, 144, 146–7, 157,
    170, 190, 212, 214
  geographic statistics, 64–5, 66, 67–8
  goals, 18, 24, 30, 157
  poverty contexts, 54
Geneva, 40–1, 42–7
geographic locations, xi, 1–5, 8, 21–2, 39, 47,
    50–1, 59–67, 91–2, 99–100, 114, 116,
    127–8, 135–6, 138, 154–6, 171, 181–2,
    203–5, 213–14, 218–19, 221–2
  see also individual locations
  risk, 91–2
Georgia, 204–5
German Development Bank (KfW), 34–5,
    37–8, 176–7
Germany, 12–14, 29, 37–8, 40–1, 121, 164,
    203–5
Ghana, 164
global financial crisis from 2007, 36, 201–3,
    205, 207
Global Partnership for Financial Inclusion
    (GPFI), 23–4, 228
global partnerships, 4, 6, 23–4
glossary, 229–31
government bonds, 193–4, 205–6
governments, 24, 25, 37–9, 44, 76–7, 134, 154,
    193–5
  see also public–private partnerships
Grameen Bank, 13, 14, 17, 87, 136
  historical background, 13, 14
'green loans,' 147
group loans, 85–6, 99–100, 101–3, 105–6,
    115
  see also loans

haircuts, 111–12
  see also restructured loans
Hattha Kaksekar Ltd (HKL), 149

health, 3–6, 11–12, 15–18, 24, 28, 30, 45, 51–3,
55–8, 67, 73–4, 85, 87, 144, 155–6, 162–3,
178, 212–13, 225
goals, 16, 17–18, 24, 30, 45, 49, 51,
55–7, 155–6, ,
loan benefits, 57, 67, 85, 154–6, 212, 213
micro entrepreneurs, 57
statistics, 57–8
hedge funds, 191, 193–5, 197–8, 207
hedging, 35, 185–7, 206–7, 208
HIV/AIDS, 4
homelessness, 230
Honduras, 162–3
house maps, 219
housing, 17, 28, 52, 65, 149–51,
162–3, 219, 225
human concerns, types, 230
human rights, 27, 44
hunger, 3–4, 6–7, 14, 52–6, 225

Imon International, 142–3
impact investments, ix, x, xi, 7, 8–9, 11–12,
15–16, 20–1, 25–9, 41, 47, 51, 59, 61,
133–58, 161–72, 213–15
see also double bottom line; financial
performance; microfinance. . .; social
performance
definition, ix, xi, 8, 15–16, 25–6, 28
imports, statistics, 204–5
Incofin, 40–1
income, 1–3, 14–17, 49–50, 56–9, 73, 129–30,
162–3, 201–9, 225
see also disposable income; sales
breakdown, 162–3, 225
buffers, 17
pyramid, 2–3, 23–4, 31, 54–5
sources, 1–2, 14–17, 49–51, 56–9, 126,
129–30, 162–3, 225
statistics, 1–3
INDECOPI, 110–12
India, 17, 59–61, 165, 203–5, 206
individual needs, Maslow's hierarchy of
needs, 54–7
Indonesia, 14, 61
industrial countries, 4–7, 11, 12–3, 24, 87, 101,
116, 119–121, 164, 180–81, 194, 203–4
commitment needs, 5–7, 171
industrialization, 6
industry-type statistics, 6, 8–9, 28, 30, 49–51,
60–1, 64–5, 68, 204–5
inequalities, 3–4, 6, 11–12, 16, 21–4, 54, 212
see also financial inclusion

inflation, 110, 164, 205–6
infrastructure needs, 6–7
innovations, 17, 43–6, 81–2, 133, 157, 213–15
institutional investors, 5–6, 7, 21–2, 34–7,
110–12, 176–98, 212–15
see also banks; foundations; insurance
companies; investments; pensions
background, 34–7, 176–7, 197, 212–15
statistics, 176–7
insurance companies, 5, 18, 34–5, 74, 75–6,
197
insurance services, 15–16, 17–18, 22, 29–30,
57–8, 71–3, 76, 85–6, 87–8, 144–6, 165,
203, 207–8, 213
see also credit risk; health; life
types, 87–8, 145–6, 165, 207–8
Inter-American Development Bank, 38
interest rate risk, 180, 185–6
interest rates, 12–13, 23, 25, 34–45, 81–4, 85–6,
96, 100–1, 111–12, 114–16, 119–32,
138–40, 161, 185–90, 205
components, 120–7, 130–2, 163–4
critique, 119, 120–3, 161, 163–4
determinants, 119, 120–1, 130–2, 163–4
high rates, 119, 120–3, 161, 163–4
historical background, 12–13
inflation rates, 164
statistics, 82–4, 120–32, 163–4
sustainable rates, 127
internal investment committees, 185,
186–7, 196–7
international equity/debt, 79–84, 96, 201–9
International Finance Corporation (IFC)
23–4, 34–5, 38
International Labour Organization (ILO)
43–4
International Monetary Fund (IMF) 3–4
inventories, 222, 223–4
investments, ix, x, xi, 5–6, 7, 8–9, 11–12, 15–16,
20–1, 24–31, 34–48, 79–84, 147, 156–8,
175–99, 201–9, 211–15
see also conventional. . .; development
finance institutions; foundations; fund
managers; impact. . .; institutional. . .;
portfolios; retail. . .
default rates, 180–1
definition, 230
incentives in microfinance, 195–8
microfinance in the overall portfolio,
191–5, 197–8
processes, 180, 181–7
regulations, 36–7, 207–9

investments (*Continued*)
   shortfalls, 5–6, 15–16
   statistics, 5–6, 20–1, 156–7, 176–98
   types, 5–6, 7, 20–1, 26–31, 34–5, 38–9,
      175–98
   value chain, 34–48, 176–98, 212–15
Ireland, 12–13
iStock.com, 243

Jim Yong Kim, xi
joint ventures, 214
J.P. Morgan, 44, 181
justice needs, 6–7

Kenya, 125–7, 146–7, 204–5
Kenya Women Microfinance Bank Limited
   (KWFT), 146–7
Kirgizstan, 2–3

land degradation, 6
late payments, loans, 108–10, 164, 165
Latin America, 1, 3, 14, 21, 38, 49–50, 58–9,
   61–4, 66, 67–8, 82, 94, 128, 143–6, 149,
   166, 183–4
   see also individual countries
leases, 144
legal systems, 73–6, 89, 101, 123, 165,
   168–9
   see also civilian law; commercial law;
      property law; regulations
liabilities, breakdown, 78–9, 162–3, 203,
   223
Libor, 195
life insurance, 18, 57, 65–7, 67, 76, 87
LifeBank foundations, 51
liquidity premiums, 121–2
liquidity requirements, 37, 85–6, 88–9, 90–1,
   92–6, 108–9, 121–2, 196–7, 205–7
LiveBank foundation, 95, 198
living standards, ix, 17, 19–23, 24, 54–7, 74,
   134–5, 150–1, 155–7, 167–70
loan agreements and pricing policies,
   investments, 187–90
loan officers, 37–8, 96, 111–12, 113–14, 127,
   147, 154–6, 162–3, 221–6
   see also credit bureaus
   profiles, 113
   roles, 112, 113–14, 127, 162–3
loan pricing, 119–32, 138–40, 148, 187–90
   see also interest rates
loan registers, 37

loans, ix, x, 8, 12–14, 16–18, 20–3, 29–30,
   34–48, 49–68, 71–96, 99–117, 187–90,
   207–9, 217–19, 221–6
   see also banks; capital; group. . .; microloans;
      progressive. . .
   applications, 37–8, 113–14, 217–19
   balances per region, 62–3
   bilateral contracts, 187–90, 197–8
   costs, 119–32
   coupons, 188–90
   covenants, 188–90, 197–8
   definition, 7, 85–6
   historical background, 12–14, 81–3
   methodologies, 99–116
   range, 56–9
   rural/urban client contrasts, 64–5, 86–7,
      104–7, 124–5, 145–7
   statistics, 7, 13–15, 20–1, 47, 51, 56–67,
      79–84, 104–10, 120–32, 142–58, 163–4,
      202–9, 214
   terms, 12–14, 20–1, 37, 85–6, 104–8, 111–12,
      138–40, 163–4, 170, 187–90, 207–8, 226
   types, 56–9, 85–6, 99–108, 135–40, 141–9
Lord, Richard, 243
Luxembourg, 41

M-CRIL social rating agency, 151–3, 157, 166
M-Pesa, 124–7
Madagascar, 61
malaria, 4
mandatory insurance, 87
mandatory savings, definition, 86–7
marine resources, 6
market efficiencies, 25, 148, 171, 211
market entry barriers, 37, 91–2
market gardeners, 104–5
market overview, 39–46, 110–12, 176–7, 201–9
   see also assets under management
   Peru, 110–12
market participants, microfinance, 24–5, 34–47,
   121–32, 134–5, 154–6, 176–98
market research, 154–6
market risk *see* systematic risk
market stalls, 51, 58, 131
Markowitz, Harry M., 191–5
Maslow's hierarchy of needs, 54–5
maternal health, 4
Máxima, Queen of the Netherlands, 119
mean-variance portfolios, 192–5
meetings with MFIs, 99, 101, 104, 107–8,
   113–14, 115

mergers and acquisitions, 214
micro enterprises, 8, 24, 30, 47, 59–67,
  81–4
micro entrepreneurs, 8, 12–13, 33–48, 49–69,
  71–2, 80–4, 92–6, 99–100, 104–16, 134–5,
  138–58, 203–9, 212–15, 221–6
  definition, 35–6, 49–51
  geographic statistics, 59–67
  loan types, 56–9
  needs and requirements, 49, 51, 52–9,
    106–8, 150–1
  rural/urban client contrasts, 64–5, 86–7,
    104–8, 124–5, 145–7
  statistics, 49–50, 59–67, 204–9
  success stories, 167, 214
  willingness to repay, 129–30, 165
Micro Finance Transparency (MFTransparency),
  140, 144–5
micro-, small-and medium-sized enterprises
  (MSMEs), 22, 28, 34–48, 169–70
Microcredit Summit Campaign Report, 14
microcredits, 13–14, 16, 20–1
microfinance, ix, x, xi, 7, 9, 11–32, 33–48, 49,
  50–1, 54–7, 71–97, 119–32, 133–58,
  175–6, 201–9, 211–15
  see also financial services; fund managers;
    impact investments; value chain
  administrators, 34–48, 122–3
  critique, 5, 161–72, 211–15
  definition, ix, xi, 11–18, 29–30, 54–5, 81,
    133–4, 155, 176–7
  goals, 15–19, 24, 25–6, 37, 49, 54–7, 72–3,
    81, 83–4, 119–20, 133–58, 165–7, 211–15
  historical background, 12–15, 42–6,
    76–7, 81–3
  statistics, 7, 13–15, 20–1, 28–9, 39–41,
    46–7, 56–67, 79–80, 142–58,
    176–98, 202–3
  trust, 99–100, 101–3, 113, 114–17, 212, 215
  types, 15–17, 56–9, 99–104
Microfinance Information Exchange Market
  (MIX Market), 62–4, 82–4, 108, 122, 124,
  128, 140, 208
microfinance institutions (MFIs), 6–8, 13–18,
  23–4, 29–31, 34–8, 46–7, 49–50, 56–63,
  71–97, 99, 100–1, 104, 119–20, 121–32,
  134–58, 165, 175–6, 181–7, 201–9,
  213–15, 221–6
  see also development finance institutions;
    Grameen Bank
  bottom-up selection processes, 181–7, 197–8

  definition, 14–15, 16, 23–4, 35, 36–7, 71–3,
    94–6, 119–20
  goals, 72–3, 83–4, 94–5, 119–20,
    133–58, 165–7
  historical background, 13–14, 76–7, 81–3
  non-financial services, 15, 16, 29–30, 71–2,
    85, 87–8, 94–5, 111–12, 141–9, 153–8
  ratings, 185, 186–7
  returns, 84
  selection processes, 181–7, 197–8
  service types, 85–8, 94–5
  statistics, 13–15, 28–9, 58–63, 76–80, 82–4,
    142–58, 165, 184–7, 202–9
  types, 73–6, 89–90, 95–6
microfinance investment vehicles (MIVs), vii,
  xi, 24–5, 30, 34–48, 64–5, 133, 153–4,
  176–98, 212, 227
  see also assets under management;
    investments
  definition, 25, 35, 36, 177–9
  interest rates, 25, 34–5
  possible pitfalls, 180–1
  statistics, 39–41, 46–7, 176–98
  types, 177–9
MicroFinanza social rating agency, 151, 152,
  153, 157, 166
microloans *see* loans
MicroRate social rating agency, 151, 152–3,
  157, 166
Middle East, 21, 62–4, 82, 128, 166, 183
Millennium Development Goals (MDGs), ix,
  3–7, 16, 29–30, 59, 212, 227
  critique, 5
minimum capital requirements, 90–2
mission, microfinance institutions (MFIs),
  133–59, 165–7, 170–1, 196–7
mission drift, microfinance institutions
  (MFIs), 170–1
MIX Market *see* Microfinance Information
  Exchange Market
mobile phones, 124–7, 130–2, 145, 211, 212–13
money laundering, 90
money lenders/relatives, 23, 74, 81, 82,
  130–2, 165
Mongolia, 60–1, 172, 203–5, 214
monitoring processes, investments, 185, 187
Montenegro, 148
Moody's credit rating agency, 186
moral hazard, 94, 100–1, 107–8, 114
Morningstar government bond index, 194–5
mortality rates, 4

MSCI EM, 194–5
MSCI World, 194–5
multilateral DFIs, 37–9
mutual monitoring, 35–6, 38–9, 99, 101–2, 103, 115

Nash equilibrium (NE), 102–3, 227
net asset values (NAVs), 179
Netherlands, 37–8, 40–1, 119
Nicaragua, 204–5, 206
Nigeria, 59–63
non-bank financial institutions (NBFIs), 21, 72–3, 74, 148, 227
non-deposit taking MFIs, regulations, 89–92
non-financial services, 15, 16, 29–30, 71–2, 85, 87–8, 94–5, 111–12, 141–9, 153–8
see also education; gender issues; health; technical assistance
non-governmental organizations (NGOs), 42–6, 72, 73–97, 110–12, 140, 143
see also microfinance institutions
definition, 73–4
non-prudential regulation, definition, 90–1, 92
Northern Africa, 21, 62–4, 128, 166, 183

OECD, 3–4, 21, 227
Oikocredit, 40–1
OPEC Fund for International Development, 38
open-end funds, 178, 179
operating costs, 119–32, 163–4, 170, 206, 211, 212–15, 225
geographic locations, 127–8, 163–4
statistics, 120–7, 128, 163–4, 206
operations, 222
over-indebtedness of clients, 108–10, 112, 116, 138–40, 144–5, 165, 171
Overseas Private Investment Corp. 38
overview of the book, ix, x, xi, xii, 8–9

Pakistan, 86, 104–6, 204–5
pawnshops, 12–13
pensions, 5, 34–5, 36–7, 65, 71–2, 87, 147, 176–7, 197
Peru, 58–9, 110–12, 163, 204–5
philanthropy, 25–6, 28–9, 31, 46
see also charities; venture. . .
Philippines, 8, 47, 50–1, 95, 150–1, 198
photo credits, 243
physiological needs, 54–6, 66
see also clothing. . .; food; water
Planet Rating social rating agency, 151, 153, 157, 166

plant diseases, 110
politics, 81–2, 168, 180–3, 202
pornography, 27
portfolio at risk (PAR), 108–10, 116
portfolios, xi, 9, 78–80, 88–96, 108–10, 124, 128, 155–6, 171, 175–98, 211–15
see also investments
microfinance in the overall portfolio, 191–5, 197–8
modern portfolio theory (MPT), 191–5, 197–8, 227
sample portfolios, 193–5
top-down selection processes, 181–7, 191–5, 197–8
Portman, Natalie, 49
postal banks, 72–3, 74, 75, 76
poverty, x, xi, 1–9, 11–18, 23–4, 25, 29–31, 38–9, 49–68, 71–2, 83–4, 95–6, 133–58, 161–72, 211–15
see also extreme. . .; moderate. . .
definitions, 2, 52–4, 66
fighting poverty, 2–7, 14–18, 29–31, 38–9, 59, 71–2, 83–4, 95–6, 119, 133–58, 211–15
future prospects, 211–15
levels, 1–2, 52–9, 66, 150–1, 166–7, 211–15
needs and requirements, 49, 51, 52–9, 150–1
pyramid, 2–3, 23–4, 31, 54–5
statistics, xi, 1–5, 53–4, 57–8, 59, 136, 150–1, 166–7
poverty assessment tool (PAT), definition, 136, 151, 166–7, 228
Prasac, 164
prejudices and reservations, 161–72
prevention measures, default rates, 110–12, 116, 207–8
principal–agent problems, 100–1
PRIs *see* United Nations Principles for Responsible Investment
privacy of client data, 138–40, 144–5
private equity, 178–81, 212–14
product design, definition, 138–9, 144–5
profit-oriented MFIs, 80–4, 96, 107, 120–32, 146–9
profits, 80–4, 95–6, 107, 119–20, 121–32, 146–9, 178–81, 202–9, 211–15
see also financial performance; returns
statistics, 123, 129–30, 178–81, 202–9
Progress Out of Poverty Index (PPI), definition, 136, 149–51, 166–7, 228

progressive loans, 99, 101–2, 103–4, 115
property law, 101
protagonists, 24–5, 34–47, 50–1, 121–32,
    134–5, 154–6, 176–98
providers, liabilities, 78–9, 223
prudential regulation, definition, 90–1
public–private partnerships, ix, 5–7, 18–19,
    34–5, 44, 179, 197

Raiffeisen, Friedrich Wilhelm, 12–14
Raiffeisen Group, 12–14, 163, 164
Rania al-Abdullah, Queen of Jordan, 11
real economy, 9, 201–9
    definition, 201–3
    local influencing factors, 201, 203–5, 208
real estate insurance, 87
recovery rates, investment defaults, 181
referees, 218, 221
references/reading list, 233–41
regional DFIs, 38–9
regulations, 36–7, 73–6, 77–9, 86–7, 88–96,
    110–12, 165, 168–9, 207–9
    see also supervision
    central aspects, 89–92
    goals, 88–90
    international standards, 37, 89
    reasons, 88–9, 168–9, 207
    value chain, 36–7, 110–12, 207–9
remuneration, 36, 141–9
renewable energy, 27, 147, 213
repayments, 14, 20, 36, 81–2, 85–6, 100–3,
    104–10, 125–7, 129–30, 153, 162–3,
    164–5, 170, 188–90, 204–5, 226
    see also collateral
    willingness to repay, 129–30, 165
ResponsAbility, 40–1, 44
restructured loans, 111–12
    see also haircuts
retail investors, 177
retail liabilities, 223
return on assets (RoA), statistics, 84
return on equity (RoE), statistics, 84
returns ix, x, xi, 7, 9, 11–12, 15–16, 18–21,
    26–9, 34–5, 39, 84, 107, 175–98,
    202–9, 211–15
    see also financial. . .; profits; risk-adjusted. . .;
    social. . .
rice agriculture, 50–1
risk management, 22, 26–9, 39, 57, 90–6,
    100–1, 107, 121–32, 154–6, 171, 181–7,
    189–90, 203, 206–7
risk types, investments, 191–5

risk-adjusted returns, 26, 175–6, 178–81, 191–5
    see also returns
risk-aversion properties, women, 107
risk-return ratios, investments, 175–6, 178–81,
    189–90, 191–5, 196–7, 211–15
risk-sharing benefits, public–private
    partnerships, 179, 197
rural clients, 63–5, 104–7, 124–5, 145–7

Sachs, Jeffrey, 71
Safaricom, 125–7
safety/security needs, 6, 54–6
sales, 221, 224–5
    see also income
sanitation, 6, 18, 52–3, 87, 147–9
satellite data, 211, 212–13
Sauty, Johann, 243
savings, 12–14, 16–17, 22, 24–5, 29–30, 65–7,
    67, 71–3, 74–6, 77–9, 85–9, 124–7, 142–4,
    162–3, 222
    historical background, 12–14
    product types, 86–7
savings cooperatives, 72–3
SBS, 110–12, 228
Scheurle, Patrick, ix, xii, xv
Schulze-Delitzsch, Hermann, 12–14
Schumpeter, Joseph, 201
self-actualization needs, Maslow's hierarchy of
    needs, 54–6
self-determination goals, microfinance, 16–17,
    30–1, 54–5
self-esteem, 52
self-regulation trends, 92–3, 171
shame thresholds, gender issues, 107
Share Microfin, 17
shareholders, 188–90
    see also equity; investments
Sharpe ratios, 193–5
Shutterstock.com, 243
sketch house maps, 219
Smart Campaign, 135, 138–40, 141,
    151–3, 165–6
    definition, 138, 141, 165
SMEs *see* micro-, small-and medium-sized
    enterprises
social capital, 87–8
social impact, definition, 134–5
social intermediation, 88
social needs, Maslow's hierarchy of needs, 54–6
social performance, ix, x, xi, 7, 11–12, 15–21,
    26–9, 30–1, 72–4, 84, 133–59, 165–7,
    196–7, 212–15

social performance (*Continued*)
see also education; food; health; housing;
poverty; technical assistance; Universal
Standards. . .
critique, 165–7
definition, 19–21, 134–5, 165
measures, 133, 135–58, 165–7
statistics, 20–1, 156–8
Social Performance Impact Reporting and
Intelligence Tool (SPIRIT), 148–9, 228
Social Performance Task Force (SPTF), 19–20,
31, 134–7, 140–1, 152, 157, 165–6, 228
social rating agencies, 151–3, 157–8, 166–7
socially neutral investing (SNI), 26–7, 228
socially responsible investments (SRIs),
definition, 26–9, 196–7
socio-economic factors, loans, 37–8, 99–100,
104–7, 115–16, 221–6
solar panels, 149
Somalia, 126
South Asia, 1, 2–3, 8, 14, 21, 47, 49–50, 59–64,
82, 94, 102, 128, 166, 183, 203–5
see also individual countries
specialized MFI banks, 74, 75, 213
sponsors, 12, 24, 25, 44, 78–9, 134–5,
176–7, 189–90
Standard & Poor's credit rating agency,
152, 186
startup MFIs, 77–9
state banks, 72, 74, 75, 77–9, 81–3, 95–6
Staudacher, Andrea, 243
Stearns, Rich, 133
Stiglitz and Weiss' model of credit rationing,
100–1, 114
Sub-Saharan Africa, 21, 59–64, 128, 166, 183
subsidies, 78–9, 80–3, 87–8
Sudan, 126
suicides in India, 165
supervision, 33–48, 73–6, 81–2, 88–96, 110–12,
127, 155–6, 162–3, 168–9, 171, 207–9
see also regulations
supply channels, 28
sustainable development, ix, 4, 5–7, 11–12, 25,
26–9, 43–6, 73, 80–4, 148–9, 212–14
see also environmental impacts
background, 5–7, 43–6, 80–1
Sustainable Development Goals
(SDGs), 5–7, 228
Sustainable Finance Geneva (SFG), 46, 228
sustainable interest rates, 127
sustainable investing (SI), definition, 26–9

Swift, Jonathan, 12–13
Swiss Investment Fund for Emerging Markets
(SIFEM) 37–8
Swiss Sustainable Finance (SSF), 46, 228
Switzerland, 29, 37–8, 40–1, 42–7, 121,
195–7, 203–5
SWOT analysis, 154
Symbiotics, 40–1, 43, 44, 176
Symbiotics Microfinance Index (SMX), 43,
193–5, 202, 228
synergy effects, 45
systematic risk, 191–5

Tajikistan, 2–3, 30, 126, 142
Tameer Bank, 105–6
Tanzania, 61
taxes, 25, 90, 120–1, 123–4, 127, 130–2, 225
technical assistance (TA), vii, 39, 143, 153–6,
157–8, 228
see also training
definition, 39, 153–4
technologies, 124–7, 130–2, 144, 154–6, 171,
211, 212–15
telecommunications, 124–7, 130–2, 144,
211, 212–13
thematic funds, 178
tiers of MFIs, 2, 77–9, 95–6
tobacco, 27
total expense ratio (TER), 178–9, 228
trade balances, statistics, 203–4
training, 35, 56–9, 87–8, 110, 124,
141–9, 153–6
see also education; technical assistance
transaction banks, 74, 75, 76
transaction services, 74, 75, 76, 85–6, 87–8
transnational companies, 5–6
transparency, 44, 90, 138–45, 150–1, 164,
168–9, 171
Triodos, 40–1
triple bottom line (TBL)
see also double. . .; impact investments;
microfinance
definition, ix
Triple Jump, 40–1
trust, loans, 99–100, 101–3, 113, 114–16, 212, 215
TVs, 150

Uganda, 126
ultra-high net worth individuals (UHNWIs), 177
United Nations Conference on Trade and
Development (UNCTAD), 5–6, 42–6, 228

United Nations Environment Programme
(UNEP), 44–5, 228
United Nations Finance Initiative
(UNEP FI), 44–5
United Nations Global Compact, 44–5
United Nations Principles for Responsible
Investment (UN PRIs), 44–6, 228
United Nations (UN), ix, 3–6, 42–7, 196
see also Millennium Development Goals;
Sustainable Development Goals
Rio de Janeiro summit in 1992, 44
Rio de Janeiro summit in 2012, 5
Universal Standards of Social Performance
Measurement (USSPMs), 135–49,
151–3, 228
definition, 135–7, 139–2
overview, 137, 141
University of Zurich's Center for
Microfinance, 195–6
unsystematic risk, 191–5
see also diversification
urban clients, 63–5, 86–7, 104–7, 124–5
USA, 14, 38, 39–41, 44, 136
USAID, 136, 151

value chain, 24–5, 33–48, 50–1, 101, 134–5,
154–6, 171, 176–98, 207–9, 212–15
see also United Nations. . .

venture philanthropy, 26, 29
Vietnam, 203–5
volatilities
see also risk. . .
voluntary savings, definition, 86–7

washing machines, 150
water, 4, 6–7, 52–3, 54–5, 56, 87, 149,
150, 165, 225
weapons/nuclear energy, 27
well-being, 6
willingness to repay, loans, vii, 129–30, 165
women *see* gender issues
World Bank, xi, 1, 2, 3–4, 17, 21, 23–4, 35,
38–9, 53, 55, 61, 126, 164, 166,
176–7, 207
World Business Council for Sustainable
Development (WBCSD), 45
World Economic Forum (WEF), ix, x, 45, 228
World Trade Organization (WTO),
44, 204, 228
WWB Colombia, 115, 131, 167, 190

XAC Bank, 60, 138, 172

Yunus, Muhammad, 7, 13, 14, 99, 211

Zurich, 40, 44, 46, 125, 195–7